BLIZZARD'S WIZARD WOODWORK

BLIZZARD'1

WIZARD
WOODWORK

RICHARD BLIZZARD

GUILD PUBLISHING LONDON

■ **Credits**

Plans: **Peter Farley and
Mervyn Hurford**

Photographs: **David Brittain**

Line illustrations: **William Giles**

This book accompanies the BBC
Television series **Blizzard's Wizard
Woodwork** first broadcast on BBC 1 in
Spring 1985

Series introduced by Richard Blizzard
and produced by Peter Ramsden

Published to accompany a series of
programmes prepared in consultation
with the BBC Continuing Education
Advisory Council

This book is set in 10 key on 11 point
News Gothic by Transcript, London WC1
Printed and bound in England by
Purnell and Sons (Book Production)
Limited, Paulton, Bristol

This edition published 1985
by Book Club Associates
by arrangement with BBC Publications

CONTENTS

ACKNOWLEDGEMENTS

■ Acknowledgements

Creating a television series and book would be quite impossible without the team effort of many gifted men and women. I am most grateful to all of you for help, encouragement, advice and ideas, and the patience you have all shown me while we have been working together. I trust that our combined efforts will bring much pleasure and enjoyment to many homemakers.

Sheila Innes and **Peter Riding** for piloting my programme proposals through the corridors of power.

Peter Ramsden, Ann Curtis and **Paula Gilder** whose combined talents made the production possible.

Peter Farley and **Mervyn Hurford** whose drawing talents turned my wooden objects into working drawings.

Jenny Spring who transformed my untidy handwriting into a tidy script.

Glyn Davies for organising and designing the layout of the book, and waiting so patiently for the last few chapters!

David Brittain for all the superb photographs in the book.

Syon Park Garden Centre, Brentford, for the loan of plants for the garden photography.

Dixons Ltd for the loan of electrical equipment for the indoor photography.

All the companies who helped with the supply of both hand and power tools enabling me to have two complete workshops, one at home, the other in the studio.

Roger Pitchfork of Bahco Record Tools for dowling jigs, planes, spokeshaves, chisels, etc.

John Costello of Black & Decker Ltd, for personal help and assistance with power tools.

Peugeot UK for electric power tools.

Derek Parsons of Elu for electric power tools.

Tony Merrett of Robert Bosch Ltd for electric jig-saw and router.

Marie Jennings and **Paul Wright** of Stanley Tools for planes, screwdrivers, hand routers and cabinet scrapers.

Norman Collier of A.E.G. for jig-saws, electric screwdrivers, etc.

Mary Spencer who designed my Pebble Mill Workshop.

Phil Thicket Floor Manager, BBC Pebble Mill.

Stan Royle Assistant Floor Manager.

Janet Pearce who advised on the flowers and enthused about the gardening section!

Peter Westley who painted floral decorations on the garden furniture.

Richard Crouch and **Paz** for such happy introductory music for the television series.

Sue Farr Graphic Designer, Pebble Mill, for the series opening titles.

David Fisher of Strand Public Relations.

Simon and **Owen Papps** for wielding measuring tape, screwdrivers and brushes!

Mr Davies and his men of W.H. Davis, Nailsworth, Stroud, Gloucestershire, for moving the furniture for the series all over the country and doing it so willingly.

Ron Hatton, Ray and the staff of **Pebble Mill** for their help.

Jennie Allen at BBC Educational Publications for her assistance and advice with the book text.

Caroline Earl of Dryad for her invaluable advice and assistance with the loom.

Paul Kriwaczek for warping up the loom.

Last, but by no means least, **Valerie,** my wife who helped us all.

INTRODUCTION

■ Foreword

We have seen already the splendid variety of wonderful wooden toys for juniors which Richard Blizzard has made: now it is the turn of seniors to be delighted.

Within recent memory our understanding of our world has been profoundly altered, and a revolution in both our ways of thinking and our daily lives has taken place. How good it is therefore that we can cling to something that is constant. God made the tree and man has grafted and crafted to contrive things of utility and beauty from it.

Richard Blizzard takes his place in this progression. His ingenuity and skill of hand provide for us, whatever our age, beautiful things to look at and use. 'I too will something make and joy in the making.'

Moreover he invites us, those of us who catch even a part of his enthusiasm, to join him in the making. We are guided, helped and advised at all levels along the way.

He makes it all so possible.

Tom Job
Abergavvenny 1984

■ Introduction

The twentieth century is an exciting time to live in. Hardly a week passes without us discovering something fresh about the world around us, or indeed what it was like to live thousands of years ago. Carbon dating has removed the speculation as to how old the archaeologists' findings are and these bring to light so much about how our ancestors lived. It would seem that man, both ancient and modern, like his Maker, is never more content than when he is actively engaged in creating things. What is more, these creations are not only of a purely functional nature. Even the ancient cave dweller enjoyed painting and whittling bone to form jewellery.

Man is the only creature who makes tools and he acquires great skill in the use of them. In today's world of the microchip these 'low technology' skills are the things that give pleasure and a sense of wellbeing to those who practise them, whether potter, weaver, stone-mason, cooper or wood turner. In all these activities there is something to show for our labours, something to look at that will last and be passed on with pride to future generations.

There has never before been a time when we have had such a choice of tools. The introduction of the electric power tool has given many the ability to tackle jobs around the home and garden that only ten years ago would not have been considered. It is my hope that this book will encourage you too to make something, and even if you work carefully from the plans provided you will be surprised and delighted to discover that, once made, it will possess something of your own character and personality.

I have created the designs in the hope that by showing you how joints are cut and things are put together, you will master the basic skills and begin to design and make for yourself – so hindering the spread of standardisation. My wish is that this book will help you discover the truth behind the poet Robert Bridges' words:
'I too will something make, and joy in the making.'

Richard E. Blizzard
September 1984

Wall Plate Rack
Page 67

Cotswold Clock
Page 71

**Platter and
Carving Set**
Pages 75, 77

Rocking Chair
Page 17

Refectory Table and Benches
Opposite

REFECTORY TABLE AND BENCHES

A quick glance at the photograph of this table may fill you with foreboding as to its complexity, but look a little closer and you will be relieved to find that only one traditional woodworking joint has to be mastered — the mortice and tenon. The popularity of this style of table is not surprising because there is plenty of room to seat a large family or accommodate guests. Noticeable features of my design are the twin stretcher rails and the benches, the legs of which fit inside the table legs to give maximum space in the kitchen when the table is not in use.

I have designed and built the table in oak, but various other hardwoods or softwoods would also be suitable. If you want to cut the cost of the table top, then a sheet of chip-board covered with Formica fitted with a suitable edging strip will serve just as well.

Having got your timber sorted out, mark face side and face edge on all the pieces as appropriate. Mark out all the mortice and tenons for the table. Pieces which are identical, such as the leg rails, should be marked out in pairs. While I am marking out I use a 'G'-cramp to hold the pieces together—it's simpler and makes for greater accuracy. My normal practice is to mark everything in pencil first and then double-check since mistakes in timber can be very costly.

■ Cutting a mortice

1 You will need a good quality sash mortice chisel for this task (not one which has been used to open paint tins!). Take the mortice gauge and adjust it to the width of the mortice chisel. With the mortice gauge set you can now mark all the mortice and tenons.

Don't forget always to work from the face side and edge marks. Marking out takes quite a time but it is essential that it is done carefully and double-checked before any cutting is done. Don't be tempted to mark just one mortice and then cut it out. Mark out everything— lay it out on the workshop floor and make sure that once all the pieces are cut out they will fit together.

2 Cutting a mortice is not difficult providing that you have a good chisel and mallet (no hammers please), and a firm surface to work on. A good stout work-table is essential as any 'bounce' from the work surface will make the cutting of the mortice very difficult.

Clamp the piece of timber firmly to the work-table making sure that you fix it so that you are standing directly behind or in front of the timber. You will then be able

to keep the chisel at 90° to the work-table as you 'chop' the mortice. Don't try to cut all the mortice hole at once, 'chop' carefully along the full length, cutting to a depth of approximately ⅜" (1 cm). The sash mortice chisel is designed in such a way that as you 'chip' along the marked section the chippings will start to eject automatically. This process has to be repeated until the required depth has been reached. It is helpful to mark a pencil line on the back of the chisel indicating the depth to which you have to cut. The way in which the sash mortice chisel raises the 'chippings' from the mortice hole as work proceeds makes the task of cutting the mortice hole much easier than you would expect.

■ Cutting a tenon

1 The tenon is the 'peg' section of the joint that fits into the mortice hole. The tenon width is marked out with the mortice gauge, thus ensuring a good fit. The advantage of marking out the whole job together as explained earlier can now be appreciated. The length of the tenon is marked very carefully with a marking knife. Don't attempt to 'make do' with a pencil line. The function of the marking knife is to cut cleanly through the wood fibres, helping you to get a good clean cut. A good cut is essential as this is a part that will show when the joint is assembled.

2 To cut the joint use a tenon saw as this has a steel or brass strip along the back which stiffens the thin blade. If you have a choice, the brass-backed saw is better as the added weight of the brass assists the cutting operation. A sharp tenon saw is essential for cutting large tenons.

The first cut to make with a tenon saw is down the mortice gauge line. With the wood firmly fixed in the vice follow the gauge lines and cut right down to the marking gauge line. It is necessary to fix the wood being sawn at a 45° angle in the vice and turn it round halfway through the operation.

3 Once the side 'cheeks' have been cut down the next task is to cut them off, leaving the 'peg' to fit into the mortice. The wood has now to be placed flat on the work-bench. To stop it sliding around while cutting a sawing block should be used. With great care saw the shoulders of the tenon.

I have described the cutting of the mortice and tenon joint in general terms. If you look at the drawings you will discover variations of this joint, but the method for cutting all of them is basically the same. Now let's look at the various reasons for the different mortice and tenon joints used.

■ The double tenon

This is used on all the table and bench legs because of its strength. If we cut a long thin tenon then the joint is correspondingly weak. Therefore I have used this double tenon joint in all the legs, feet and top rails.

■ Wedged mortice and tenon

1 This joint is used to hold the legs together in both benches and table. Once the tenon has been cut, two vertical saw cuts are made down the outside edges of the tenon.
2 On the face side of the leg the through mortice hole is enlarged to a taper to take the wedge when it is driven in. When the table framework is assembled the wedges are driven into the saw cuts. This has the effect of opening the tenon out and preventing the rails from ever coming out.
3 After gluing, the protruding tenon and wedge are cut off and planed flush with the face side of the leg.

■ Twin stub tenons

These joints are used on all the top rail and tie bars. Once again the width of the top tie bars makes a single tenon impractical, so twin stub tenons are used. The stub tenons do not go right through so they do not show from the face side of the top rail. The top tie bars are for the support of the table top.

■ The table top

Once the basic frameworks have been made for benches and table you have a choice of tops. For a very busy kitchen often occupied by youngsters with sticky fingers it is worth considering the use of chipboard faced with Formica. This can look quite attractive, particularly if you take the trouble to fix a hardwood strip round the edges.

However, if you decide to make the top from 'solid' material a little more skill and time are needed. You will have to join planks together to form the top. There are several methods of jointing planks, but before you do anything you must ensure that the plank edges are flat and square. Traditionally a very long plane called a jointer is used for this purpose. The long sole of the plane takes out all the unevenness in the edge of the planks, which a shorter plane simply won't do. I strongly recommend that you have this 'truing' done when the timber is purchased, otherwise the loan of a jointer plane for the evening will be essential.

■ Jointing the planks

Once the edges of the planks have been trued some way of holding them together is needed. There are several methods:
1   'Plough' a groove along all the inside edges of the boards and cut plywood 'tongues' to be glued into the grooves.
2   Using a rebate plane cut rebates on one plank edge to fit into a corresponding groove on the other.
3   Use an electric router to cut tongues and grooves in the planks.
4   A simpler method, and one that is very strong, is to use dowel rods and glue.

The planks to be joined are placed side by side and marked at intervals where the dowels are to be inserted. Mark the centre of each plank thickness and then drill a hole to take the dowel rod. Careful alignment of the holes is essential. Now cut a number of dowel rods to fit into the holes. It is important to make 'score' marks along the sides of the dowels, as this will allow any excess glue that may get trapped in the holes to escape. Sash cramps must be used when gluing up the table top and the gluing-up operation must take place on a flat surface.

Whichever method of jointing you use, the solid table top has to be planed up, the ends cut off square and the edges nicely rounded off. This work can be done with a spokeshave. You will find the use of a cabinet scraper invaluable when attempting to achieve a good finish on any solid wood surface.

■ Attaching the table top to the framework

Wood, however old and however well seasoned, will always move and this has to be taken into consideration when designing the table. To allow for movement we use 'buttons' made of wood! You will have cut the mortice holes on the top tie bars before final assembly. It is into these holes that the lips of the buttons are pushed. A screw passes through the middle of the button into the table top so that any movement of the table is compensated for by the buttons. If you use oak don't forget to use brass screws as the tannin in oak attacks steel wood screws.

■ Final shaping of table underframe

1   Once all the joints have been cut, the shaping of the table legs and feet can start. Saw and plane the feet to shape.

Using a bow or coping saw (or an electric jig-saw if you have one), cut the shaping of the legs. Use a spokeshave to remove all the saw cuts from the shaped sections.
2   All sharp edges should be removed by cutting a chamfer with a spokeshave. The chamfer should be approximately 3/16 (5mm) wide. This chamfering of the edges changes the whole appearance of the table framework and enhances its appearance.

■ Gluing up

Once all the individual pieces have been cleaned up and chamfers have been cut, you can start gluing the framework together.
1   Glue both the feet, legs and top rails first.
2   Fit top and bottom tie rails. Drive in wedges through tenons.
3   Make and fit table top.
4   Follow exactly the same procedure for making the two benches.

■ Finishing

1   If you have used a good quality timber then it deserves a good finish. Today there are many finishes available. Perhaps the simplest to apply and get a good result is polyurethane. In a dry, warm, dust-free atmosphere use a piece of clean, lint-free cloth and wipe the polyurethane onto the wood.
2   Leave it for 24 hours then lightly work over the whole surface with a very fine glasspaper. Remove any dust created and repeat the whole sequence four times. Using this method an amateur can achieve a very good finish. *Warning* Follow the manufacturer's instructions very carefully and make sure adequate ventilation is provided when using polyurethane finishes.

Photographs: pages 8, 26-27

■ CUTTING LIST

Table

Leg	2 off	660 x 224 x 32 mm (26 x 9 x 1¼ in)	timber
Top rail	2 off	686 x 74 x 32 mm (27 x 3 x 1¼ in)	timber
Foot	2 off	686 x 105 x 32 mm (27 x 4⅛ x 1¼ in)	timber
Top tie bar	2 off	1320 x 71 x 25 mm (52 x 2⅞ x 1 in)	timber
Bottom or lower tie bar	2 off	1352 x 76 x 25 mm (53¼ x 3 x 1 in)	timber
Button	16 off make from	660 x 25 x 22 mm (26 x 1 x ⅞ in)	timber
Table top	1 off	1575 x 736 x 22 mm (62 x 29 x ⅞ in)	timber

Bench — quantities per bench

Leg	2 off	508 x 150 x 32 mm (20 x 6 x 1¼ in)	timber
Top rail	2 off	375 x 50 x 32 mm (14¾ x 2 x 1¼ in)	timber
Foot	2 off	375 x 60 x 32 mm (14¾ x 2⅜ x 1¼ in)	timber
Top tie bar	2 off	1244 x 47 x 25 mm (49 x 1⅞ x 1 in)	timber
Bottom or lower tie bar	2 off	1276 x 44 x 25 mm (50¼ x 1¾ x 1 in)	timber
Button	14 off make from	578 x 25 x 22 mm (22¾ x 1 x ⅞ in)	timber
Bench top	1 off	1575 x 380 x 22 mm (62 x 15 x ⅞ in)	timber

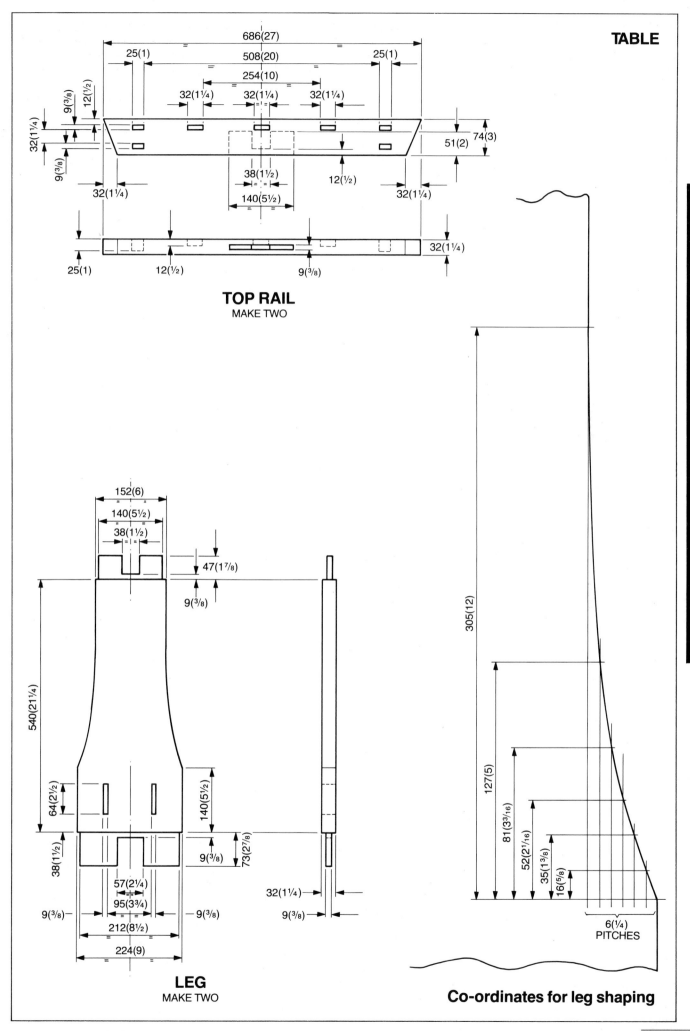

686(27)

25(1)

508(20)

25(1)

254(10)

9(3/8)

12(1/2)

32(1¼)

32(1¼)

32(1¼)

74(3)

32(1¼)

51(2)

9(3/8)

38(1½)

12(1/2)

32(1¼)

32(1¼)

140(5½)

32(1¼)

25(1)

12(1/2)

9(3/8)

TOP RAIL
MAKE TWO

152(6)

140(5½)

38(1½)

47(1⁷/₈)

9(3/8)

305(12)

540(21¼)

127(5)

64(2½)

140(5½)

81(3³/₁₆)

38(1½)

9(3/8)

73(2⁷/₈)

52(2¹/₁₆)

57(2¼)

35(1³/₈)

95(3¾)

32(1¼)

16(⁵/₈)

9(3/8)

9(3/8)

9(3/8)

212(8½)

6(¼)
PITCHES

224(9)

LEG
MAKE TWO

Co-ordinates for leg shaping

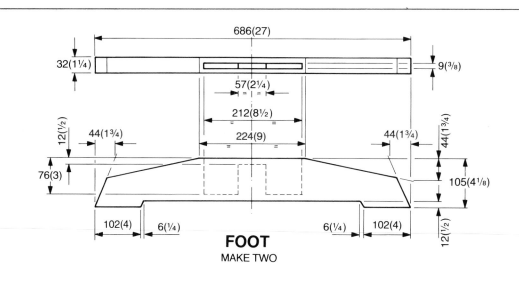

FOOT
MAKE TWO

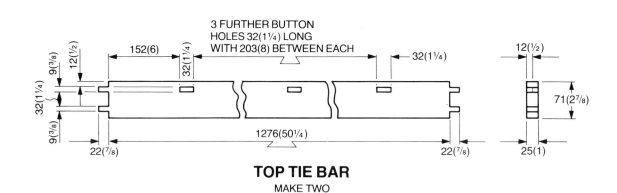

3 FURTHER BUTTON
HOLES 32(1¼) LONG
WITH 203(8) BETWEEN EACH

TOP TIE BAR
MAKE TWO

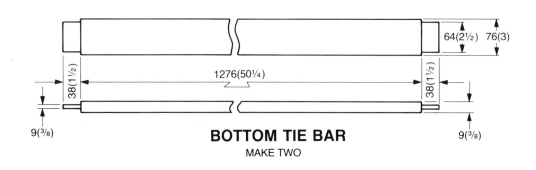

BOTTOM TIE BAR
MAKE TWO

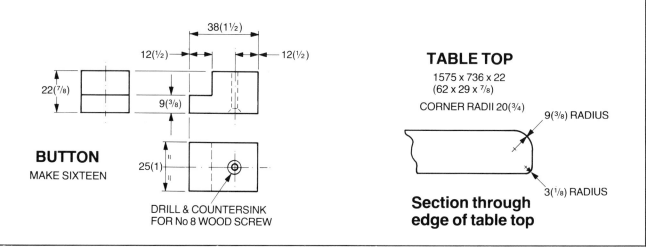

BUTTON
MAKE SIXTEEN

DRILL & COUNTERSINK
FOR No 8 WOOD SCREW

TABLE TOP
1575 x 736 x 22
(62 x 29 x ⅞)

CORNER RADII 20(¾)

9(⅜) RADIUS

3(⅛) RADIUS

**Section through
edge of table top**

12

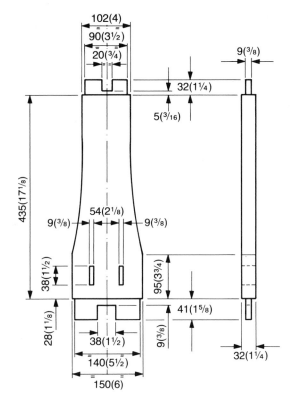

102(4)
90(3½)
20(¾)
9(⅜)
32(1¼)
5(³⁄₁₆)
435(17⅛)
54(2⅛)
9(⅜)
9(⅜)
38(1½)
95(3¾)
28(1⅛)
41(1⅝)
38(1½)
9(⅜)
140(5½)
32(1¼)
150(6)

LEG
MAKE TWO

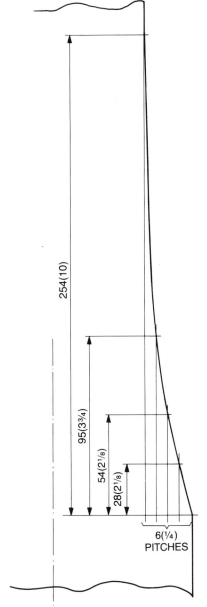

254(10)
95(3¾)
54(2⅛)
28(2⅛)
6(¼)
PITCHES

Co-ordinates for leg shaping

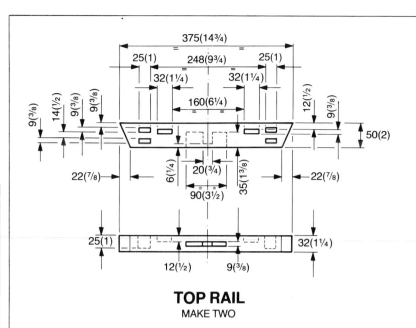

TOP RAIL

MAKE TWO

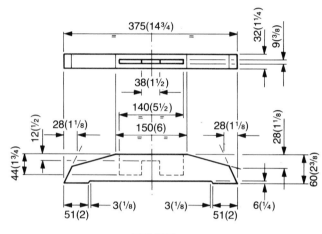

FOOT

MAKE TWO

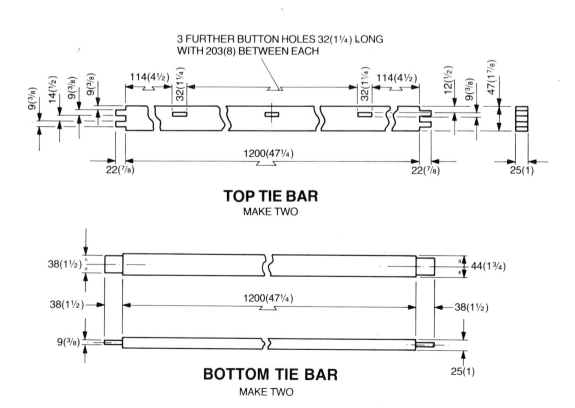

3 FURTHER BUTTON HOLES 32(1¼) LONG
WITH 203(8) BETWEEN EACH

TOP TIE BAR

MAKE TWO

BOTTOM TIE BAR

MAKE TWO

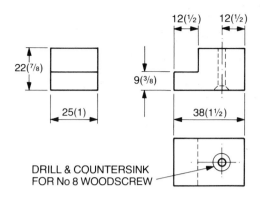

22($^7/_8$)

25(1)

12($^1/_2$)   12($^1/_2$)

9($^3/_8$)

38($1^1/_2$)

DRILL & COUNTERSINK
FOR No 8 WOODSCREW

BUTTON
MAKE FOURTEEN

BENCH TOP

1575 x 380 x 22
(62 x 15 x $^7/_8$)

CORNER RADII 20($^3/_4$)

9($^3/_8$) RADIUS

3($^1/_8$) RADIUS

Section through edge
of bench top

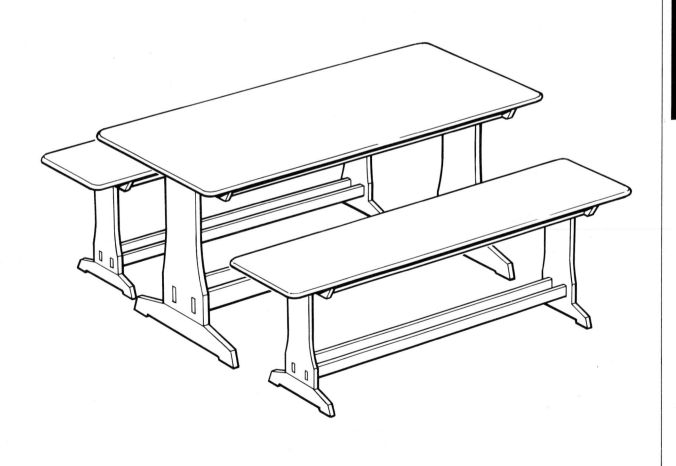

Most of us have some household possession that we treasure. Mine is my rocking chair in which I comfortably contemplate the day's happenings. If you have not tackled any traditional woodwork before, you will not find this the easiest item to make, but determination and a little practice in cutting the mortice and tenon joint will ensure success. I find rocking chairs very rewarding to make, for however difficult the task of construction there is always somewhere to sit when you have finished!

1 The first and most important job is to draw one side frame of the rocking chair full size on a sheet of hardboard. Now lay your prepared pieces of timber on the full-size drawing and transfer onto these the positions of joints, angles, etc. Great accuracy at this stage is essential. Remove the timber from the hardboard and transfer the joint positions, angles, etc. onto your pieces for the other side.

2 You may find it useful to make a template for the rockers before marking them out by drawing the shape full size on card and cutting it out. Then draw round your template straight onto the timber. The long 'toe' at the back of the rocker will prevent the chair tipping over backwards.

3 Now work over all the pencil lines for the joints with a marking knife and cut them out. This is the most difficult part of this project as all the joints are at angles. When cutting the mortice holes you may find it easier to fix the timber in a vice at the required angle, so that you can then cut down in the normal way.

4 Before cutting the mortices on the rockers you will have to cut and shape these. Cut the angle on the top of each rocker and complete the curved upper section with a spokeshave. But don't cut the curve on the bottom yet as the flat base is needed for cramping up.

5 Once all the mortices and tenons have been cut, fit all the joints together and make any necessary adjustments to get a good fit. It is sometimes necessary to trim the shoulders of the tenons. If so, do it very sparingly.

6 Now fit together both the side frames, which should be exactly the same size. If all is well, glue up the frames using four cramps for each one.

7 When these have dried, shape the bottom of the rockers and then place both frames together in a vice. If there is any unevenness work carefully with a very sharp spokeshave to remove the bumps.

8 The side frames are held together by rails that have twin stub tenon joints. Once these joints have been cut, the chair framework can be assembled.

9 The seat of the chair is a mortice and tenon framework on which the chair cushion rests. Fix it to the chair frame by screwing it onto the two cross rails.

10 The back of the chair is unusual in that it provides full support for your back since the spars run vertically. Place all the spars together and mark the shoulder lines. The mortices to take the spars should be staged in a semi-circle. Chamfer off the inside edge of each spar to give a smooth curve for the chair cushion to fit into. Constructing a chair back in this way allows the maker to alter the angle of the back to suit himself. Fix the back in position with two screws at the top and two at the bottom.

11 Cut the arm rests from solid pieces of timber. Shape the inner edges with a spokeshave, and then glue them onto the side frames. Hold the arms on with 'G' cramps while the glue sets.

12 You can either use loose cushions on the chair, which will allow more of the wood to show, or you can have it upholstered as illustrated. (See Useful Addresses, page 140).

Photographs: pages 8, 26-27

■ **CUTTING LIST**

Rocking chair

Main frame			
Rear vertical	2 off	1080 x 38 x 32 mm (42½ x 1½ x 1¼ in)	timber
Front vertical	2 off	539 x 38 x 32 mm (21¼ x 1½ x 1¼ in)	timber
Upper side bar	2 off	686 x 57 x 32 mm (27 x 2¼ x 1¼ in)	timber
Lower side bar	2 off	635 x 89 x 32 mm (25 x 3½ x 1¼ in)	timber
Rocker	2 off	990 x 152 x 32 mm (39 x 6 x 1¼ in)	timber
Front tie bar & seat support	1 off	532 x 57 x 22 mm (20⅞ x 2¼ x ⅞ in)	timber
Rear tie bar	1 off	532 x 89 x 22 mm (20⅞ x 3½ x ⅞ in)	timber
Rear seat support	1 off	492 x 38 x 32 mm (19⅜ x 1½ x 1¼ in)	timber
Arm rest	2 off	727 x 67 x 35 mm (28⅝ x 2⅝ x 1⅜ in)	timber
Rear vertical tie bar	1 off	532 x 38 x 28 mm (20⅞ x 1½ x 1⅛ in)	timber

Back assembly			
Lower rail	1 off	556 x 64 x 28 mm (21⅞ x 2½ x 1⅛ in)	timber
Upper rail	1 off	559 x 64 x 28 mm (22 x 2½ x 1⅛ in)	timber
Spars	11 off	784 x 28 x 22 mm (30⅞ x 1⅛ x ⅞ in)	timber

Seat assembly			
Front & rear cross bar	2 off	435 x 57 x 22 mm (17⅛ x 2¼ x ⅞ in)	timber
Sides	2 off	511 x 60 x 22 mm (20⅛ x 2⅜ x ⅞ in)	timber
Slats	5 off	435 x 28 x 22 mm (17⅛ x 1⅛ x ⅞ in)	timber

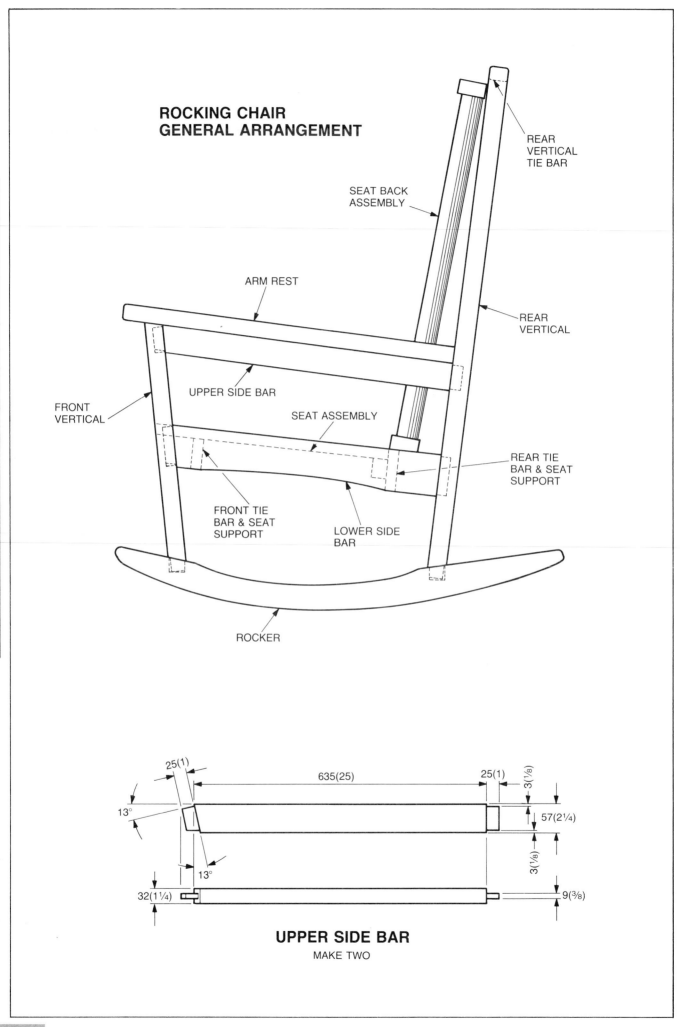

ROCKING CHAIR
GENERAL ARRANGEMENT

REAR
VERTICAL
TIE BAR

SEAT BACK
ASSEMBLY

ARM REST

REAR
VERTICAL

UPPER SIDE BAR

SEAT ASSEMBLY

FRONT
VERTICAL

REAR TIE
BAR & SEAT
SUPPORT

FRONT TIE
BAR & SEAT
SUPPORT

LOWER SIDE
BAR

ROCKER

25(1)

635(25)

25(1)

3(¹⁄₈)

13°

57(2¹⁄₄)

13°

3(¹⁄₈)

32(1¹⁄₄)

9(³⁄₈)

UPPER SIDE BAR
MAKE TWO

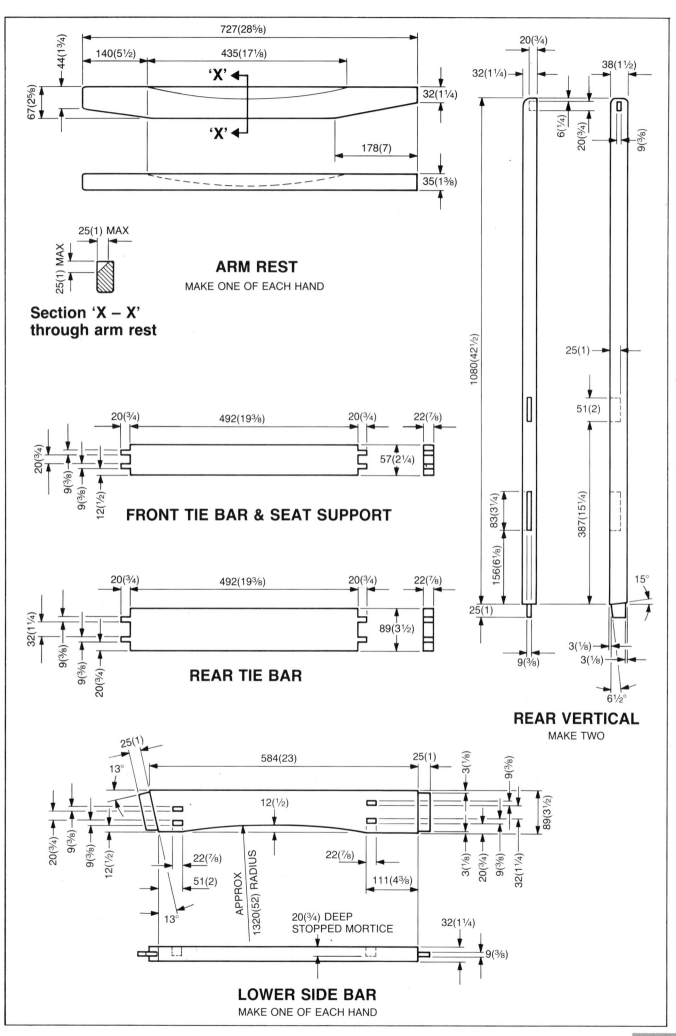

ARM REST
MAKE ONE OF EACH HAND

**Section 'X – X'
through arm rest**

FRONT TIE BAR & SEAT SUPPORT

REAR TIE BAR

REAR VERTICAL
MAKE TWO

LOWER SIDE BAR
MAKE ONE OF EACH HAND

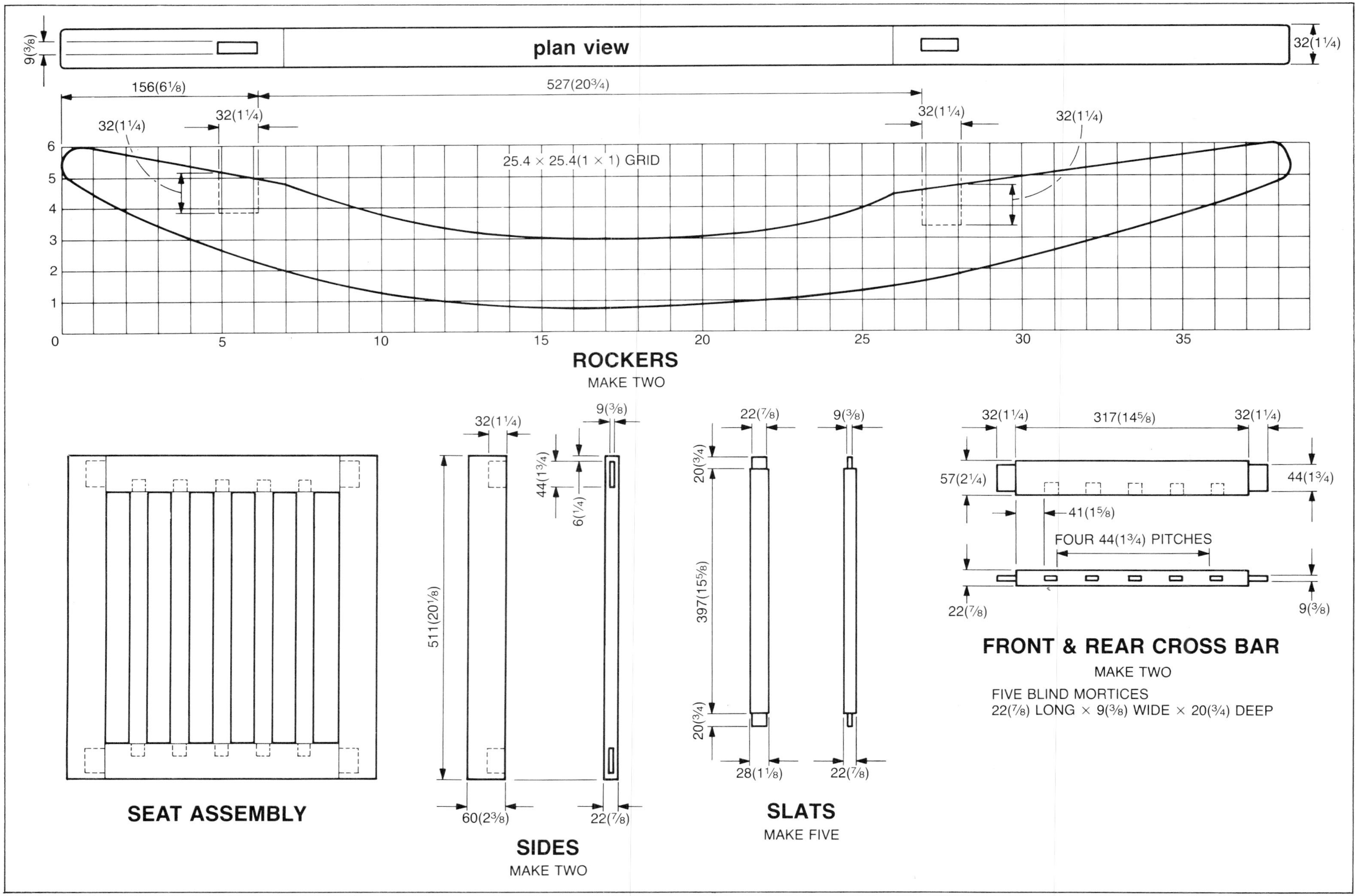
plan view
9(3/8)
32(1¼)
156(6⅛)
527(20¾)
32(1¼)
32(1¼)
32(1¼)
32(1¼)
25.4 × 25.4(1 × 1) GRID
0
5
10
15
20
25
30
35
1
2
3
4
5
6
ROCKERS
MAKE TWO
SEAT ASSEMBLY
32(1¼)
511(20⅛)
60(2⅜)
9(3/8)
44(1¾)
6(¼)
22(⅞)
SIDES
MAKE TWO
22(⅞)
20(¾)
397(15⅝)
20(¾)
28(1⅛)
9(3/8)
22(⅞)
SLATS
MAKE FIVE
32(1¼)
317(14⅝)
32(1¼)
57(2¼)
44(1¾)
41(1⅝)
FOUR 44(1¾) PITCHES
22(⅞)
9(3/8)
FRONT & REAR CROSS BAR
MAKE TWO
FIVE BLIND MORTICES
22(⅞) LONG × 9(⅜) WIDE × 20(¾) DEEP

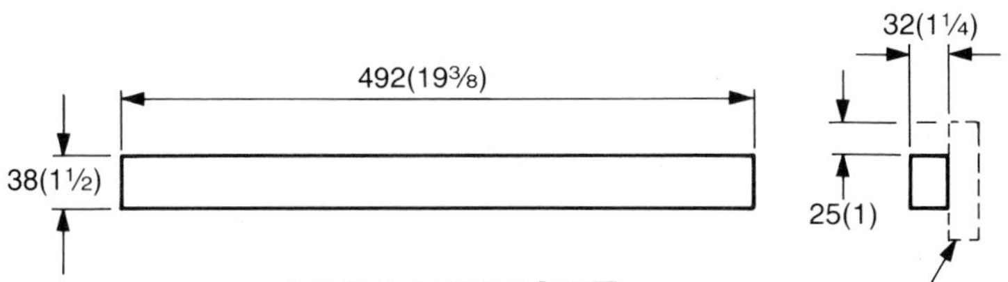
492(19 3/8)
38(1 1/2)
32(1 1/4)
25(1)
REAR TIE BAR

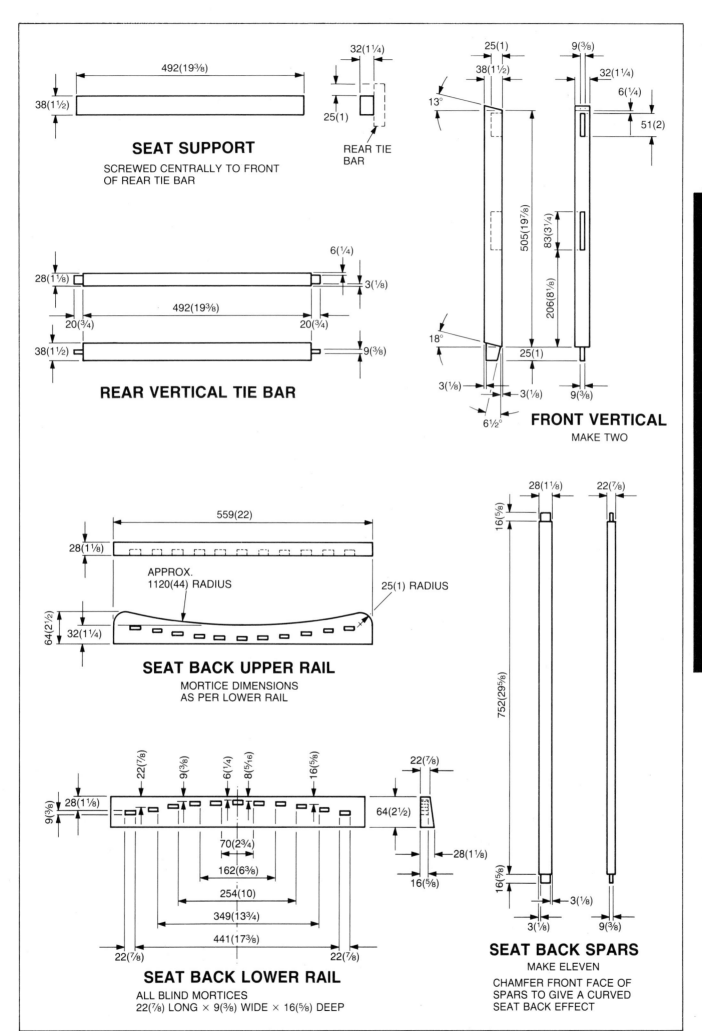

SEAT SUPPORT

SCREWED CENTRALLY TO FRONT OF REAR TIE BAR

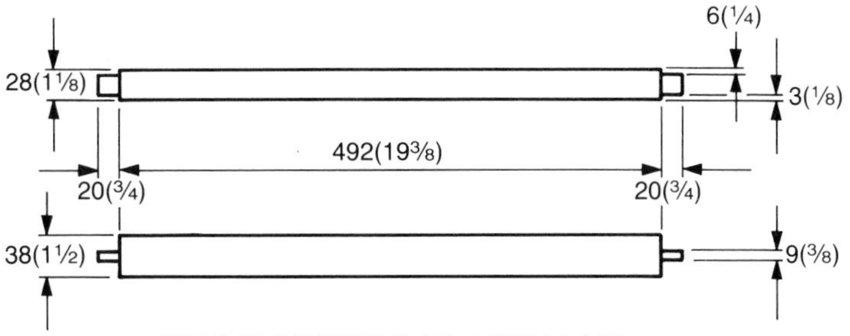
6(1/4)
28(1 1/8)
3(1/8)
492(19 3/8)
20(3/4)
20(3/4)
38(1 1/2)
9(3/8)

REAR VERTICAL TIE BAR

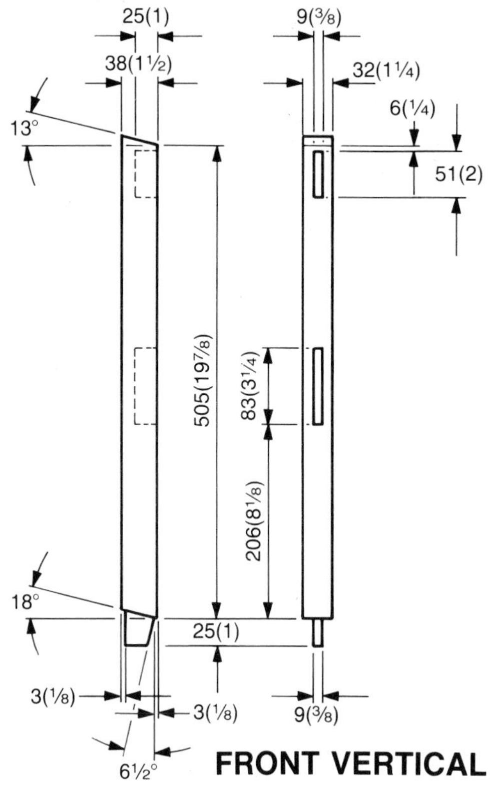
25(1)
38(1 1/2)
9(3/8)
32(1 1/4)
6(1/4)
51(2)
13°
505(19 7/8)
83(3 1/4)
206(8 1/8)
18°
25(1)
3(1/8)
3(1/8)
9(3/8)
6 1/2°

FRONT VERTICAL

MAKE TWO

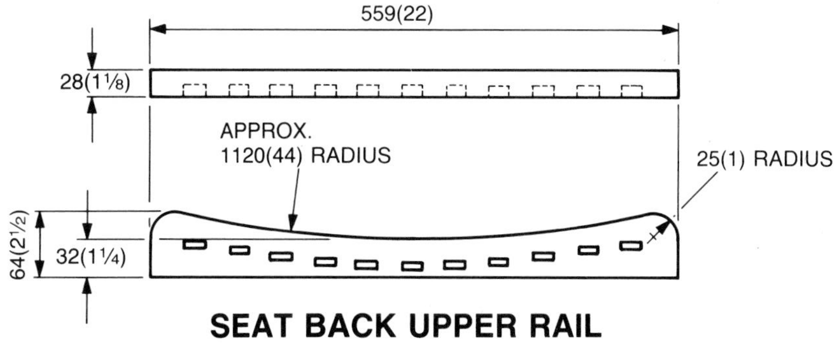
559(22)
28(1 1/8)
APPROX.
1120(44) RADIUS
25(1) RADIUS
64(2 1/2)
32(1 1/4)

SEAT BACK UPPER RAIL

MORTICE DIMENSIONS AS PER LOWER RAIL

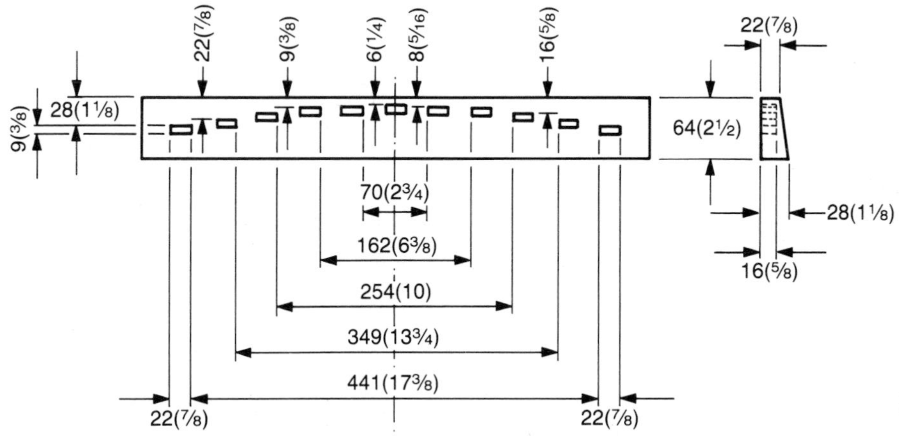
22(7/8)
9(3/8)
6(1/4)
8(5/16)
16(5/8)
22(7/8)
9(3/8)
28(1 1/8)
64(2 1/2)
28(1 1/8)
16(5/8)
70(2 3/4)
162(6 3/8)
254(10)
349(13 3/4)
441(17 3/8)
22(7/8)
22(7/8)

SEAT BACK LOWER RAIL

ALL BLIND MORTICES
22(7/8) LONG × 9(3/8) WIDE × 16(5/8) DEEP

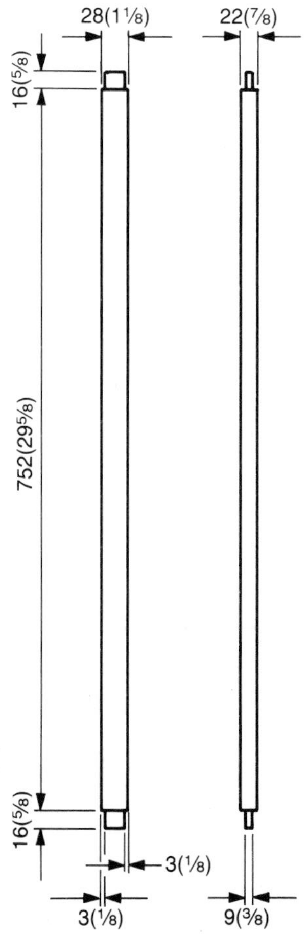
28(1 1/8)
22(7/8)
16(5/8)
752(29 5/8)
16(5/8)
3(1/8)
3(1/8)
9(3/8)

SEAT BACK SPARS

MAKE ELEVEN

CHAMFER FRONT FACE OF SPARS TO GIVE A CURVED SEAT BACK EFFECT

I felt it was essential when designing these units that you should be able to use the full width of the shelves for books and video tapes and not get tangled up with jointing blocks in the corners. I therefore decided to use wooden dowels to joint the pieces together. The doors for the small book case and video and record player units are all fitted with piano hinge and stand 'proud' of the carcass units. I suggest you use man-made board for these units and if you have never worked with this before you should turn to page 135 for some useful advice. Some boards come in different lengths and widths so it's worth acquainting yourself with what is available.

1   Once you have chosen your board, careful marking out is essential. If you don't mark out the board accurately at the very beginning then nothing will fit together at a later stage. Similarly, in all the particular units I have designed, cutting accurately and squarely is essential. So it is a good idea to make yourself a wooden T-square to use for marking accurately across the boards. You should also allow for the width of the saw cut. Once you have 'pencilled in' all the pieces, double-check all your dimensions.

2   Cutting man-made boards can in some ways be more difficult than cutting traditional board and unless you are prepared with the correct blades you will end up with a horrible shattered mess. Once again you should turn to page 135 for some hints to help you avoid this. As with the marking-out stage it is essential that you cut accurately and squarely. It is also absolutely essential to support the work well before you start cutting. *Planning* the cutting operation is an essential part of the job.

I actually prefer to cut the unit pieces a fraction larger than required and then plane them off — just to be on the safe side. The doors for the book case, video and record player units, and also the front of the drawer, however, should be cut a fraction smaller as the iron-on veneer will add to their dimensions all round.

3   Once the boards have been cut to size check pieces for squareness and mark the face side and face edge marks in pencil. Dowel jointing is an easy operation providing that you have a good dowling jig. The Record dowling jig is ideal for these jobs as it has extension bars and once the technique of using it has been mastered, it is an invaluable piece of equipment for any workshop. You must always work from the face side or face edge marks on all the pieces, otherwise the dowels will not line up when you try to assemble the unit. Mark out on the boards every dowel position in pencil, checking that everything lines up before drilling any holes.

4   Cut to length all the dowels you will need. Cut the dowels a little shorter than the combined depth of the two holes and scribe a line along their length. This scribed line allows glue to squeeze out at the sides and prevents it being trapped at the bottom of the dowel hole.

5   Now make up the 'carcasses'. I found when doing this that it was simpler to glue all the dowels into the top, bottom and shelf sections first. While the glue was setting I fitted a countersink in the drill and very slightly countersunk all the other holes the dowels had to go into. This helps tremendously when assembling and gives the dowels a 'start' into each of the holes. Cramps must be fitted to pull all the joints up tight and the glue left overnight to set.

6   Veneer the edges of the carcasses and all round the doors and drawer unit. Iron-on veneer is best bought at the same time as you buy the board to ensure that you get a good colour match. There is no need to feel apprehensive about this job — it really isn't difficult. Just place the strip of veneer on the edge of the piece of board, allowing a tiny overlap at each end, and work slowly along it with a warm iron. It is a good idea to practise this using scrap pieces first to make sure that the iron temperature is right and to help you get used to the technique. Allow the glue to cool down before trimming off the surplus. The Stanley knife is an ideal tool for this job. Once the surplus veneer has been cut off, glasspaper the edge to remove any traces of roughness.

7   Now hang the doors. In traditional carpentry door hinges are recessed, but this is not necessary if you use piano hinge. Piano hinge can be bought in long lengths from ironmongers and D.I.Y. shops, and this is definitely the most economical way to buy hinges. First cut the appropriate length of hinge and screw the hinge onto the cabinet. Brass cabinet stays should now be attached and, while you are buying these, look at the variety of brass handles, knobs etc that are available. All the door units should be fitted in this way.

8   The drawer for the record player unit is made by dowling the four pieces of board together. To make the drawer slide easily and smoothly I bought a piece of 'L' section plastic channel and glued it onto the bottom of the drawer unit. The 'L' shaped section is best as it provides friction-free movement on both sides and bottom. The inside of the drawer I fitted with dividers to house standard cassette tapes.

9   All the backs of the units are plywood and are screwed in place. Plastic insets can be fitted to allow for the adjustable shelf unit; these are available from most D.I.Y. shops. Before applying any varnish finishes, give all the units a good glasspapering all over.

Photographs: opposite

■ CUTTING LISTS

Wide bookcase

Side	2 off	1220 x 254 x 20 mm (48 x 10 x ¾ in)	veneered blockboard
Top and fixed shelves	4 off	806 x 254 x 20 mm (31¾ x 10 x ¾ in)	veneered blockboard
Adjustable shelves	as required	806 x 254 x 20 mm (31¾ x 10 x ¾ in)	veneered blockboard
Kicking strip	1 off	806 x 89 x 20 mm (31¾ x 3½ x ¾ in)	veneered blockboard
Back	1 off	1220 x 846 x 6 mm (48 x 33¼ x ¼ in)	mahogany-faced plywood

Ancillaries

	9 mm (⅜ in) diam dowelling x 762 mm (30 in) long	
2 off	Plastic corner blocks	
as required	Plastic shelf supports	

Narrow bookcase

Side	2 off	1220 x 254 x 20 mm (48 x 10 x ¾ in)	veneered blockboard
Top and fixed shelves	4 off	578 x 254 x 20 mm (22¾ x 10 x ¾ in)	veneered blockboard
Adjustable shelves	as required	578 x 254 x 20 mm (22¾ x 10 x ¾ in)	veneered blockboard
Kicking strip	1 off	578 x 89 x 20 mm (22¾ x 3½ x ¾ in)	veneered blockboard
Door	1 off	616 x 356 x 20 mm (24¼ x 14 x ¾ in)	veneered blockboard
Back	1 off	1220 x 616 x 6 mm (48 x 24¼ x ¼ in)	mahogany-faced plywood

Ancillaries

	9 mm (⅜ in) diam dowelling x 762 mm (30 in) long
1 off	25 x 25 mm (1 x 1 in) x 57 mm (22½ in) long piano hinge
1 off	Handle
1 off	Spring-loaded ball catch
1 off	Brass door stay
2 off	Plastic corner blocks
as required	Plastic shelf supports

Video centre

Side	2 off	578 x 400 x 20 mm (22¾ x 15¾ x ¾ in)	veneered blockboard
Top and shelves	3 off	482 x 400 x 20 mm (19 x 15¾ x ¾ in)	veneered blockboard
Kicking strip	1 off	482 x 89 x 20 mm (19 x 3½ x ¾ in)	veneered blockboard
Door	1 off	522 x 254 x 20 mm (20½ x 10 x ¾ in)	veneered blockboard
Back	1 off	578 x 522 x 6 mm (22¾ x 20½ x ¼ in)	mahogany-faced plywood

Ancillaries

	9 mm (⅜ in) diam dowelling x 610 mm (24 in) long
1 off	25 x 25 mm (1 x 1 in) x 476 mm (18¾ in) long piano hinge
1 off	Handle
1 off	Spring-loaded ball catch
1 off	Brass door stay
2 off	Plastic corner blocks

Record player and cassette storage unit

Side	2 off	578 x 400 x 20 mm (22¾ x 15¾ x ¾ in)	veneered blockboard
Top and shelves	3 off	762 x 400 x 20 mm (30 x 15¾ x ¾ in)	veneered blockboard
Kicking strip	1 off	762 x 89 x 20 mm (30 x 3½ x ¾ in)	veneered blockboard
Dividers	2 off	335 x 305 x 20 mm (13¼ x 12 x ¾ in)	veneered blockboard
Door	1 off	800 x 346 x 20 mm (31½ x 13⅝ x ¾ in)	veneered blockboard
Back	1 off	800 x 578 x 6 mm (31½ x 22¾ x ¼ in)	mahogany-faced plywood
Drawer			
Front	1 off	800 x 121 x 20 mm (31½ x 4¾ x ¾ in)	veneered blockboard
Side and divider	6 off	372 x 95 x 20 mm (14¾ x 3¾ x ¾ in)	veneered blockboard
Back	1 off	755 x 95 x 20 mm (29¾ x 3¾ x ¾ in)	veneered blockboard
Divider	2 off	179 x 95 x 20 mm (7¼ x 3¾ x ¾ in)	veneered blockboard
Bottom	1 off	715 x 372 x 6 mm (28¼ x 14¾ x ¼ in)	mahogany-faced plywood
Bottom support	make from	2200 x 9 x 9 mm (87 x ⅜ x ⅜ in)	timber

Ancillaries

	9 mm (⅜ in) diam dowelling x 610 mm (24 in) long
1 off	25 x 25 mm (1 x 1 in) x 755 mm (29¾ in) long piano hinge

CONTINUED ►

NEVER TRUST
A SMILING CAT!

LIFE IS
ONE BIG THRILL
AFTER ANOTHER!

BUNK BED COMPLEX

PAGE 51

COMPUTER WORKSTATION
PAGE 35

2 off	25 x 25 mm (1 x 1) x 400 mm (15¾ in) plastic angle section
4 off	Handles
1 off	Spring-loaded ball catch
1 off	Brass door stay
2 off	Plastic corner blocks

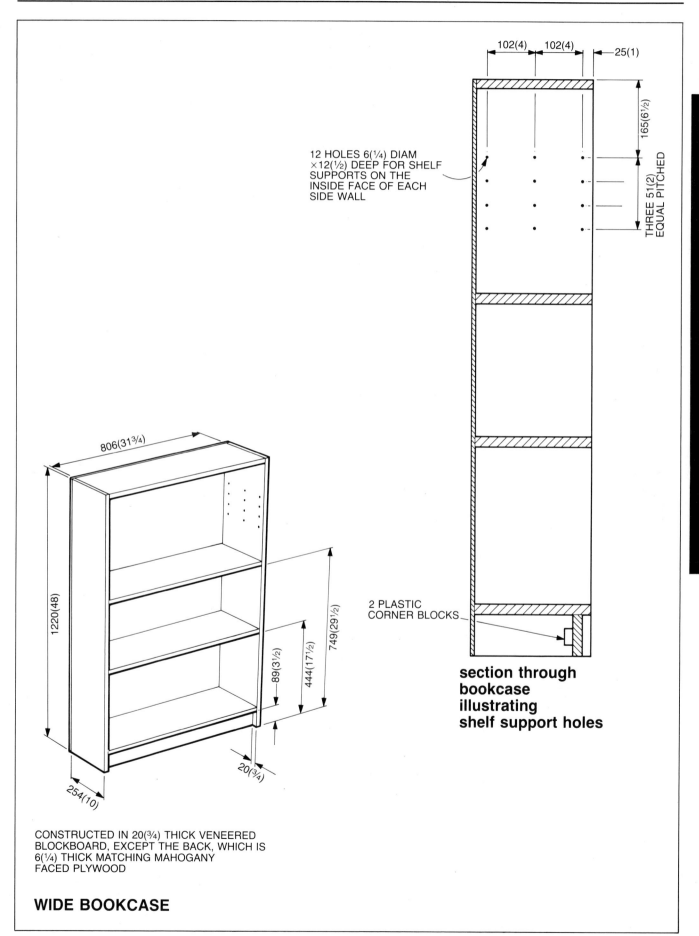

102(4) 102(4) 25(1)

165(6½)

THREE 51(2)
EQUAL PITCHED

12 HOLES 6(¼) DIAM
×12(½) DEEP FOR SHELF
SUPPORTS ON THE
INSIDE FACE OF EACH
SIDE WALL

2 PLASTIC
CORNER BLOCKS

**section through
bookcase
illustrating
shelf support holes**

806(31¾)

1220(48)

749(29½)

444(17½)

89(3½)

20(¾)

254(10)

CONSTRUCTED IN 20(¾) THICK VENEERED
BLOCKBOARD, EXCEPT THE BACK, WHICH IS
6(¼) THICK MATCHING MAHOGANY
FACED PLYWOOD

WIDE BOOKCASE

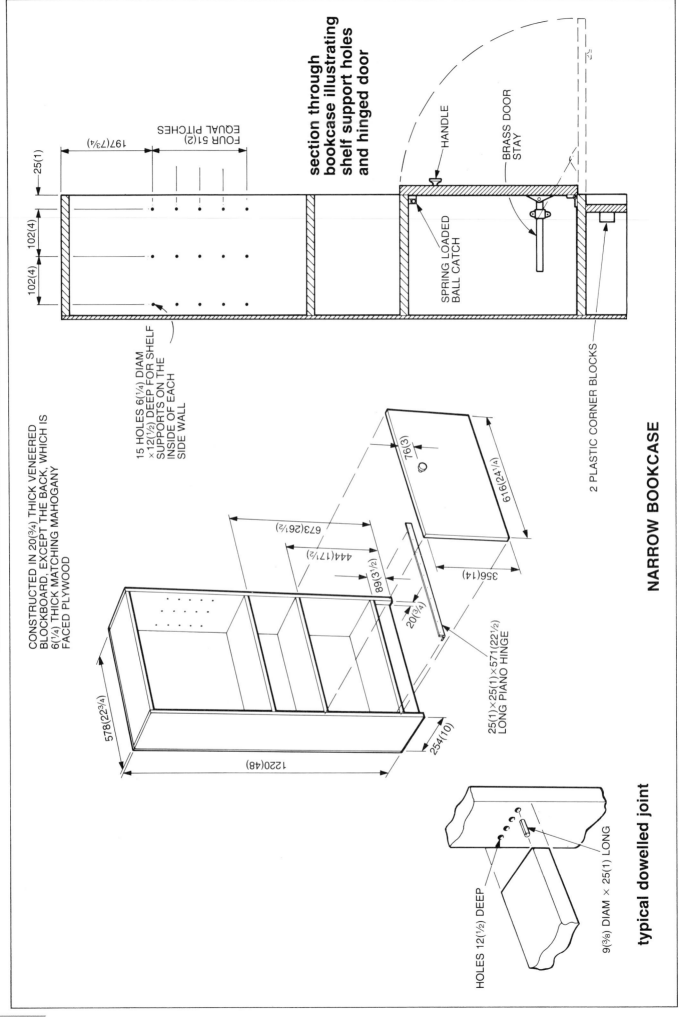

section through bookcase illustrating shelf support holes and hinged door

HANDLE

BRASS DOOR STAY

SPRING LOADED BALL CATCH

2 PLASTIC CORNER BLOCKS

25(1)

197(7¾)

FOUR 51(2) EQUAL PITCHES

102(4)

102(4)

15 HOLES 6(¼) DIAM × 12(½) DEEP FOR SHELF SUPPORTS ON THE INSIDE OF EACH SIDE WALL

CONSTRUCTED IN 20(¾) THICK VENEERED BLOCKBOARD, EXCEPT THE BACK, WHICH IS 6(¼) THICK MATCHING MAHOGANY FACED PLYWOOD

76(3)

616(24¼)

356(14)

673(26½)

444(17½)

89(3½)

20(¾)

25(1)×25(1)×571(22½) LONG PIANO HINGE

578(22¾)

254(10)

1220(48)

NARROW BOOKCASE

HOLES 12(½) DEEP

9(⅜) DIAM × 25(1) LONG

typical dowelled joint

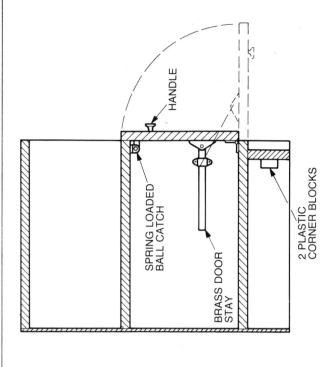

HANDLE

SPRING LOADED
BALL CATCH

BRASS DOOR
STAY

2 PLASTIC
CORNER BLOCKS

**section through
unit illustrating
door fixing and
fitments**

CONSTRUCTED IN 20(¾) THICK VENEERED
BLOCKBOARD, EXCEPT THE BACK, WHICH IS
6(¼) THICK MATCHING MAHOGANY
FACED PLYWOOD

VIDEO CENTRE

64(2½)

522(20½)

254(10)

343(13½)

89(3½)

20(¾)

482(19)

400(15¾)

578(22¾)

25(1)×25(1)×476(18¾)
LONG PIANO HINGE

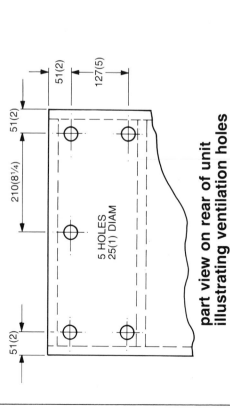

51(2)

127(5)

51(2)

51(2)

210(8¼)

5 HOLES
25(1) DIAM

51(2)

**part view on rear of unit
illustrating ventilation holes
and recorder cable entry hole.**

RECORD PLAYER AND CASSETTE STORAGE UNIT

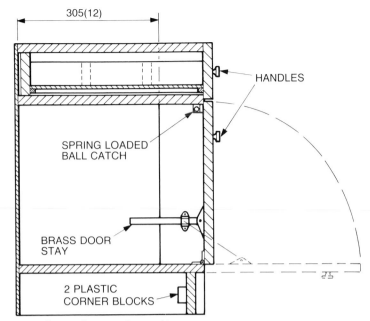

305(12)

HANDLES

SPRING LOADED
BALL CATCH

BRASS DOOR
STAY

2 PLASTIC
CORNER BLOCKS

**section through unit
illustrating dividing wall,
drawer layout and door fixing
and fitments**

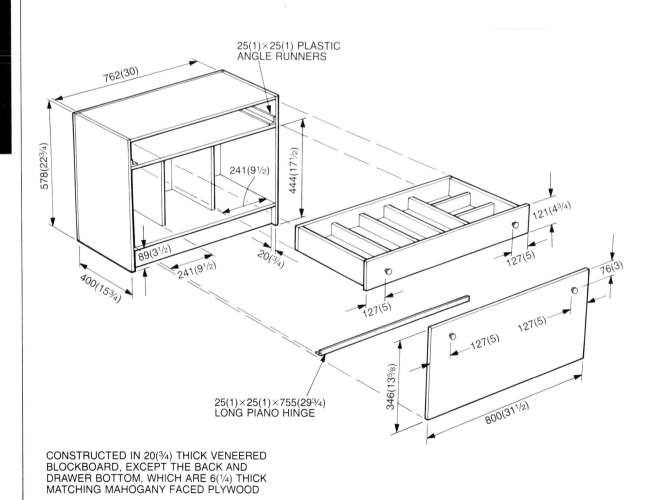

25(1)×25(1) PLASTIC
ANGLE RUNNERS

762(30)

578(22³⁄₄)

444(17¹⁄₂)

241(9¹⁄₂)

89(3¹⁄₂)

20(³⁄₄)

241(9¹⁄₂)

400(15³⁄₄)

121(4³⁄₄)

127(5)

127(5)

76(3)

127(5)

127(5)

127(5)

346(13⁵⁄₈)

25(1)×25(1)×755(29³⁄₄)
LONG PIANO HINGE

800(31¹⁄₂)

CONSTRUCTED IN 20(³⁄₄) THICK VENEERED
BLOCKBOARD, EXCEPT THE BACK AND
DRAWER BOTTOM, WHICH ARE 6(¹⁄₄) THICK
MATCHING MAHOGANY FACED PLYWOOD

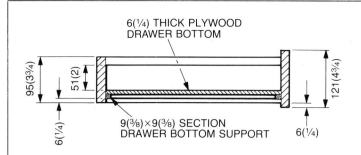

6(¼) THICK PLYWOOD
DRAWER BOTTOM

95(3¾)

51(2)

121(4¾)

9(⅜)×9(⅜) SECTION
DRAWER BOTTOM SUPPORT

6(¼)

6(¼)

section through drawer

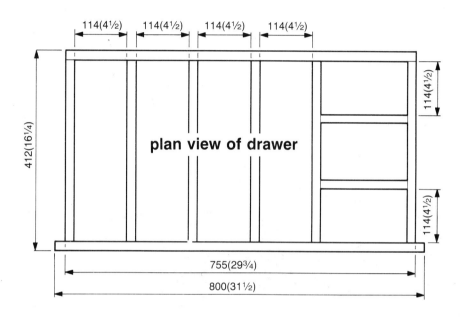

114(4½)   114(4½)   114(4½)   114(4½)

114(4½)

412(16¼)

plan view of drawer

114(4½)

755(29¾)

800(31½)

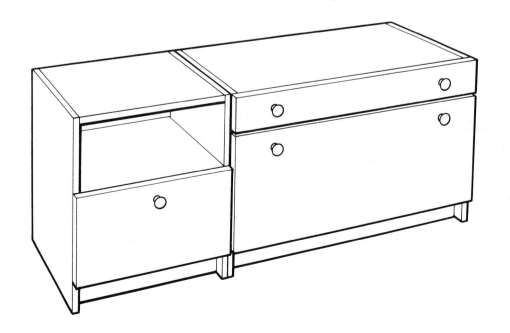

Once you have recovered from the initial excitement of unpacking and assembling your computer, not many minutes will pass before you are wondering where to put it, and what piece of spare furniture is available to house it and all its extras. The only answer is to build a purpose-built desk. Now many boffins (high tech types) will hold up their hands (soldering irons) in horror when faced with the humble task of building a desk for themselves (very low tech). So if attempting such a project seems to you rather daunting, rest assured that I have avoided using any special woodworking skills in designing and making this desk. All that is necessary to make a really professional-looking job is the ability to cut boards squarely – no traditional joints are used throughout the entire construction.

The storage compartments in this design can be varied to meet individual needs. In my particular design I decided to have my printer on the right-hand side (sometimes this is determined for you by the lead length – so check!). The paper is stored in the compartment and is fed up to the printer by a slot cut in the top of the desk. The compartment is divided by a shelf which I felt should be adjustable for height. In the top of this compartment I also fitted a sliding work surface. This does not go back to the full depth of the desk as otherwise it would interfere with the paper being fed to the printer.

The left-hand storage compartment has a drawer in the top and a cupboard below with yet another shelf adjustable for height. This compartment need not be so wide as the other as its purpose is the storage of books, floppy discs, tapes, etc. The drawer unit is constructed from simple, glued butt joints and runs smoothly on plastic channels. The space between the two compartments has a sliding work surface supported entirely on plastic channel. To prevent this shelf from being pulled out completely a length of cord is attached to the back of the desk and the shelf.

Storage compartments

1   It is absolutely essential to mark the storage compartments out accurately, and for this purpose I used a wooden T–square. Cutting out must be undertaken with the same care, otherwise extreme difficulty will be experienced when you try to assemble the various units. If you don't possess an electrically powered circular saw then it is worth considering buying or hiring one as this tool will make things far quicker and simpler.

2   Once the compartment sides, top, bottom and back have been cut out, assemble dry (i.e. without glue) and check that things fit. If they don't you will have to work very carefully on the edges with a hand plane. Only remove a very little at a time, be patient and you will get it to fit.

3   The pieces for both compartments are not jointed in any way and rely entirely on glue and wood screws. However it is essential to have a set of cramps to hold the pieces together while drilling the necessary pilot holes for the screws and once this has been done to provide extra cramping pressure while the glue sets. The ideal cramp for this purpose is lighter in weight than the traditional carpenter's sash cramps and has a small nylon pad fixed over the steel cramp head. Without cramps you would find it almost impossible to cramp, glue and screw the compartments together.

4   For this particular project I did not countersink the screw heads but used cup washers. The advantage of these is that they put extra pressure on the side of the panel and make a feature of the screw rather than trying to hide the screw head. Both compartments are made in this way.

Leg units

1   For the legs you will need to obtain some aluminium tube. This is available in a variety of sizes and a fairly large diameter is necessary to give stability. Cut and shape up the supports into which the tubing will fit. These are exactly the same dimensions for both top and bottom.

2   Now, using a centre bit in an electric drill, bore holes in the supports to take the tube. It is essential to have the drill fixed in a drill stand for this as otherwise you will find great difficulty in drilling the holes at a 90° angle to the base.

3   While the drill is in the stand, bore holes in the top supports to take the bolts that fix the leg units onto the bottom of the desk. First drill a large counter bore hole (the centre bit you used for the tube is probably ideal). This hole will allow you to fit a ring spanner or socket over the end of the nut. Now change the centre bit to one that fits the diameter of the coach bolt you are using and finish drilling the holes.

4   Assemble the aluminium tube into the wooden supports and check that all fits well and that the aluminium tube has been cut to the right length. I polished the tube before gluing, but made certain that no traces of polish were left on the ends of the tube I was going to glue into the wooden supports. Epoxy resin is best for bonding aluminium to wood, and once this has been done, lightly cramp the supports to the tube for about 20 minutes.

Assembling the desk

1   Once the leg units have been finished they can be bolted onto the bottoms of the storage compartments. The head of the bolt is kept inside the compartment, the nut being fixed and tightened in the counterbored hole in the leg support.

2   Now both compartments have to be fixed together with a back piece. The back is screwed on using cup washers and screws. It is essential to check with a spirit level that both compartments being joined are at 90° to the ground before finally tightening up all the screws. With this part of the operation complete the desk is now taking shape.

3   The next items to be fitted are the plastic drawer and work shelf runners. Now there are a large variety of thicknesses and shapes of plastic runner

available. I found the simplest way to check that I was buying what I wanted was to take offcuts of plywood to the D.I.Y. store so that I could 'offer up' the wood to the plastic channel and get it right first time. I found that as a general rule the most suitable plastic section for the drawer runners was an 'L' section. The sliding work surfaces require the strongest 'U' section available, and if they have provision for screws in the bottom of the 'U' section this is the most suitable of all. The plastic channel will have to take quite a weight, especially when the shelf is being worked on so I feel it best to glue and screw the plastic sections in place. The glue for this particular job should be an impact adhesive. Apply impact adhesive to both sides of the sections you want to fix. Leave both pieces for approximately 10 minutes until the surfaces feel dry. It is vital that you position both pieces exactly before you fix them together. Now fix the screws into the channel making sure that you have countersunk the screw heads.

4 Traditionally the cabinet maker had a chance to display his skills when he came to making the drawers. However this drawer unit is constructed using glue and plastic corner blocks – wood engineering! The plastic corner blocks are easy to use and also give you an accurate 90° angle when screwing the second side on. The bottom is made from the same thickness material as the sides and fitted inside. Gluing the drawer unit together as well makes it very strong, even if the old cabinet maker would wring his hands in despair!

It is always a good idea to leave the drawer unit a little larger than the drawer opening, as you can always plane and glasspaper a little off, but you can't put it on as easily. The drawer unit will slide very smoothly in the compartment if fitted like this.

5 Provision should be made at this stage of construction for the adjustable shelf units in each compartment. Small plastic 'buttons' are available which can be attached to the sides of the compartment to take the shelf unit. These are best attached by a small screw. The easiest method of positioning them is to mark a line with a set square at both back and front of the compartment. Now, measuring from the top, put a pencil mark on the line where you want the screw holding the plastic button to go. Repeat this four times and you will find that, after fixing the buttons, the shelf unit will not wobble when in position.

6 The hinged doors on both compartments are fitted at the bottom with piano hinge. This is available in long lengths and has to be cut to the right length with a small hack-saw. One of the advantages of using a piano hinge is that you don't have to recess the hinge into the cabinet. Brass stays are fitted to support the hinged doors when they are open. The doors are kept closed by ball catches which are available in a range of sizes and shapes. The compartment housing the paper supply for the printer needs the ball catch fitted on the side in the top right hand corner. It is not possible to fit the catch at the top in the conventional place as the sliding working surface is there.

■ Desk top

Once all the insides of the compartments are finished it's time to make the desk top. I decided to use a contrasting wood for the top, but it's entirely a matter of choice.

1 It is necessary to cut a slot in the top to allow the paper to feed from below into the printer. The slot can be cut with a keyhole saw or, if you have one, a jig-saw. After cutting the slot, fit plastic channel in place to prevent any snagging of the paper as it is fed into the printer.

2 Attach the desk top to the compartments below with screws. Now this was one of the places I did not want the screw head to show, so I used a plug cutter (available from all good tool shops). This cuts out a circular plug of wood which is then glued over the head of the screw. The screw must therefore fit into a counterbore hole exactly the same size as the wood plug, so counter sinks and plug cutters are usually sold as a matching pair.

3 Now provision has to be made on the top of the desk for various pieces of equipment. I made a very simple 'tray' which holds the monitor above the keyboard. The tray also makes provision for one interface and the Telecom equipment. The printer is mounted on top of the tray.

Throughout this whole project I used iron-on veneer edging which I found very simple to use and most effective. After ironing on, the excess is trimmed off with a Stanley knife. Final finishing is done with a fine glasspaper.

■ Stool

It seems nowadays that children are more conversant with computers than many adults. I therefore felt it important to make an adjustable stool so that all ages and heights could make themselves comfortable. Study the drawings carefully and you will see that the construction is very simple.

1 Fix one block of the foot assembly and the main leg in the vice together and screw another block onto the first one, using the centre leg as a positioning guide. Repeat this procedure with the other two blocks. Now fix together the two jointed sections. Plane a few fine shavings off the centre leg to get it to fit well into the middle of the finished foot assembly.

2 Drill holes for the adjustable peg, one in the foot assembly and the others in the centre leg. I found it easier to drill the hole right through the foot assembly first, then fit the centre leg and, using the existing hole as a guide, drill the holes in the centre leg at various heights.

3 The seat is held in place by four pieces of wood which mirror the foot assembly unit. Cut the circular seat out with a jig-saw. Before attaching it to the top support blocks, fix it in the vice and cut a length of veneer that will go round the seat. The veneer goes on quite well using a hot iron but a little more care is necessary to get the adhesive to stick. I found it helpful to press the veneer on firmly with my fingers after I had used the iron on it and wait a very short time until the glue had cooled off. The veneer has shown no signs of peeling off.

4 Now fix the blocks to the support beneath with screws. Once again I used the plug cutter and counterbored the screw head. The plugs were glued over the screw heads and any roughness glasspapered off.

5 The peg for adjusting the stool height is a standard piece of ramin dowel rod fitted with a square knob to give the fingers a good grip.

6 The desk and stool should be finished with three coats of polyurethane varnish.

Photographs: pages 28, 34

■ CUTTING LIST

Computer desk

Top	1 off	1143 x 559 x 12 mm (45 x 22 x ½ in)	veneered plywood

Left hand cupboard

Rear	1 off	559 x 254 x 20 mm (22 x 10 x ¾ in)	veneered blockboard
Side	2 off	559 x 432 x 20 mm (22 x 17 x ¾ in)	veneered blockboard
Shelf	2 off	412 x 254 x 20 mm (16¼ x 10 x ¾ in)	veneered blockboard
Top bar	1 off	254 x 114 x 20 mm (10 x 4½ x ¾ in)	veneered blockboard
Door	1 off	356 x 292 x 20 mm (14 x 11½ x ¾ in)	veneered blockboard
Drawer rear	1 off	208 x 146 x 20 mm (8¼ x 5¾ x ¾ in)	veneered blockboard
Drawer side	2 off	406 x 146 x 20 mm (16 x 5¾ x ¾ in)	veneered blockboard
Drawer base	1 off	386 x 208 x 20 mm (15¼ x 8¼ x ¾ in)	veneered blockboard
Drawer front	1 off	292 x 178 x 20 mm (11½ x 7 x ¾ in)	veneered blockboard
Drawer backstop	1 off	102 x 51 x 12 mm (4 x 2 x ½ in)	plywood
Handle	2 off	286 x 32 x 22 mm (11¼ x 1¼ x ⅞ in)	timber
Adjustable shelf	1 off	406 x 250 x 20 mm (16 x 9⅞ x ¾ in)	veneered blockboard

Right hand cupboard

Rear	1 off	340 x 336 x 20 mm (13⅜ x 13¼ x ¾ in)	veneered blockboard
Side	2 off	533 x 340 x 20 mm (21 x 13⅜ x ¾ in)	veneered blockboard
Shelf	1 off	437 x 336 x 20 mm (17¼ x 13¼ x ¾ in)	veneered blockboard
Top bar front	1 off	336 x 114 x 20 mm (13¼ x 4½ x ¾ in)	veneered blockboard
Top bar rear	1 off	336 x 44 x 20 mm (13¼ x 1¾ x ¾ in)	veneered blockboard
Door	1 off	375 x 279 x 20 mm (14¾ x 11 x ¾ in)	veneered blockboard
Handle	1 off	368 x 32 x 22 mm (14½ x 1¾ x ⅞ in)	timber
Sliding panel	1 off	381 x 330 x 20 mm (15 x 13 x ¾ in)	veneered blockboard
	1 off	279 x 32 x 20 mm (11 x 1¼ x ¾ in)	timber
	1 off	330 x 12 x 12 mm (13 x ½ x ½ in)	timber
Adjustable shelf	1 off	457 x 333 x 12 mm (18 x 13⅛ x ½ in)	veneered plywood

Leg assembly

Head and foot block	4 off	400 x 70 x 41 mm (15¾ x 2¾ x 1⅝ in)	timber

Centre section

Sliding panel	1 off	540 x 419 x 12 mm (21¼ x 16½ x ½ in)	plywood
	1 off	375 x 32 x 22 mm (14¾ x 1¼ x ⅞ in)	timber

Monitor tray

Top	1 off	902 x 387 x 20 mm (35½ x 15¼ x ¾ in)	veneered blockboard
Legs	2 off	387 x 102 x 20 mm (15¼ x 4 x ¾ in)	veneered blockboard
	1 off	279 x 102 x 20 mm (11 x 4 x ¾ in)	veneered blockboard

Ancillaries

		20 x 20 mm (¾ x ¾ in) x 2310 mm (92 in) long plastic angle
		20 x 12 mm (¾ x ½ in) x 1115 mm (44 in) long plastic 'U' section channel
		25 x 12 mm (1 x ½ in) x 785 mm (31 in) long plastic 'U' section channel
	12 off	Plastic shelf support blocks
	12 off	Plastic shelf support pins
	2 off	28 mm (1⅛ in) diam x 198 mm (7⅞ in) long steel tube
	2 off	28 mm (1⅛ in) diam x 417 mm (16½ in) long steel tube
	2 off	Spring-loaded door catch
	2 off	Brass door stay
		25 x 25 mm (1 x 1 in) x 580 mm (22¾ in) long piano hinge
		'Iron-on' veneer edging strip

Computer desk stool

Seat	1 off	318 x 318 x 20 mm (12½ x 12½ x ¾ in)	veneered blockboard
Upper leg support block	4 off	162 x 98 x 20 mm (6⅜ x 3⅞ x ¾ in)	veneered blockboard
Foot	4 off	250 x 203 x 20 mm (9⅞ x 8 x ¾ in)	veneered blockboard
Leg	1 off	533 x 57 x 57 mm (21 x 2¼ x 2¼ in)	timber
Support pin	1 off	16 mm (⅝ in) diam x 228 mm (9 in)	long dowel
	1 off	47 x 35 x 22 mm (1⅞ x 1⅜ x ⅞ in)	timber

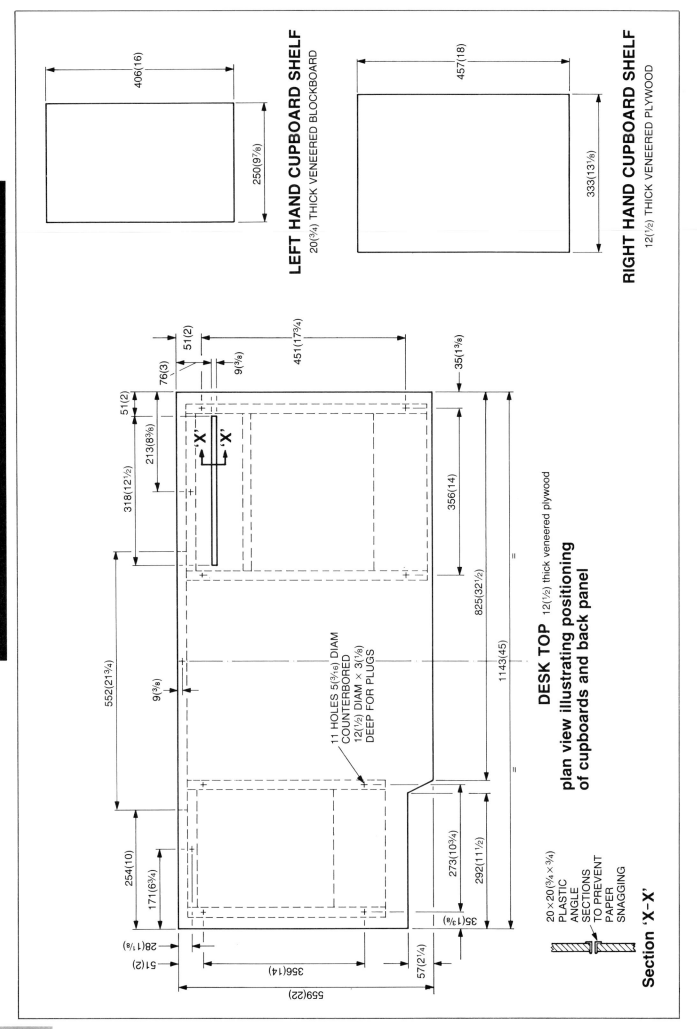

LEFT HAND CUPBOARD SHELF 20(³⁄₄) THICK VENEERED BLOCKBOARD

406(16)

250(9⁷⁄₈)

RIGHT HAND CUPBOARD SHELF 12(¹⁄₂) THICK VENEERED PLYWOOD

457(18)

333(13¹⁄₈)

51(2)

76(3)

9(³⁄₈)

451(17³⁄₄)

35(1³⁄₈)

51(2)

213(8³⁄₈)

318(12¹⁄₂)

356(14)

'X'   'X'

825(32¹⁄₂)

552(21³⁄₄)

9(³⁄₈)

1143(45)

11 HOLES 5(³⁄₁₆) DIAM
COUNTERBORED
12(¹⁄₂) DIAM × 3(¹⁄₈)
DEEP FOR PLUGS

254(10)

171(6³⁄₄)

273(10³⁄₄)

292(11¹⁄₂)

35(1³⁄₈)

28(1¹⁄₈)

51(2)

356(14)

57(2¹⁄₄)

559(22)

DESK TOP 12(¹⁄₂) thick veneered plywood

**plan view illustrating positioning
of cupboards and back panel**

20 × 20 (³⁄₄ × ³⁄₄)
PLASTIC
ANGLE
SECTIONS
TO PREVENT
PAPER
SNAGGING

Section 'X–X'

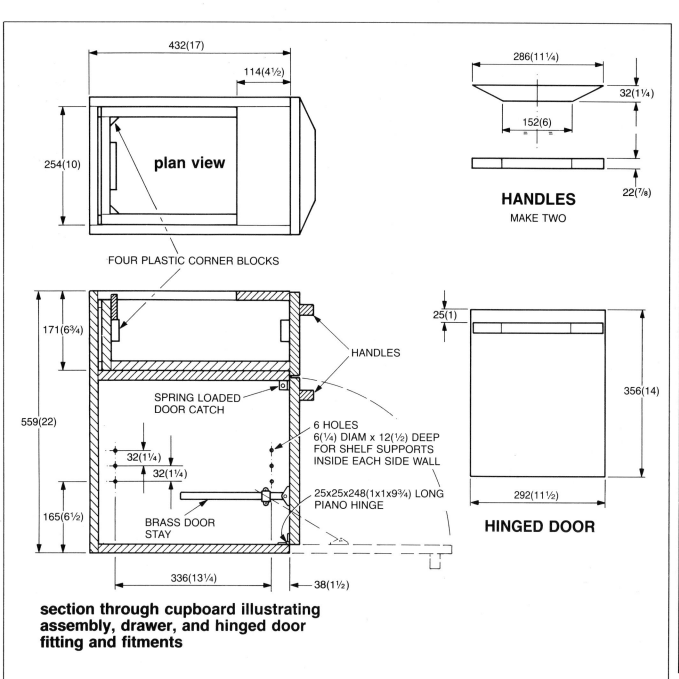

432(17)

114(4½)

254(10)

plan view

FOUR PLASTIC CORNER BLOCKS

171(6¾)

559(22)

32(1¼)

32(1¼)

165(6½)

SPRING LOADED
DOOR CATCH

HANDLES

6 HOLES
6(¼) DIAM x 12(½) DEEP
FOR SHELF SUPPORTS
INSIDE EACH SIDE WALL

BRASS DOOR
STAY

25x25x248(1x1x9¾) LONG
PIANO HINGE

336(13¼)

38(1½)

**section through cupboard illustrating
assembly, drawer, and hinged door
fitting and fitments**

286(11¼)

32(1¼)

152(6)

22(⅞)

HANDLES

MAKE TWO

25(1)

356(14)

292(11½)

HINGED DOOR

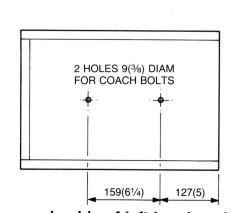

2 HOLES 9(⅜) DIAM
FOR COACH BOLTS

159(6¼)

127(5)

view on underside of left hand cupboard

LEFT HAND CUPBOARD ASSEMBLY
AND DETAILS

20(¾) VENEERED BLOCKBOARD
EXCEPT HANDLES IN 22(⅞) TIMBER
AND BACK STOP 12(½) PLYWOOD

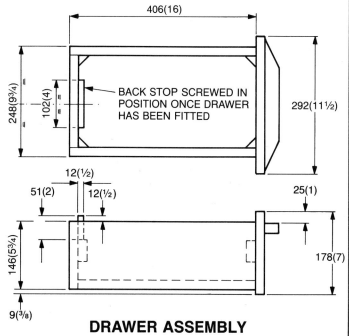

406(16)

248(9¾)

102(4)

BACK STOP SCREWED IN
POSITION ONCE DRAWER
HAS BEEN FITTED

292(11½)

12(½)

51(2)

12(½)

25(1)

146(5¾)

178(7)

9(⅜)

DRAWER ASSEMBLY

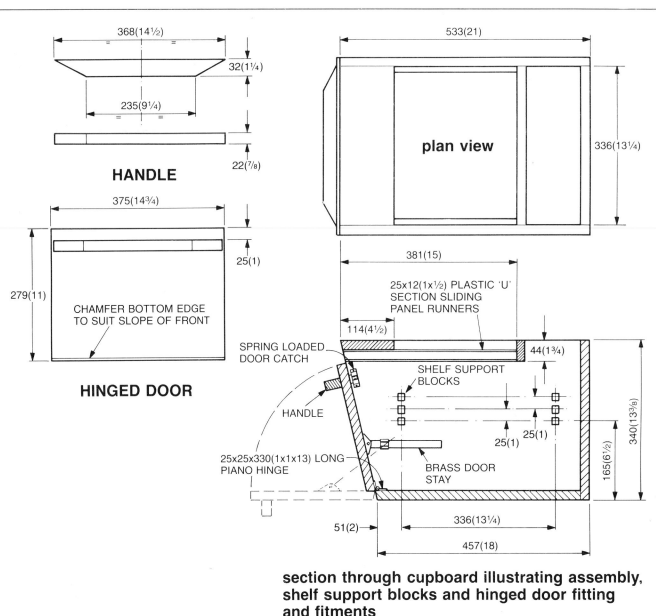

368(14½)

235(9¼)

32(1¼)

22(⅞)

HANDLE

375(14¾)

279(11)

25(1)

CHAMFER BOTTOM EDGE
TO SUIT SLOPE OF FRONT

HINGED DOOR

533(21)

plan view

336(13¼)

381(15)

25x12(1x½) PLASTIC 'U'
SECTION SLIDING
PANEL RUNNERS

114(4½)

44(1¾)

SPRING LOADED
DOOR CATCH

SHELF SUPPORT
BLOCKS

HANDLE

25(1) 25(1)

340(13⅜)

165(6½)

25x25x330(1x1x13) LONG
PIANO HINGE

BRASS DOOR
STAY

51(2)

336(13¼)

457(18)

**section through cupboard illustrating assembly,
shelf support blocks and hinged door fitting
and fitments**

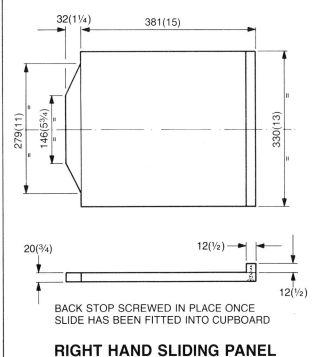

32(1¼)

381(15)

279(11)

146(5¾)

330(13)

20(¾)

12(½)

12(½)

BACK STOP SCREWED IN PLACE ONCE
SLIDE HAS BEEN FITTED INTO CUPBOARD

RIGHT HAND SLIDING PANEL

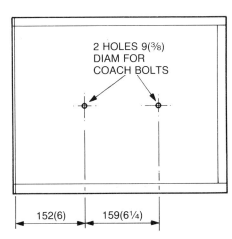

2 HOLES 9(⅜)
DIAM FOR
COACH BOLTS

152(6) 159(6¼)

view on underside of right hand cupboard

**RIGHT HAND CUPBOARD ASSEMBLY
AND DETAILS**

20(¾) VENEERED BLOCKBOARD EXCEPT HANDLE
22(⅞) TIMBER, AND SLIDING PANEL HANDLE
20(¾) TIMBER AND BACK STOP 12(½) × 12(½) TIMBER

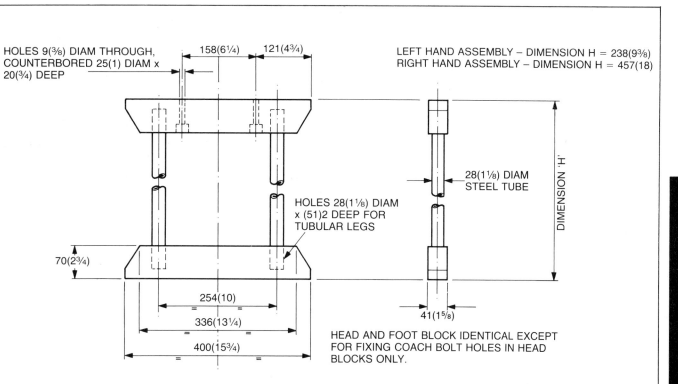

HOLES 9(⅜) DIAM THROUGH, COUNTERBORED 25(1) DIAM x 20(¾) DEEP

158(6¼) 121(4¾)

LEFT HAND ASSEMBLY – DIMENSION H = 238(9⅜)
RIGHT HAND ASSEMBLY – DIMENSION H = 457(18)

28(1⅛) DIAM STEEL TUBE

HOLES 28(1⅛) DIAM x (51)2 DEEP FOR TUBULAR LEGS

DIMENSION 'H'

70(2¾)

254(10)

336(13¼)

400(15¾)

41(1⅝)

HEAD AND FOOT BLOCK IDENTICAL EXCEPT FOR FIXING COACH BOLT HOLES IN HEAD BLOCKS ONLY.

SUPPORT LEG ASSEMBLY

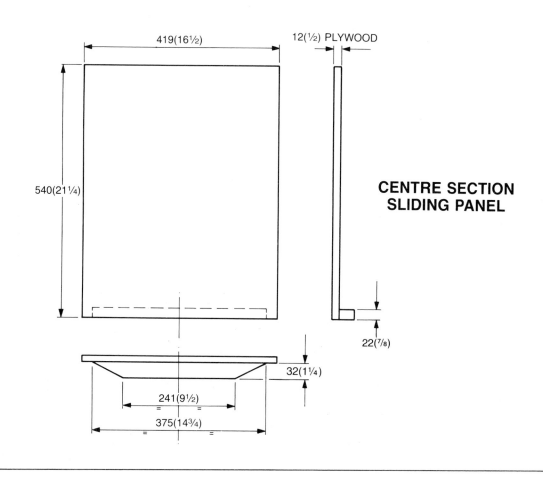

419(16½)

12(½) PLYWOOD

540(21¼)

CENTRE SECTION SLIDING PANEL

22(⅞)

32(1¼)

241(9½)

375(14¾)

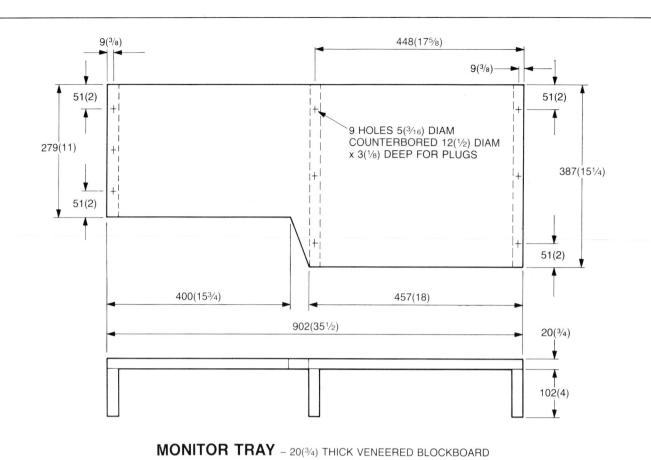

9 HOLES 5(³/₁₆) DIAM
COUNTERBORED 12(¹/₂) DIAM
x 3(¹/₈) DEEP FOR PLUGS

MONITOR TRAY – 20(³/₄) THICK VENEERED BLOCKBOARD

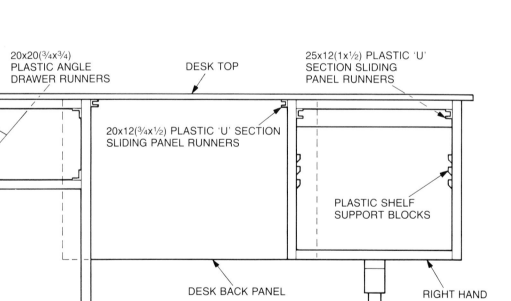

20x20(³/₄x³/₄)
PLASTIC ANGLE
DRAWER RUNNERS

DESK TOP

25x12(1x¹/₂) PLASTIC 'U'
SECTION SLIDING
PANEL RUNNERS

20x12(³/₄x¹/₂) PLASTIC 'U' SECTION
SLIDING PANEL RUNNERS

PLASTIC SHELF
SUPPORT BLOCKS

DESK BACK PANEL

RIGHT HAND
CUPBOARD

LEFT HAND
CUPBOARD

RIGHT HAND
SUPPORT LEG

LEFT HAND
SUPPORT LEG

ASSEMBLED DESK, FRONT VIEW
DRAWER, SLIDING PANELS AND HINGED DOOR
REMOVED TO ILLUSTRATE FITTINGS

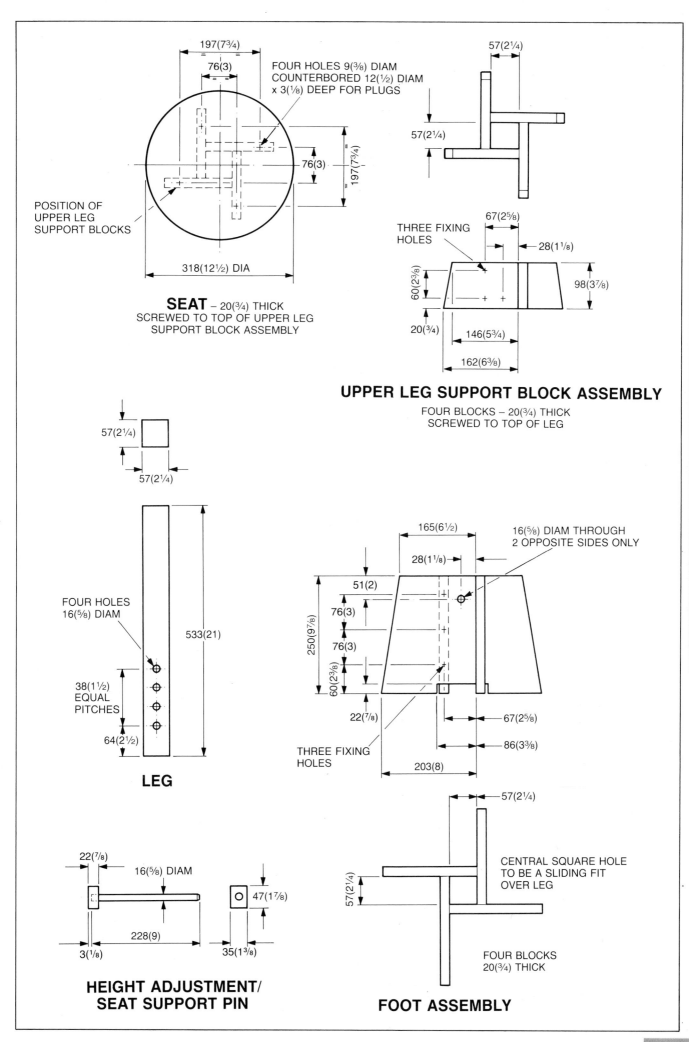

197(7¾)

76(3)

FOUR HOLES 9(⅜) DIAM
COUNTERBORED 12(½) DIAM
x 3(⅛) DEEP FOR PLUGS

76(3)

197(7¾)

POSITION OF
UPPER LEG
SUPPORT BLOCKS

318(12½) DIA

SEAT – 20(¾) THICK
SCREWED TO TOP OF UPPER LEG
SUPPORT BLOCK ASSEMBLY

57(2¼)

57(2¼)

THREE FIXING
HOLES

67(2⅝)

28(1⅛)

60(2⅜)

98(3⅞)

20(¾)

146(5¾)

162(6⅜)

UPPER LEG SUPPORT BLOCK ASSEMBLY

FOUR BLOCKS – 20(¾) THICK
SCREWED TO TOP OF LEG

57(2¼)

57(2¼)

FOUR HOLES
16(⅝) DIAM

533(21)

38(1½)
EQUAL
PITCHES

64(2½)

LEG

165(6½)

16(⅝) DIAM THROUGH
2 OPPOSITE SIDES ONLY

28(1⅛)

51(2)

76(3)

250(9⅞)

76(3)

60(2⅜)

22(⅞)

67(2⅝)

86(3⅜)

THREE FIXING
HOLES

203(8)

22(⅞)

16(⅝) DIAM

47(1⅞)

228(9)

3(⅛)

35(1⅜)

**HEIGHT ADJUSTMENT/
SEAT SUPPORT PIN**

57(2¼)

57(2¼)

CENTRAL SQUARE HOLE
TO BE A SLIDING FIT
OVER LEG

FOUR BLOCKS
20(¾) THICK

FOOT ASSEMBLY

Considering the degree of high technology which is necessary to make a computer one would have thought that it ought to have been possible to produce a machine that was compact and easily transportable. In fact, however, garlands of wires are required to connect the various pieces of equipment together and it is necessary to have two power supplies and one aerial connection to a TV monitor. Not only are all these loose wires hazardous but they also make it difficult to clean the carpet!

1   The box featured here was specifically designed around the Sinclair ZX Spectrum. If you have a different model of computer I suggest that, before you start, you place all the various essentials on a flat surface and see if the design layout will suit your model. The most important thing is to arrange all the items carefully so that they will be able to work and you can get at them easily once they have been put in the box. Once you are sure each item is correctly positioned you can measure the internal dimensions of the box. Whichever computer you have you will find the construction details for making the box the same.

2   The most suitable wood for the box is plywood. Start working on the base and rebate all round the four edges. The rebate should be the thickness of the plywood sides. It is essential to have the use of a rebate plane for this job. As plywood layers are placed with their grains running in opposite directions it is essential that you should first pencil in the position of the rebate you want to cut and then also score the line deeply with a marking knife or a Stanley knife. If you don't do this then you will get nasty splinters as the cutter in the rebate plane starts to cut across the different layers of plywood. Some rebate planes are fitted with a little spur which is lowered before you start ploughing to cut the cross grain. However, the essential operation is to score deeply with a sharp knife before any cutting takes place .

3   Once the rebates have been cut, the sides are fitted into them. There are no rebates on the sides and they are simply glued to each other. Before applying any glue assemble all the pieces and check that they fit.

4   Since the contents of the box are precious and the whole idea of the box is to allow the computer to be easily transported, it is a good idea to give the bottom and sides as much rigidity as possible. To achieve this I used four corner

brackets. Many of you will be familiar with the corner blocks which are used when fastening two pieces of wood together at an angle of 90°. They are used for constructing drawers, for example. The corner brackets differ in that they not only hold two sides together at 90°, but also hold the base in place. They are triangular in shape and are often used in the back of cupboards where they are fixed to wall surfaces. Position the corner brackets and mark through the holes where the screws will go with a pencil. Drill small pilot holes for the screws. Now glue the sides in place. It always helps to have some cramps available when gluing up. Now screw the corner brackets into the box. I often find it helpful to position all the corner brackets and only finally tighten all the screws in the brackets when I have checked that the box is square. Once this is done the most difficult part of making the box is over.

5   As you can see from the drawings, the lid is made of a thinner plywood than the bottom and sides. However, for strength, the thicker plywood is screwed along the back and two sides of the top of the lid. This also provides the anchorage points for the side clasps that keep the lid closed. Glue and screw the plywood onto the lid and countersink all screw heads. Fix the lid on and plane carefully round the sides with the lid firmly clamped in position.

6   Fix the clasps to hold the lid in place. These clasps are generally only available from a tool shop or ironmonger's which stocks a little more than the common range of 'bubble packs' hardware. However, should you get that blank look when explaining what you want, this is one of those cases when the customer is right and 'they' do still make them. Once you are happy that the lid fits well it's time to 'fit out' the inside.

7   I found that it was easiest to gather up all the festoons of wire into tidy 'yarns' and position them at the back of the box.

I glued small blocks in the back to provide anchorage points for the plywood casing and drilled extra holes in the anchorage blocks so that if I ever wanted to run extra wires into the case it would be easy. After cutting the plywood casing and taking note of where the wires ran, I positioned screws to avoid the wires. The casing might be something that you would want to remove so I put the cup washers under the screw heads.

8   What wires you have to accommodate depends on the type of computer that you are using and its accessories. If a power supply is needed for both computer and a program data recorder then a junction box will have to be fitted. If you don't know what you are doing ask a qualified electrician to help, as it is better to be safe and not sorry. Remember that children's fingers get into everything and be sure that you have the junction box wired correctly. Power comes into the box from a standard three-pin power socket (check that the fuse rating in the plug is correct) and is then fed into the junction box. From the junction box power is taken to the computer and the recorder. All this should be checked very carefully to be certain that it is safe.

9   The cable and plug are stored in the box at the back. To keep the plug in its place I cut three holes to allow the plug pins to be inserted. The cable is coiled in clips. The clips can also be used to hold the TV aerial lead.

10   The aerial socket for the coax cable is fitted in a convenient place which I found to be the top right-hand side of the box. Your local TV shop will be able to provide you with a length of coax cable and the small adaptor necessary to plug the aerial into the box.

11   I found it necessary to glue several dividers in the box to keep things tidy. I also used Velcro on the bottoms of the microdrive and printer to hold them securely. A small block of wood is fitted at the back of the computer and also one at the side of the recorder. Provision is also made for the tapes and discs, or a second microdrive can take the place of the tapes. I then used self-adhesive green baize to line most of the box. You should find at this stage that things fit snugly and don't move about. As it is essential that things should not move around while the box is being carried, I also glued a sheet of foam rubber onto the underside of the lid. Before fixing this I found there was also sufficient space to store the manual and other instruction books in the box.

12 I glued plastic channel onto the lid to hold the manuals in place. To stop them falling out I drilled holes through the plastic and fitted tie tapes to hold them.

13 Now fit the lid in place. You may find that it is necessary to cut some of the foam away with a sharp Stanley Knife to get a good snug fit. 'Pressure points' will show up on the foam when the lid is closed and a little foam may have to be cut away from these places. Finish the outside of the box with polyurethane and fix on a good strong carrying handle.

NB All electrical connections and fuse ratings should be checked before this equipment is connected to the mains.

Photograph: page 44

■ CUTTING LIST

Sinclair ZX computer box

Base section

Side walls	2 off	420 x 84 x 12 mm (16½ x 3¼ x ½ in)	plywood
Front wall	1 off	581 x 42 x 12 mm (22⅞ x 1⅝ x ½ in)	plywood
Rear wall	1 off	581 x 84 x 12 mm (22⅞ x 3¼ x ½ in)	plywood
Base	1 off	605 x 420 x 12 mm (23⅞ x 16½ x ½ in)	plywood

Cable stowage compartment

Front	1 off	581 x 44 x 5 mm (22⅞ x 1¾ x ³⁄₁₆ in)	plywood
Cover	1 off	581 x 60 x 5 mm (22⅞ x 2¼ x ³⁄₁₆ in)	plywood
Dividers	3 off	60 x 39 x 12 mm (2¼ x 1⁹⁄₁₆ x ½ in)	plywood

Partitions – various to suit actual computer equipment

	make from	84 x 12 mm (3¼ x ½ in)	plywood

Lid

Top	1 off	605 x 420 x 5 mm (23⅞ x 16½ x ³⁄₁₆ in)	plywood
Front strip	1 off	581 x 42 x 12 mm (22⅞ x 1⅝ x ½ in)	plywood
Side strips	2 off	336 x 25 x 12 mm (13¼ x 1 x ½ in)	plywood
Rear strip	1 off	605 x 84 x 12 mm (23⅞ x 3¼ x ½ in)	plywood
Motif	make from	51 x 22 x 5 mm (2 x ⅞ x ³⁄₁₆ in)	plywood
	2 off	76 x 5 x 5 mm (3 x ³⁄₁₆ x ³⁄₁₆ in)	plywood

Ancillaries

	1 off	605 x 420 x 25 mm (23⅞ x 16½ x 1 in) rubber foam
		20 x 20 mm (¾ x ¾ in) x 800 mm (31½ in) long plastic 'U' section channel
	4 off	Plastic corner joint blocks
	4 off	Chromed lid catches
	1 off	Chromed handle
	4 off	Feet 22 mm (⅞ in) diam dowel x 12 mm (½ in) thick
	1 off	Mains lead connector
	1 off	Co-axial socket
	2 off	Terry clips
		6 mm (¼ in) wide black elastic
		1 metre (39 in) co-axial cable
		1 metre (39 in) three core mains cable
	1 off	Electrical terminal block connector strip
	1 off	610 x 610 mm (24 x 24 in) green felt

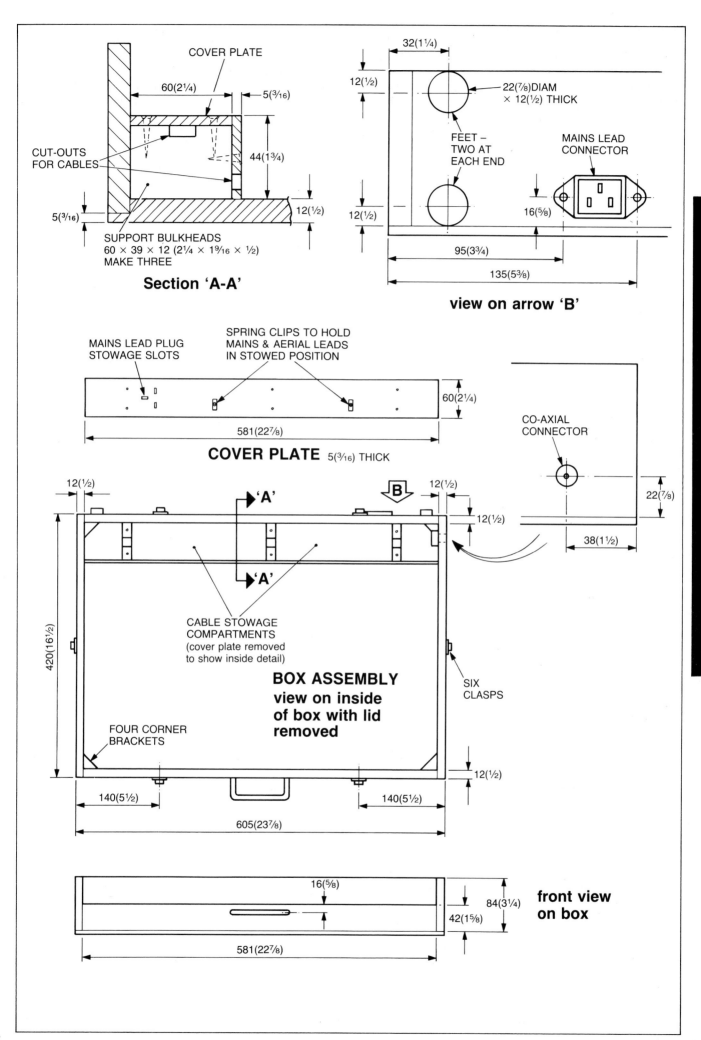

COVER PLATE

60(2¼)

5(³⁄₁₆)

44(1¾)

CUT-OUTS
FOR CABLES

5(³⁄₁₆)

12(½)

SUPPORT BULKHEADS
60 × 39 × 12 (2¼ × 1⁹⁄₁₆ × ½)
MAKE THREE

Section 'A-A'

32(1¼)

12(½)

22(⁷⁄₈)DIAM
× 12(½) THICK

FEET –
TWO AT
EACH END

MAINS LEAD
CONNECTOR

12(½)

16(⁵⁄₈)

95(3¾)

135(5³⁄₈)

view on arrow 'B'

MAINS LEAD PLUG
STOWAGE SLOTS

SPRING CLIPS TO HOLD
MAINS & AERIAL LEADS
IN STOWED POSITION

60(2¼)

581(22⁷⁄₈)

COVER PLATE 5(³⁄₁₆) THICK

CO-AXIAL
CONNECTOR

22(⁷⁄₈)

38(1½)

12(½)

'A'

B

12(½)

12(½)

12(½)

CABLE STOWAGE
COMPARTMENTS
(cover plate removed
to show inside detail)

'A'

420(16½)

**BOX ASSEMBLY
view on inside
of box with lid
removed**

SIX
CLASPS

FOUR CORNER
BRACKETS

12(½)

140(5½)

140(5½)

605(23⁷⁄₈)

16(⁵⁄₈)

84(3¼)

**front view
on box**

42(1⁵⁄₈)

581(22⁷⁄₈)

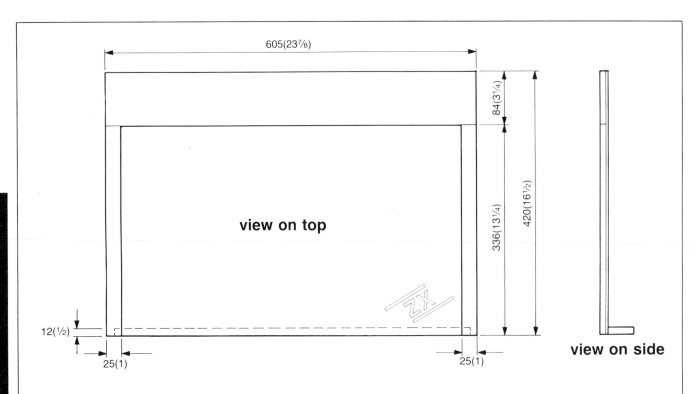

605(23⁷/₈)

84(3¹/₄)

420(16¹/₂)

336(13¹/₄)

view on top

12(½)

25(1)   25(1)

view on side

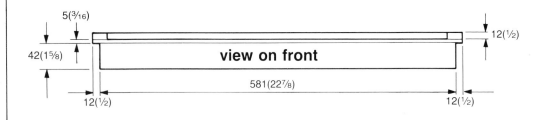

5(³/₁₆)

12(½)

42(1⁵/₈)

view on front

581(22⁷/₈)

12(½)   12(½)

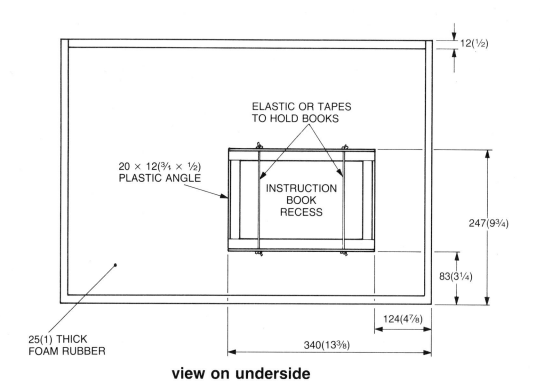

12(½)

ELASTIC OR TAPES
TO HOLD BOOKS

20 × 12(¾ × ½)
PLASTIC ANGLE

INSTRUCTION
BOOK
RECESS

247(9¾)

83(3¼)

25(1) THICK
FOAM RUBBER

124(4⅞)

340(13⅜)

view on underside

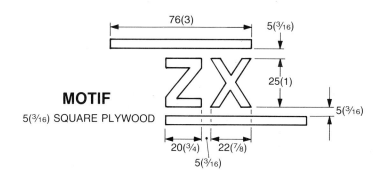

76(3)

5(³⁄₁₆)

MOTIF

25(1)

5(³⁄₁₆) SQUARE PLYWOOD

5(³⁄₁₆)

20(¾)   22(⅞)

5(³⁄₁₆)

BUNK BED COMPLEX
COMPRISING DESK AND WARDROBE

All parents will at some stage be aware not only of the physical growth of their children, but also of the growth of their possessions. Somewhere must be found for their homework to be done, and to store those large Christmas games, football kit, hockey stick and violin! The area of a bedroom taken up by a bed is largely wasted space and only used when the occupant is asleep. However, if you raise the bed up and use the space underneath for a work area then the room is used to far greater advantage. The construction entails the use of only two traditional joints, the mortice and tenon and halving joint. The finished structure looks fairly impressive, but when split into sections it is not too difficult to build.

■ Main frames

1   Start by marking out the three frames that hold the bed up and provide a framework for the drawers and wardrobe unit. Mark in pencil where the rails go for the drawer units.
2   Before you start cutting anything find a large flat surface and put down all the pieces you have marked out, and make sure that the various joints line up and that once cutting has begun the pieces will fit. Don't proceed any further until you have thought each stage through.
3   Once you are sure everything will fit, cut out the halving joints on the three main frames. The three frames are held together at the top by a rack that runs full length and provides support for the plywood on which the mattress rests. The rack is held together by mortice and tenon joints and fits into the halving joints in the three main frames. Once this part is completed you can start work on the individual units, knowing that when final assembly is attempted the parts will fit.

■ Drawers and shelf unit

1   To make a sturdy base unit for the drawers it is necessary to mortice and tenon the rails. This is the only piece of traditional woodworking involved in this project.
     Drawer units and the rails the drawers run on are always very complicated and time-consuming to make. Once the front and side rails have been cut and the whole unit glued together, the rails for the drawers should be cut to fit very tight between front and back rails.
2   The drawer runner rails should now be glued into place. In order to get these large drawers to run smoothly I cut and glued 'L' section plastic strip on the

bottom and top of the rails. Make sure you glue the plastic strip to the rails accurately as any slight tapering of the plastic runner towards the back will make it impossible to close the drawers.
3   Once the plastic strip has been fitted you can take measurements for the width and height of the drawers. It is a good idea to allow a small fraction oversize for the drawer units as it is always possible to glasspaper the sides down for a good fit. Good D.I.Y. shops keep a large variety of plastic jointing blocks. I found the triangular type designed for the backs of cabinets best to use at the bottom of the drawers. The triangular blocks also provide screw holes for fixing on the drawer base. At the top edges of the drawers I used a smaller jointing block. To avoid the difficulty of trying to assemble two sides and two ends plus plastic blocks and screws, I assembled one side and end first. It helps a lot at this stage to have an assistant, or a good method of clamping the wood, otherwise a fairly simple task becomes a problem. As each side is jointed to the end, check for squareness.
4   When sides and ends have been glued and screwed, bring both pieces together for the remaining corner blocks and screws. You will find that the corner blocks are of great help and keep things square as the drawer is made.
5   Once all the sides are fitted, cut and glue in the drawer bottom.
6   Drawer handles can be bought, but I think it's a great deal better to shape and fit your own. As the drawer is large and deep, a wooden handle will need to have a good grip provided, and to be glued and screwed onto the the drawer front. The shaping of the handles is a matter of choice, but I have given the shape and dimensions of my design so you can follow this if you wish.

■ Desk

From the drawings, cut and fit the desk top and book shelf. The various spaces and different shelf units possible are a matter of individual choice. However, it is important to fit 'book ends' to stop everything falling off. It will also be necessary to fit some form of lighting and you should get a competent electrician to do this job for you.

■ Wardrobe

1   The other two main frames are now fitted together and form the framework for the wardrobe. This part of the job is like constructing a large wooden box which is clad in plywood. You will find that a good tight-fitting rail and a good wood glue are all that are necessary, as the plywood covering the frame will bind it all together to form a very strong construction. To use the plywood economically you will find, as I did, that the width of the sheet finishes a few inches short of the top. Cut a rail and glue it into the frame, leaving an overlap to which you can fasten the plywood.
2   Panel pins and glue are used to fasten the plywood to the frame. It is advisable to buy a pin punch to tap the panel pin heads just below the surface. The little hole left can then be filled before varnishing. This gives a much better finished appearance than to have dozens of little panel pin holes showing.

■ Doors

Once the framework for the wardrobe is complete and the plywood has been fitted, measurements can be taken for the doors. These are made in blockboard, and the edges best finished with iron-on wood veneer. If you have never fitted hinges before, don't worry, as there are now a variety of hinges that don't need recessing into the wood. It is just a matter of going and looking at what is available before you cut the doors.
1   To fit any door you should first offer it up to the area it has to fill and take shavings off one by one. Don't rush the job and remember it is easy to take shavings off, but impossible to stick them back on again! Fit the top hinge first and support the bottom of the door on a wedge of wood. You must allow for clearance at the

bottom of the door besides using the wedge to hold the door steady. After all the doors have been fitted one usually finds that they will settle and it is necessary to make further adjustments.

2 To keep the doors shut I used magnetic door catches. The door handles were made from offcuts of wood.

■ Rack

1 The two units, wardrobe and desk, are now held together by the rack at the top. The rack provides support for the mattress as well as holding the units together. Traditional mortice and tenon joints are used here and halving joints that fit into those on the main frames. As suggested earlier it is best if this rack is made at the same time as the main frames, but if you have been avoiding it so far, you must make it now.

2 After the rack has been glued together it has to be fitted into the halving joints on the main frames. It is important for both wardrobe and book case to be on an even surface, otherwise you will not get the joints to fit. The rack should ideally be a tight fit onto the main frames, but don't fix it in any way, as it is held in place by the top bunk side pieces.

■ Bunk

To prevent youngsters falling out while turning over in their sleep I felt it important to make high sides. A timber that it is in

plentiful supply is parana pine which is available in long wide boards and ideal for this task.

1 First cut a sheet of plywood which should be laid upon the rack, but not fitted to it.

2 Now measure carefully and cut to length the sides and ends of the bunk.

3 To fix the bunk together I used some very strong plastic corner blocks. There are some that have a bolt holding the two halves together, which are excellent and ideal for this job. At the bottom edges of the bunk I fitted triangular corner blocks to allow the bunk sides to slip over the plywood and come down over the rack. This means that the halving joints are covered up and everything held in place. The triangular corner blocks prevent the sides going any further down by acting as stops on the plywood.

4 Once this has been done fit a number of corner jointing blocks along the length of the bunk side. This will strengthen the bunk and hold the sides firmly to the plywood base.

5 At the bottom of the bed I cut an 'entry port'. This also has the advantage of allowing the ladder to fit well into the side of the bunk.

6 If the sides are still not high enough to prevent the occupant from falling out, you can fit safety rails on the sides of the bunk away from the wall.

Make up the safety rail frames and then glue and screw these to the sides of the bunk.

■ Ladder

1 The sides should be cut and cramped together and the positions of the mortice holes marked in pencil. Separate the two sides and mark the mortices with a mortice gauge.

2 Now cut the ladder rungs to length. Cramp them all together and mark the shoulder lines for the tenons.

3 Remove the cramp and, using the mortice gauge, mark the tenons. Then cut all the joints.

4 Before final fixing, round off the ladder rungs and also the sides of the ladder with a spokeshave or plane.

5 The bottom of the ladder should be cut at an angle and the tops very carefully rounded off. Do take time and care to round off the ladder tops otherwise children could hurt themselves on them.

6 You will have to buy two metal shelf brackets to fit onto the top of the ladder. The brackets then have to be bent to hook onto the bunk.

7 Make sure that all screws are well countersunk and double check that the undersides of the brackets have no sharp edges. If you find any sharp edges use a very fine file and work along the sides and around the corners.

NB The bunk bed has been designed for a mattress 2ft 6in (66.2cm) wide. If you want to allow for a mattress 3ft (91.5cm) wide then it will be necessary to re-design the rack to accommodate the extra width.

Photographs: pages 25, 50

■ CUTTING LIST

Bunk bed

Wardrobe section

Main frame verticals	4 off	1390 x 76 x 44 mm (54¾ x 3 x 1¾ in)	timber
Main frame cross members	6 off	711 x 44 x 32 mm (28 x 1¾ x 1¼ in)	timber
Main frame spacers	2 off	762 x 64 x 22 mm (30 x 2½ x ⅞ in)	timber
Under floor support bar	1 off	667 x 44 x 22 mm (26¼ x 1¾ x ⅞ in)	timber
Front & rear floor supports	2 off	610 x 44 x 22 mm (24 x 1¾ x ⅞ in)	timber
Side skin panel supports	2 off	622 x 44 x 16 mm (24½ x 1¾ x ⅝ in)	timber
Rear skin upper support	1 off	610 x 44 x 16 mm (24 x 1¾ x ⅝ in)	timber
R.H. wall skin	1 off	1346 x 714 x 3 mm (53 x 28⅛ x ⅛ in)	veneered plywood
Rear wall skin	1 off	1346 x 762 x 3 mm (53 x 30 x ⅛ in)	veneered plywood
Upper L.H. wall outer skin	1 off	686 x 714 x 12 mm (27 x 28⅛ x ½ in)	pegboard
Upper L.H. wall inner skin	1 off	708 x 622 x 3 mm (27⅞ x 24½ x ⅛ in)	plywood
Lower L.H. wall skin	1 off	660 x 714 x 3 mm (26 x 28⅛ x ⅛ in)	veneered plywood
Floor panel	1 off	762 x 711 x 6 mm (30 x 28 x ¼ in)	veneered plywood
Door	2 off	1290 x 302 x 12 mm (50¾ x 11⅞ x ½ in)	veneered plywood
Door handle	2 off	140 x 32 x 32 mm (5½ x 1¼ x 1¼ in)	timber

Desk section

Part	Qty	Dimensions	Material
Main frame verticals	2 off	1390 x 76 x 44 mm (54¾ x 3 x 1¾ in)	timber
Main frame cross members	3 off	711 x 44 x 32 mm (28 x 1¾ x 1¼ in)	timber
Desk front legs	2 off	682 x 44 x 44 mm (26⅞ x 1¾ x 1¾ in)	timber
End cross members	6 off	320 x 41 x 28 mm (12½ x 1⅝ x 1⅛ in)	timber
Front cross members	3 off	662 x 41 x 28 mm (26 x 1⅝ x 1⅛ in)	timber
Vertical	1 off	536 x 32 x 16 mm (21⅛ x 1¼ x ⅝ in)	timber
Horizontals	2 off	422 x 32 x 16 mm (16⅝ x 1¼ x ⅝ in)	timber
Upper rear wall skin	1 off	660 x 244 x 3 mm (26 x 9⅝ x ⅛ in)	veneered plywood
Front & lower rear wall skins	2 off	682 x 714 x 3 mm (26⅞ x 28⅛ x ⅛ in)	veneered plywood
End wall skin	1 off	682 x 406 x 3 mm (26⅞ x 16 x ⅛ in)	veneered plywood
Shelf bracket	4 off	241 x 152 x 20 mm (9½ x 6 x ¾ in)	timber
Upper shelf	1 off	711 x 254 x 12 mm (28 x 10 x ½ in)	veneered plywood
Desk top	1 off	736 x 520 x 12 mm (29 x 20½ x ½ in)	veneered plywood
Drawer sides	4 off	610 x 273 x 20 mm (24 x 10¾ x ¾ in)	veneered blockboard
Drawer backs	2 off	273 x 273 x 20 mm (10¾ x 10¾ x ¾ in)	veneered blockboard
Drawer front	2 off	317 x 317 x 20 mm (12½ x 12½ x ¾ in)	veneered blockboard
Drawer bottom	2 off	610 x 233 x 20 mm (24 x 9¼ x ¾ in)	veneered blockboard
Drawer handle	2 off	241 x 38 x 28 mm (9½ x 1½ x 1⅛ in)	timber
Drawer guides	8 off	654 x 44 x 20 mm (25¾ x 1¾ x ¾ in)	timber

Tie frame

Part	Qty	Dimensions	Material
Longitudinal members	2 off	1930 x 47 x 44 mm (76 x 1⅞ x 1¾ in)	timber
Cross members	3 off	672 x 44 x 32 mm (26½ x 1¾ x 1¼ in)	timber
Cross members	2 off	646 x 44 x 32 mm (25½ x 1¾ x 1¼ in)	timber
Spacer blocks	4 off	152 x 47 x 44 mm (6 x 1⅞ x 1¾ in)	timber

Bed section

Part	Qty	Dimensions	Material
Sides	2 off	1935 x 241 x 20 mm (76¼ x 9½ x ¾ in)	timber
Ends	2 off	864 x 241 x 20 mm (34 x 9½ x ¾ in)	timber
Base board	1 off	1935 x 826 x 12 mm (76¼ x 32½ x ½ in)	plywood
Ladder stringers	2 off	1780 x 44 x 28 mm (70 x 1¾ x 1⅛ in)	timber
Ladder rungs	6 off	268 x 35 x 22 mm (10½ x 1⅜ x ⅞ in)	timber

Safety rail frames

Part	Qty	Dimensions	Material
Side guard rails	2 off	1111 x 47 x 22 mm (43¾ x 1⅞ x ⅞ in)	timber
Head guard rails	2 off	908 x 47 x 22 mm (35¾ x 1⅞ x ⅞ in)	timber
Posts	4 off	546 x 47 x 22 mm (21½ x 1⅞ x ⅞ in)	timber

Ancillaries

Part	Qty	Description
	4 off	51 mm (2 in) long hinges
	2 off	Magnetic catch assemblies
	20 off	Plastic corner joint blocks
	12 off	Plastic corner/face brackets
		20 x 20 mm (¾ x ¾ in) x 4672 mm (184 in) long plastic angle
	2 off	127 x 127 mm (5 x 5 in) shelf brackets

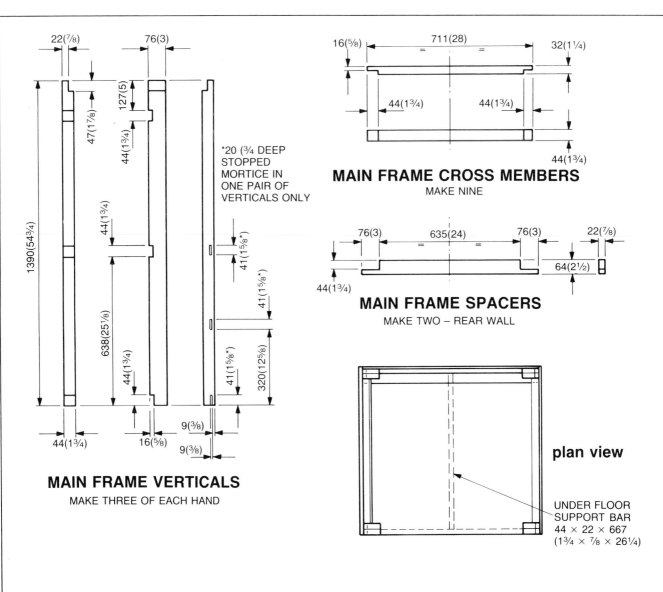

22(⁷/₈)   76(3)

127(5)

47(1⁷/₈)

44(1³/₄)

*20 (³/₄ DEEP
STOPPED
MORTICE IN
ONE PAIR OF
VERTICALS ONLY

1390(54³/₄)

44(1³/₄)

638(25¹/₈)

44(1³/₄)

41(1⁵/₈*)

41(1⁵/₈*)

41(1⁵/₈*)

320(12⁵/₈)

44(1³/₄)   16(⁵/₈)   9(³/₈)

9(³/₈)

MAIN FRAME VERTICALS

MAKE THREE OF EACH HAND

16(⁵/₈)   711(28)   32(1¹/₄)

44(1³/₄)   44(1³/₄)

44(1³/₄)

MAIN FRAME CROSS MEMBERS

MAKE NINE

76(3)   635(24)   76(3)   22(⁷/₈)

64(2¹/₂)

44(1³/₄)

MAIN FRAME SPACERS

MAKE TWO – REAR WALL

plan view

UNDER FLOOR
SUPPORT BAR
44 × 22 × 667
(1³/₄ × ⁷/₈ × 26¹/₄)

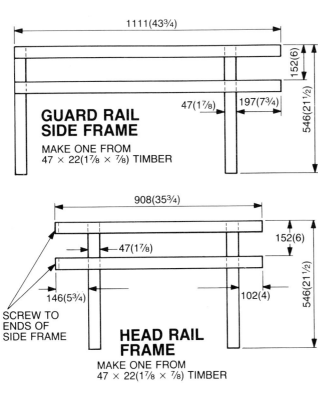

1111(43³/₄)

152(6)

47(1⁷/₈)   197(7³/₄)

546(21¹/₂)

GUARD RAIL
SIDE FRAME

MAKE ONE FROM
47 × 22(1⁷/₈ × ⁷/₈) TIMBER

908(35³/₄)

152(6)

47(1⁷/₈)

546(21¹/₂)

146(5³/₄)   102(4)

SCREW TO
ENDS OF
SIDE FRAME

HEAD RAIL
FRAME

MAKE ONE FROM
47 × 22(1⁷/₈ × ⁷/₈) TIMBER

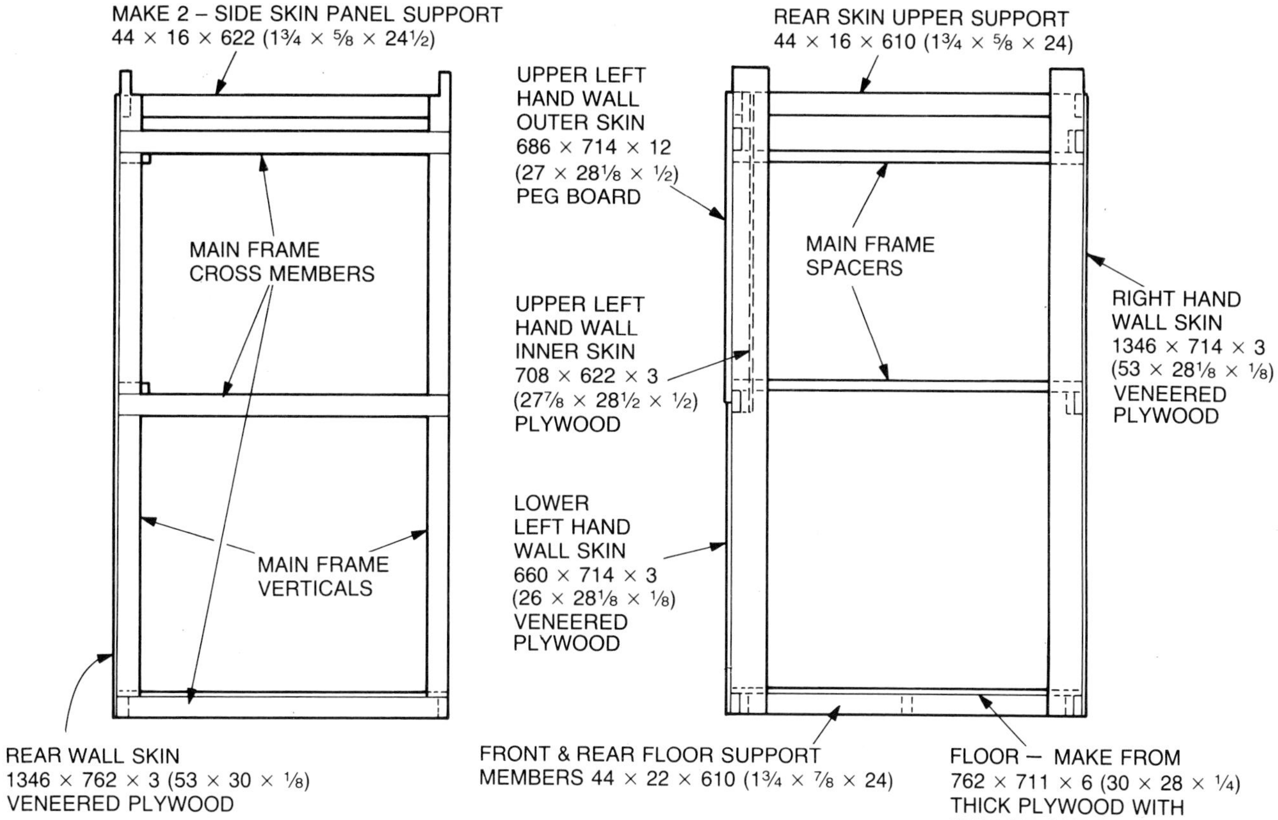
MAKE 2 – SIDE SKIN PANEL SUPPORT
44 × 16 × 622 (1¾ × ⅝ × 24½)
MAIN FRAME CROSS MEMBERS
MAIN FRAME VERTICALS
REAR WALL SKIN
1346 × 762 × 3 (53 × 30 × ⅛)
VENEERED PLYWOOD
UPPER LEFT HAND WALL OUTER SKIN
686 × 714 × 12
(27 × 28⅛ × ½)
PEG BOARD
UPPER LEFT HAND WALL INNER SKIN
708 × 622 × 3
(27⅞ × 28½ × ½)
PLYWOOD
LOWER LEFT HAND WALL SKIN
660 × 714 × 3
(26 × 28⅛ × ⅛)
VENEERED PLYWOOD
REAR SKIN UPPER SUPPORT
44 × 16 × 610 (1¾ × ⅝ × 24)
MAIN FRAME SPACERS
RIGHT HAND WALL SKIN
1346 × 714 × 3
(53 × 28⅛ × ⅛)
VENEERED PLYWOOD
FRONT & REAR FLOOR SUPPORT MEMBERS 44 × 22 × 610 (1¾ × ⅞ × 24)
FLOOR – MAKE FROM 762 × 711 × 6 (30 × 28 × ¼) THICK PLYWOOD WITH CORNER CUT OUTS FOR CLEARANCE ON MAIN FRAME VERTICALS

WARDROBE SECTION CONSTRUCTION

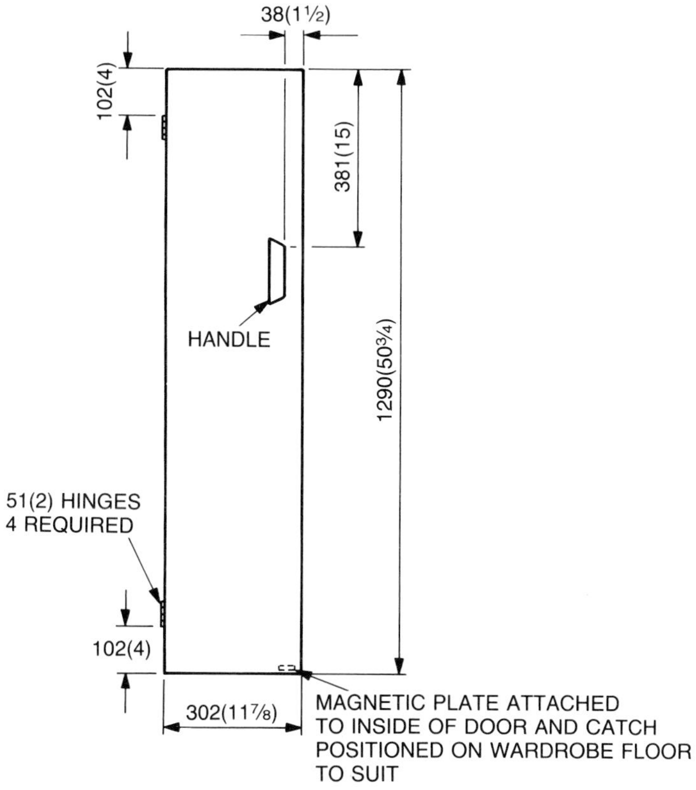
38(1½)
102(4)
381(15)
HANDLE
1290(50¾)
51(2) HINGES
4 REQUIRED
102(4)
302(11⅞)
MAGNETIC PLATE ATTACHED TO INSIDE OF DOOR AND CATCH POSITIONED ON WARDROBE FLOOR TO SUIT

WARDROBE DOOR

MAKE ONE PAIR

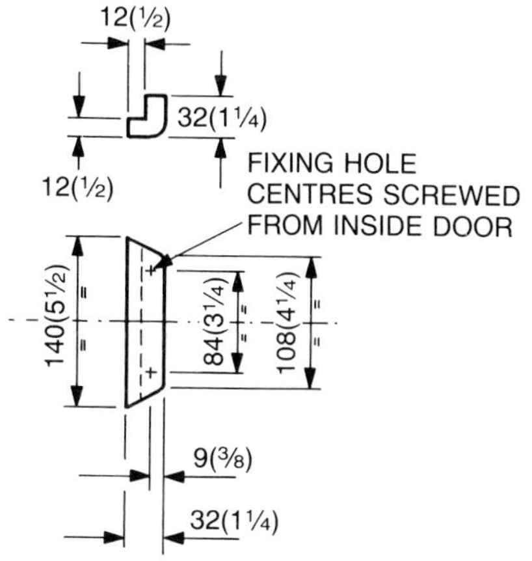
12(½)
32(1¼)
12(½)
FIXING HOLE CENTRES SCREWED FROM INSIDE DOOR
140(5½)
84(3¼)
108(4¼)
9(⅜)
32(1¼)

HANDLES

MAKE TWO

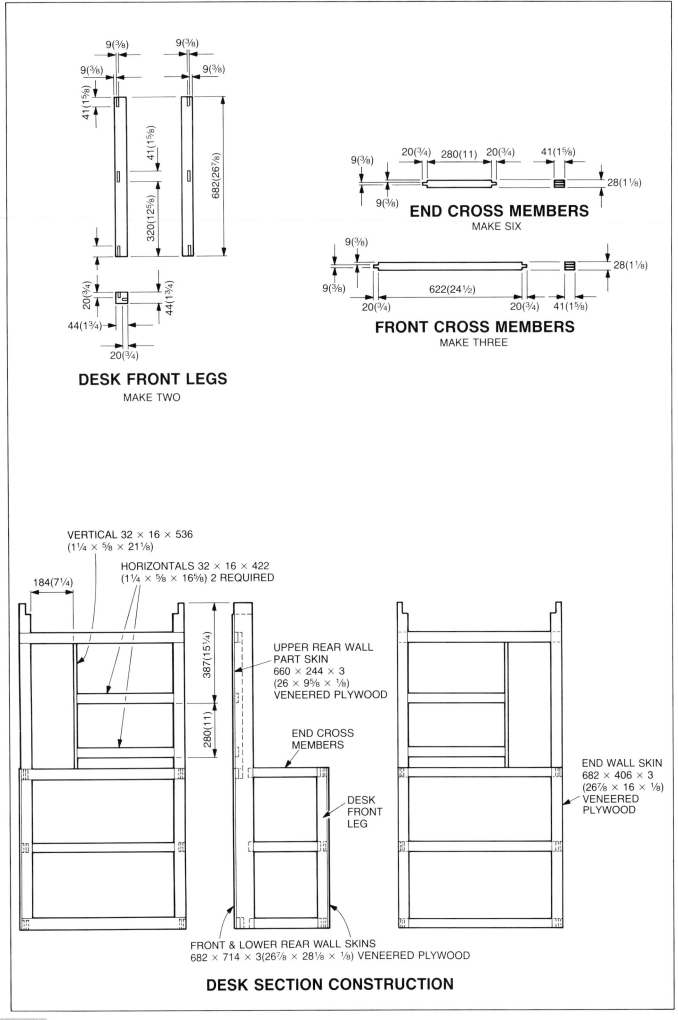

DESK FRONT LEGS
MAKE TWO

END CROSS MEMBERS
MAKE SIX

FRONT CROSS MEMBERS
MAKE THREE

VERTICAL 32 × 16 × 536
(1¼ × ⅝ × 21⅛)

HORIZONTALS 32 × 16 × 422
(1¼ × ⅝ × 16⅝) 2 REQUIRED

UPPER REAR WALL
PART SKIN
660 × 244 × 3
(26 × 9⅝ × ⅛)
VENEERED PLYWOOD

END CROSS
MEMBERS

DESK
FRONT
LEG

END WALL SKIN
682 × 406 × 3
(26⅞ × 16 × ⅛)
VENEERED
PLYWOOD

FRONT & LOWER REAR WALL SKINS
682 × 714 × 3(26⅞ × 28⅛ × ⅛) VENEERED PLYWOOD

DESK SECTION CONSTRUCTION

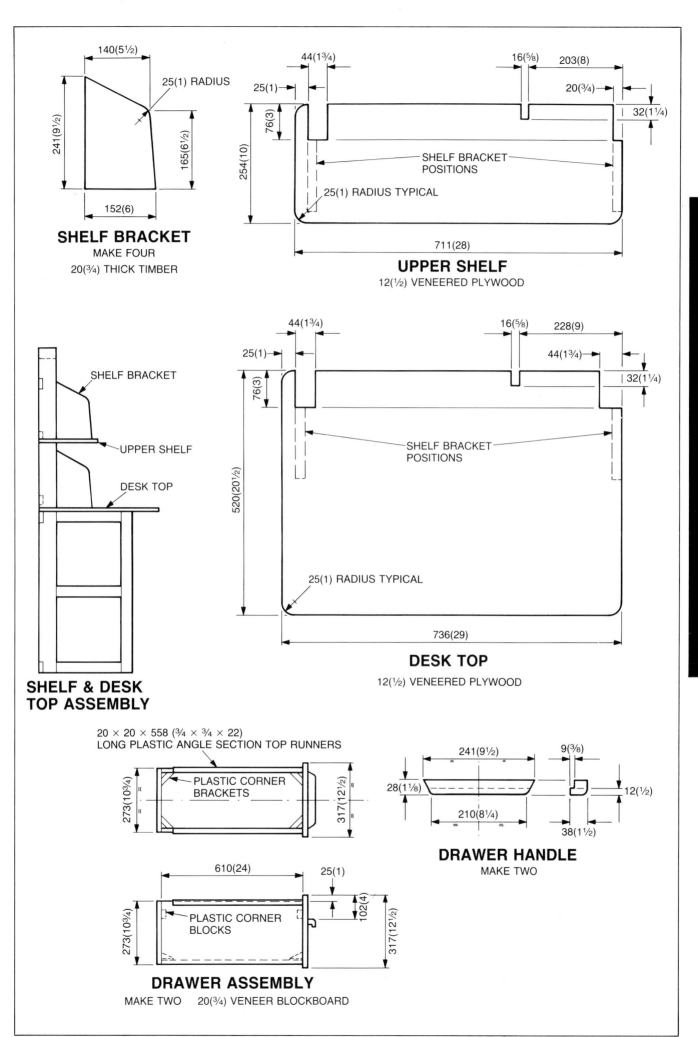

SHELF BRACKET
MAKE FOUR
20(¾) THICK TIMBER

140(5½)
25(1) RADIUS
241(9½)
165(6½)
152(6)

UPPER SHELF
12(½) VENEERED PLYWOOD

44(1¾)
25(1)
16(⅝)
203(8)
20(¾)
32(1¼)
76(3)
254(10)
SHELF BRACKET POSITIONS
25(1) RADIUS TYPICAL
711(28)

SHELF & DESK TOP ASSEMBLY

SHELF BRACKET
UPPER SHELF
DESK TOP

DESK TOP
12(½) VENEERED PLYWOOD

44(1¾)
25(1)
16(⅝)
228(9)
44(1¾)
32(1¼)
76(3)
520(20½)
SHELF BRACKET POSITIONS
25(1) RADIUS TYPICAL
736(29)

20 × 20 × 558 (¾ × ¾ × 22)
LONG PLASTIC ANGLE SECTION TOP RUNNERS
PLASTIC CORNER BRACKETS
273(10¾)
317(12½)

DRAWER HANDLE
MAKE TWO

241(9½)
9(⅜)
28(1⅛)
12(½)
210(8¼)
38(1½)

DRAWER ASSEMBLY
MAKE TWO   20(¾) VENEER BLOCKBOARD

610(24)
25(1)
PLASTIC CORNER BLOCKS
273(10¾)
102(4)
317(12½)

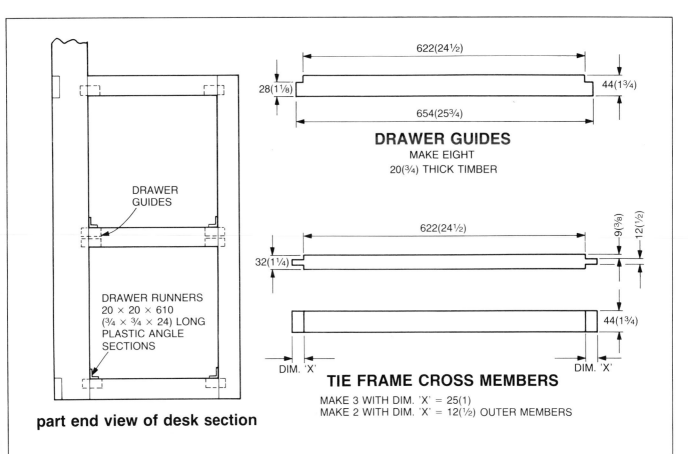

DRAWER GUIDES
MAKE EIGHT
20(¾) THICK TIMBER

TIE FRAME CROSS MEMBERS
MAKE 3 WITH DIM. 'X' = 25(1)
MAKE 2 WITH DIM. 'X' = 12(½) OUTER MEMBERS

DRAWER GUIDES

DRAWER RUNNERS
20 × 20 × 610
(¾ × ¾ × 24) LONG
PLASTIC ANGLE
SECTIONS

part end view of desk section

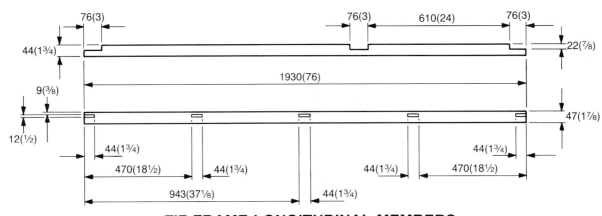

TIE FRAME LONGITUDINAL MEMBERS MAKE ONE PAIR

OUTER STOPPED MORTICE 12(½) DEEP
INTERMEDIATE ONES 25(1) DEEP

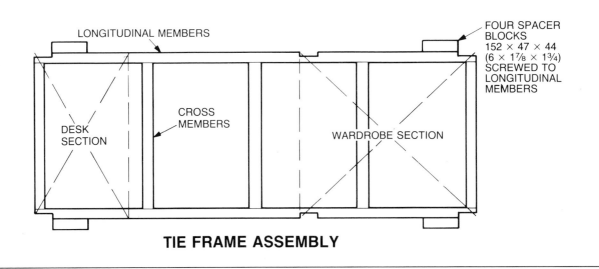

LONGITUDINAL MEMBERS

FOUR SPACER
BLOCKS
152 × 47 × 44
(6 × 1⅞ × 1¾)
SCREWED TO
LONGITUDINAL
MEMBERS

DESK
SECTION

CROSS
MEMBERS

WARDROBE SECTION

TIE FRAME ASSEMBLY

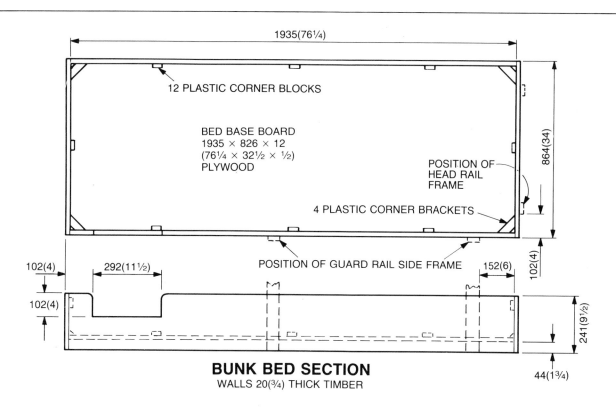

1935(76¼)

12 PLASTIC CORNER BLOCKS

864(34)

BED BASE BOARD
1935 × 826 × 12
(76¼ × 32½ × ½)
PLYWOOD

POSITION OF
HEAD RAIL
FRAME

4 PLASTIC CORNER BRACKETS

POSITION OF GUARD RAIL SIDE FRAME

102(4)

292(11½)

152(6)

102(4)

102(4)

241(9½)

44(1¾)

BUNK BED SECTION
WALLS 20(¾) THICK TIMBER

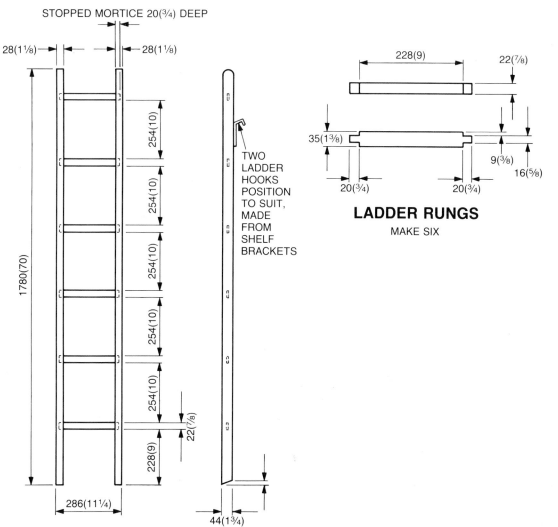

STOPPED MORTICE 20(¾) DEEP

28(1⅛)

28(1⅛)

254(10)

254(10)

254(10)

254(10)

254(10)

228(9)

22(⅞)

1780(70)

286(11¼)

TWO
LADDER
HOOKS
POSITION
TO SUIT,
MADE
FROM
SHELF
BRACKETS

44(1¾)

228(9)

22(⅞)

35(1⅜)

9(⅜)

16(⅝)

20(¾)

20(¾)

LADDER RUNGS
MAKE SIX

BED ACCESS LADDER

Most large D.I.Y. stores keep plastic-veneered chipboard in stock. This is available in a variety of widths and lengths, and the most common finishes are white or teak. From these boards the home-maker can build almost anything to suit his or her particular sized room. To fix these plastic-veneered chipboards together and to hinge the doors a whole range of jointing blocks and hinges has been devised with clear instructions on the packs as to how to use them.

There are two pieces of equipment you can buy which will help you to work successfully with this material. One is a large circular cutter for recessing the special hinges. This is an expensive item and perhaps only worth buying if you are contemplating making a whole range of cupboards. Otherwise alternative hinges are available which can be fitted in the normal way.

The second piece of equipment you could buy, and which is essential for cutting accurate hinge holes, is a vertical drill stand. Without this it is almost inevitable that you will not get the hole in the right place, or you will slip, or not bore the hole vertically in the wood. This sort of woodworking is really mechanical, the only skills necessary being to measure accurately and cut to the pencil line you have drawn.

■ Wardrobe

1 Boards of suitable size are available for the sides and doors without the need to cut to length and width. However three pieces are necessary for the top, bottom and shelf, and these should all be cut to exactly the same length, the width being the same as the sides.

2 Using a T-square and pencil mark the positions of the top, bottom and shelf.

3 Attach the top, bottom and shelf to the sides using jointing blocks. The plastic jointing blocks I favour come in two pieces. One piece is screwed onto the shelf unit, the other onto the side. Using the template provided on the packet will ensure that all the pieces line up for final assembly. Work methodically attaching blocks to the top, bottom and shelf, and then to the sides.

4 Lay one side of the wardrobe flat on the bench and fit the top, bottom and shelf in place. The two halves of the jointing block are held together with a nut and bolt. Do the bolts up, but not tightly, and then fit the other side of the wardrobe. As always, an extra pair of hands will be a great help at this stage.

5 Now do all the bolts up tight and check that the wardrobe is square. Turn the wardrobe over and prepare to fit the back.

6 With this type of construction a back is essential as it gives the unit rigidity. Use a melamine-faced hardboard, placing the white face inside the unit. Once the hardboard has been cut to size screw it onto the back. A very quick method of fixing is to use an electric staple gun.

■ Vanity unit

1 First make the box at the bottom. The method of construction is exactly the same as for the wardrobe.

2 Screw the back (which also forms the support for the mirror) onto the box at the bottom. Be sure to use fairly long 'supa screws' to get a good fixing.

3 Cut the sides of the vanity unit to length and fix them in place by screws passing through the back. Fit jointing blocks at the bottom front edge of the sides to prevent any flexing of the back.

4 Fix on the mirror. A range of different-sized mirrors are available with a variety of fixings. Some mirrors are pre-drilled in which case a special screw and rubber ferrule should be used. Insist that the shop selling the mirror also supplies the necessary fixings. Mirrors without holes drilled in them can be fitted with clips. The plastic clip fits onto the edge of the mirror and has a fixing place for the screw. Never attempt to drill holes in the mirror.

5 When the mirror is fitted attach a small strip light to a short length of

board at the top of the vanity unit with plastic corner blocks.

■ Top locker blanket box

A useful storage area is on top of the wardrobe, but unless this space is enclosed dust will gather. It's a good idea to measure from the top of the wardrobe to the ceiling and make this measurement the total height of the locker. Construct the locker in exactly the same way as the wardrobe.

■ Fitting the doors

In the past the hinge was something that required the touch of the cabinet maker to fit well. Today we have a surprisingly large array of hinges that can be used on plastic-faced chipboard and no real skill required to fit them. As I have mentioned, special hinges have been developed which require a large round hole to fit into and undoubtedly if you are making a number of units then it's worth considering the initial outlay of the cutter for this job. This hinge has the advantage of being completely hidden from the outside and being adjustable after fitting. There are other hinges which are more traditional in appearance and which do not require recesses to be cut out of the wood to take the hinge flaps. Look carefully before you buy and study the packets for fixing instructions.

1 Fitting hinges requires special 'supa screws' to get a good fixing into the chipboard. If you decide to buy a cutter for sinking the large circular hinge fixing, make sure that you follow the instructions carefully and drill a small pilot hole for the cutter point to follow.

2 Once the hinge has been fitted to the door it must be attached to the 'carcass'. I always put a block of wood with an angled wedge on top under the door to hold it, and then place a piece of thin card on top of the wedge which is the amount of clearance between the bottom of the door and the base. Fit the top hinge to the carcass first and then the bottom one. It is helpful to have someone to assist you, particularly for the large wardrobe doors.

3 Before fixing the vanity unit doors and the blanket locker you will need to veneer the 'cut edges'. This is a simpler job than it sounds. (The veneer should be bought at the same time as the board to ensure colour match.) Cut a strip of veneer slightly longer than the edge you are working on. Set an old electric iron to a fairly high temperature and, when it is hot, begin ironing down the plastic veneer. The veneer strip will be slightly wider than the board, so keep one edge aligned exactly all the way allowing the overlap on one side only. I have found that the iron can be applied directly to the veneer without any disastrous results.

4   Allow the veneer to cool down and then with a very sharp Stanley knife trim off the excess. I found that trimming off plastic veneer was more difficult than trimming off the wood veneer used on the blockboard in the hi-fi storage units (page 23). It is probably a good idea to experiment with some off-cuts so that you appreciate the difficulties involved before working on a large piece of board.

5   It only remains for you now to fit magnetic catches, door handles and a stay to the top locker and the units are finished.

■ Stool

If you need a confidence-builder before you attempt the larger items, this is an ideal project to begin with so that you can get used to the method of jointing the board.

Once the legs and uprights have been cut to length, use plastic jointing blocks to fix them together (see wardrobe fixing instructions). The shelf which has to be fixed below the top gives the stool its rigidity. Veneer the edges of the board to finish off the unit.

Photograph: page 60

■ CUTTING LIST

Wardrobe

Sides	2 off	1830 x 456 x 16 mm (72 x 18 x ⅝ in)	plastic-veneered chipboard
Top, shelf & floor	3 off	578 x 456 x 16 mm (22¾ x 18 x ⅝ in)	plastic-veneered chipboard
Doors	2 off	1748 x 305 x 16 mm (68¾ x 12 x ⅝ in)	plastic-veneered chipboard
Kicking strip	1 off	578 x 76 x 16 mm (22¾ x 3 x ⅝ in)	plastic-veneered chipboard
Back	1 off	1830 x 610 x 3 mm (72 x 24 x ⅛ in)	hardboard

Ancillaries

	14 off	Plastic corner joint blocks
	6 off	Hinges
	2 off	Magnetic catch assemblies
	2 off	Handles
	1 off	Clothes rail plus end fittings
		'Iron-on' plastic veneer edging strip. Panel pins or screws

Top locker

Sides & divider	3 off	456 x 196 x 16 mm (18 x 7¾ x ⅝ in)	plastic-veneered chipboard
Top & bottom	2 off	1143 x 456 x 16 mm (45 x 18 x ⅝ in)	plastic-veneered chipboard
Door	1 off	1143 x 228 x 16 mm (45 x 9 x ⅝ in)	plastic-veneered chipboard
Back	1 off	1143 x 228 x 3 mm (45 x 9 x ⅛ in)	hardboard

Ancillaries

	8 off	Plastic corner joint blocks
	2 off	Hinges
	2 off	Magnetic catch assemblies
	2 off	Handles
	2 off	Brass door stay
		'Iron-on' plastic veneer edging strip. Panel pins or screws

Vanity unit

Upper side panels	2 off	1226 x 152 x 16 mm (48¼ x 6 x ⅝ in)	plastic-veneered chipboard
Lower side panels	2 off	588 x 305 x 16 mm (23⅛ x 12 x ⅝ in)	plastic-veneered chipboard
Top surface	1 off	533 x 305 x 16 mm (21 x 12 x ⅝ in)	plastic-veneered chipboard
Shelf & bottom	2 off	501 x 305 x 16 mm (19¾ x 12 x ⅝ in)	plastic-veneered chipboard
Back	1 off	1830 x 533 x 16 mm (72 x 21 x ⅝ in)	plastic-veneered chipboard
Kicking & header strip	2 off	501 x 76 x 16 mm (19¾ x 3 x ⅝ in)	plastic-veneered chipboard
Doors	2 off	528 x 266 x 16 mm (20¾ x 10½ x ⅝ in)	plastic-veneered chipboard

Ancillaries

	18 off	Plastic corner joint blocks
	4 off	Hinges
	2 off	Magnetic catch assemblies
	2 off	Handles
	1 off	1200 x 450 mm (47¼ x 17¾ in) mirror
	4 off	Mirror fixing screws and caps
	1 off	305 mm (12 in) long tube light fitting
		'Iron-on' plastic veneer edging strip. Screws

HOUSEHOLD SECTION

Stool			
Sides	2 off	380 x 230 x 16 mm (15 x 9 x ⅝ in)	plastic-veneered chipboard
Top	1 off	432 x 230 x 16 mm (17 x 9 x ⅝ in)	plastic-veneered chipboard
Shelf	1 off	350 x 230 x 16 mm (13¾ x 9 x ⅝ in)	plastic-veneered chipboard

Ancillaries			
	8 off	Plastic corner joint blocks. 'Iron-on' plastic veneer edging strip	

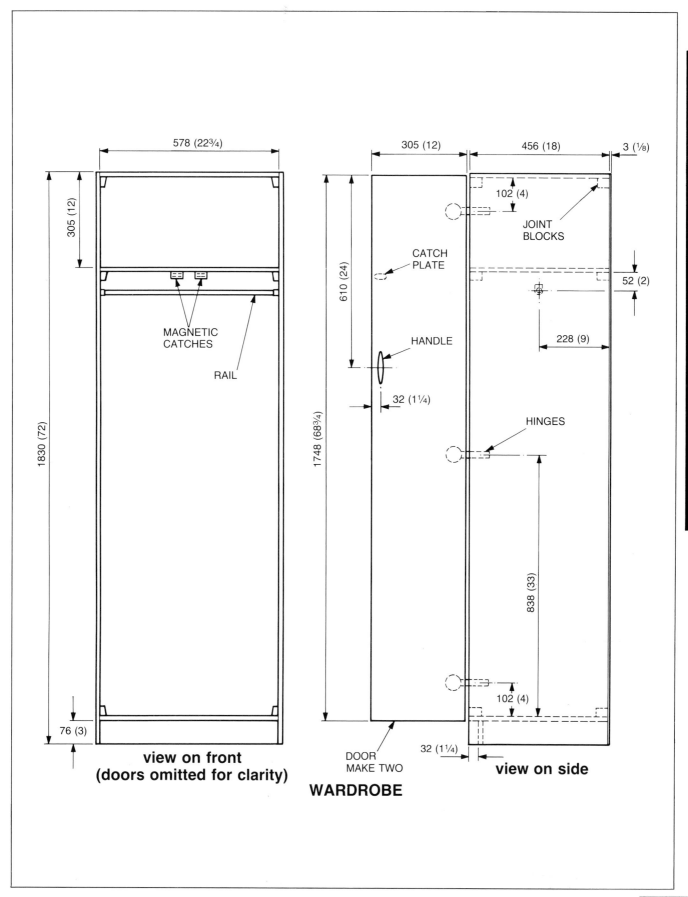

view on front
(doors omitted for clarity)

DOOR
MAKE TWO

view on side

WARDROBE

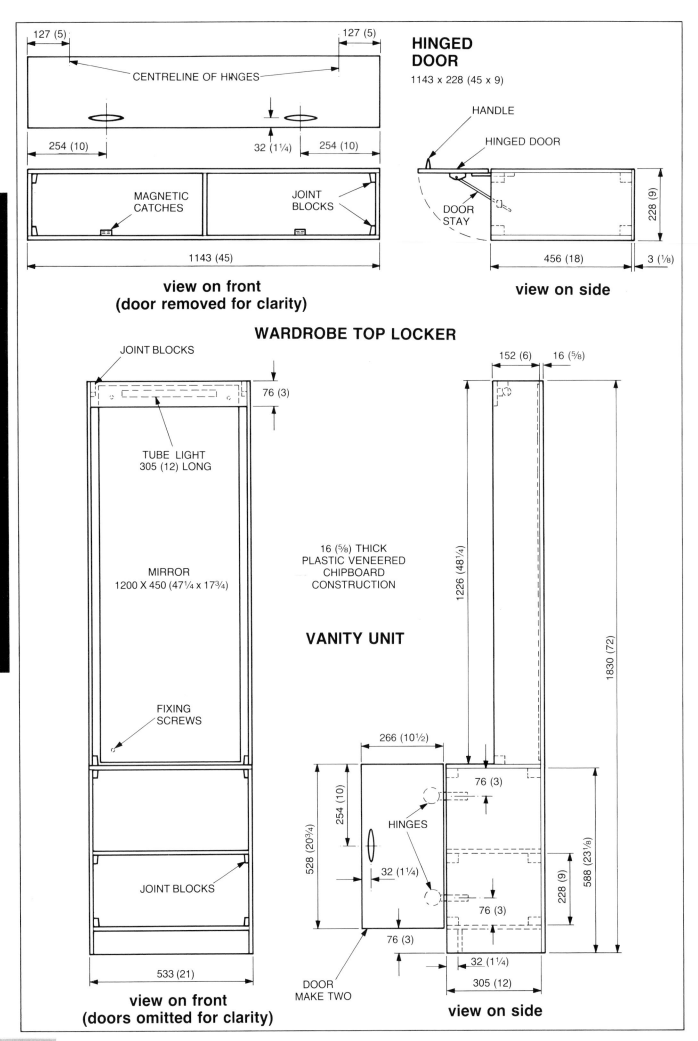

HINGED DOOR
1143 x 228 (45 x 9)

127 (5)   127 (5)

CENTRELINE OF HINGES

254 (10)   32 (1¼)   254 (10)

HANDLE

HINGED DOOR

MAGNETIC
CATCHES

JOINT
BLOCKS

DOOR
STAY

228 (9)

1143 (45)

456 (18)   3 (⅛)

**view on front
(door removed for clarity)**

view on side

WARDROBE TOP LOCKER

JOINT BLOCKS

76 (3)

152 (6)   16 (⅝)

TUBE LIGHT
305 (12) LONG

16 (⅝) THICK
PLASTIC VENEERED
CHIPBOARD
CONSTRUCTION

MIRROR
1200 X 450 (47¼ x 17¾)

1226 (48¼)

VANITY UNIT

1830 (72)

FIXING
SCREWS

266 (10½)

76 (3)

HINGES

JOINT BLOCKS

254 (10)

528 (20¾)

32 (1¼)

588 (23⅛)

228 (9)

76 (3)

76 (3)

533 (21)

DOOR
MAKE TWO

32 (1¼)

305 (12)

**view on front
(doors omitted for clarity)**

view on side

HOUSEHOLD SECTION

64

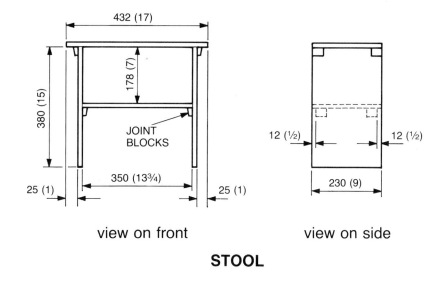

432 (17)

178 (7)

380 (15)

JOINT
BLOCKS

25 (1)

350 (13¾)

25 (1)

view on front

12 (½)

12 (½)

230 (9)

view on side

STOOL

WALL PLATE RACK

I have designed this rack to match the features used on the table and Cotswold clock. I have used chamfers on all the edges which give the finished rack a very gentle and flowing line. If you collect china objects then you may wish to alter the rack to suit your collection or add an extra shelf to it.

Stopped housing joint

The new joint to be tackled in this job is the stopped housing joint. As you can see from the illustration this joint consists basically of a trench, stopped at one end, into which the shelf fits. The stopped housing presents a neater finish than a through housing joint as it hides the joint that holds the shelf in place. The two plate support racks at the back are jointed to the ends by stub mortice and tenons. (Cutting this joint is described in the Refectory table section on page 9.)

1 As with all construction jobs, mark out the complete job before doing any cutting. Clamp together the two ends — mark the position of the joints in pencil. Clamp together the two rails and shelves and mark the shoulder lines. Check all the measurements and then use the marking knife to scribe in all the shoulder lines.

2 To make the stopped housing joint start by clamping the wood firmly to the bench top. As you have to cut across the grain it is always a good idea to scribe the trench for this deeply as this will prevent any possibility of fibres 'splitting out' and spoiling the joint.

3 With a sharp chisel cut out a small square hole at the 'stopped' end of the trench. Cut this carefully to the correct depth.

4 Using a tenon saw, insert the tip into the hole and start sawing along the deeply scribed housing trench. To begin with you will only be able to move the tenon saw backwards and forwards by a very small amount. Keep the tenon saw upright and use your thumb to guide it along the groove. The most difficult part is getting started. Now cut down to the bottom of the small square hole you have chiselled out and down to the gauge line at the back of the trench. Repeat this operation on the other side.

5 Now the waste wood in the middle of the trench has to be removed with a sharp firmer or bevel-edged chisel. Avoid taking heavy cuts otherwise the chisel will dig in. When you get near the gauge line make sure that you have the bottom of the trench flat. A little care is needed here to level things off.

Traditionally the woodworker would have used a hand router to make sure that the bottom of the trench was even all along its length, but with care this is one tool you won't have to purchase unless you intend to do quite a lot of woodwork. In the past five years the electric hand-

held router has come within the financial reach of all keen woodworkers. If you have one of these versatile electric tools then you will know how quickly and accurately they can cut housing joints.

6 The shelf will now fit into the housing joint after the small 'step' has been cut out on the front of the shelf.

7 After cutting all the joints, assemble the rack and check for fit. It is sometimes very helpful to pencil-mark each joint so that after final shaping re-locating the pairs of joints is a much easier task.

8 Now, using a plough plane, cut grooves along the front of the shelves. This can be done with a chisel, but it is not easy and would take a great deal of time.

9 Cut the bottom shelf to shape and remove the saw marks with a spokeshave. Now, using the spokeshave, shape the dish curve along the bow front. This can be done quite easily, but care must be taken to remove equal amounts of wood from either side. The shaping used is the same as on the Cotswold clock.

10 Cut the ends to shape and chamfer the sides. Chamfer the front edges of the rails and the top front shelf.

11 Attaching the rack to the wall really requires two small brass plates recessed and screwed into the top of the back rail. This makes a neat fixing point for wall mounting.

12 'Cramp up' the job dry (without glue) using sash cramps to check all is well before finally gluing. Use the cramps to hold the joints in place while the glue dries.

Photographs: opposite and pages 8, 26-27

CUTTING LIST

Wall plate rack

End	2 off	502 x 117 x 22 mm (19¾ x 4⅝ x ⅞ in)	timber
Rail	2 off	936 x 38 x 20 mm (36⅞ x 1½ x ¾ in)	timber
Top shelf	1 off	938 x 86 x 20 mm (37 x 3⅜ x ¾ in)	timber
Bottom shelf	1 off	938 x 146 x 20 mm (37 x 5¾ x ¾ in)	timber

Ancillaries

	2 off	Brass key hole hanging plates

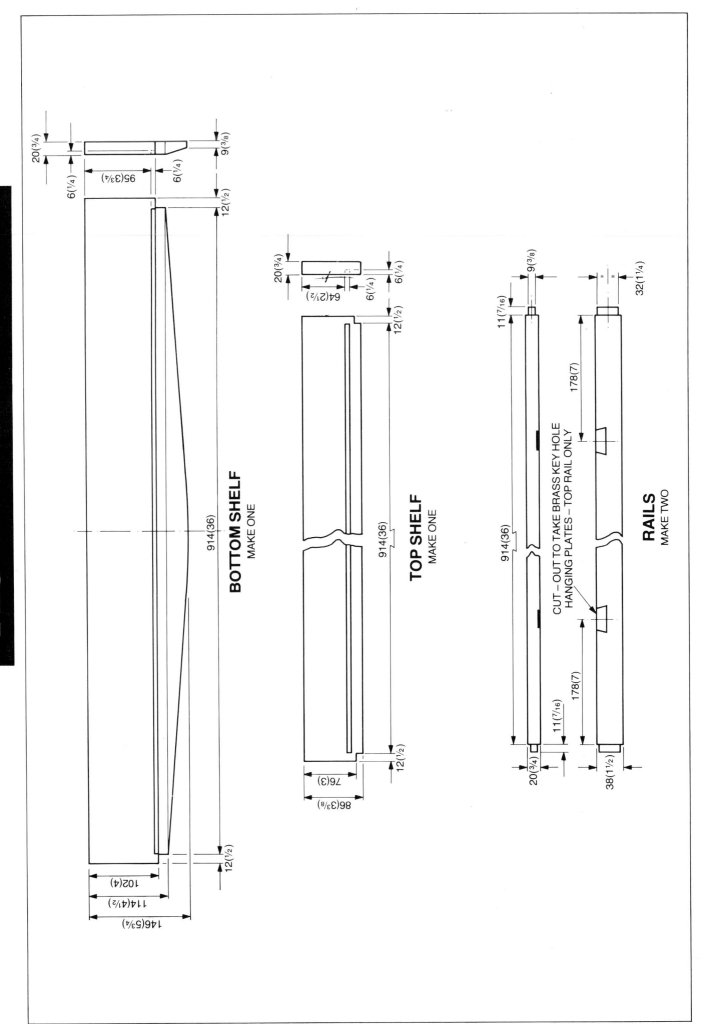

BOTTOM SHELF
MAKE ONE

TOP SHELF
MAKE ONE

RAILS
MAKE TWO

CUT – OUT TO TAKE BRASS KEY HOLE
HANGING PLATES – TOP RAIL ONLY

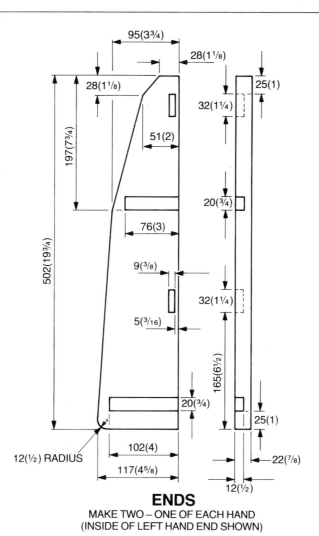

95(3¾)

28(1⅛)

28(1⅛)

25(1)

32(1¼)

197(7¾)

51(2)

20(¾)

502(19¾)

76(3)

9(⅜)

32(1¼)

5(³/₁₆)

165(6½)

20(¾)

25(1)

12(½) RADIUS

102(4)

22(⅞)

117(4⅝)

12(½)

ENDS
MAKE TWO – ONE OF EACH HAND
(INSIDE OF LEFT HAND END SHOWN)

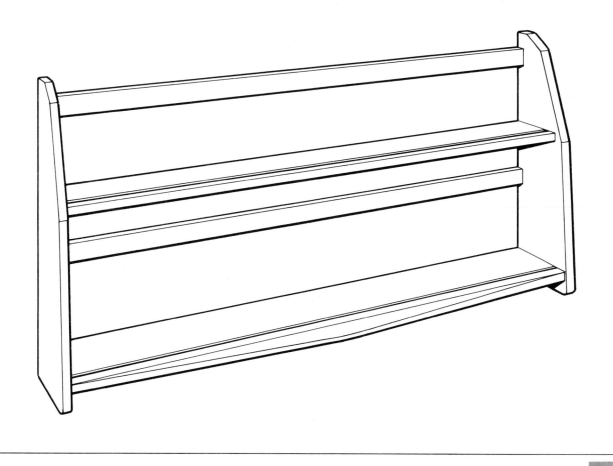

With the introduction of the quartz electronic battery clock mechanism it is now possible to construct a variety of clocks to your own style at a minimum cost. The quartz movement has a battery that lasts a year and keeps excellent time. You can have a pendulum swinging gently backwards and forwards as I have if you wish, but it no longer governs the time-keeping of the clock—it's just there for appearance!

The readily available quartz movement means that you have complete freedom of choice as to your clock design. I have used the same mechanism in two completely different clock styles just to get you started.

■ Contemporary-style wall hanging clock

If you have never made a clock before then this is a good one to start with as there are no joints to make—you only have to cut the wood to shape. If you use two contrasting woods the design will look even better. I suggest one of the African mahoganies (any one of this variety with a reddish brown colouring) for the main support, and sycamore or ash (whitish colouring) for the top and bottom. If you cannot get these woods any good quality hardwood will do.

The clock consists basically of three pieces of wood glued and screwed together. The centre piece (main support) holds the mechanism and attached to this are two pieces of wood— one at the top, the other at the bottom.

1 The first task is to cut a housing to take the clock mechanism. This has to be done in order that the spigot which holds the clock hands will protrude sufficiently to allow them to be attached. Mark in pencil round the clock mechanism, taking note of the central hole that has to be drilled to take the spigot. Mechanisms and spigots vary in shape and size, depending on who makes them, so it is always best to buy the mechanism before you try to cut the wood.

2 Drill the central hole for the spigot. Using the largest firmer or bevel-edged chisel you have, start to chip out the recess. Take light cuts over the whole area, keeping the edges 'tidy'. Great care has to be exercised when the task is nearly finished as the bottom of the recess is not very thick. When the housing is finished test to see if the mechanism fits and that the spigot clears the face sufficiently to allow for the hands to move freely over the clock face.

3 Now you must cut a hole in the bottom of the centre piece to allow the pendulum to be seen more easily. There are two ways of doing this:
i Drill a small hole and insert a coping saw blade. Re-attach the coping saw blade to its frame and, with the wood fixed in a vice, cut out the hole.
ii Use a hole-cutting attachment for your electric drill. This device is fairly new on the market and is called a hole saw. It comes complete with a set of circular hole-cutting blades.
4 With all the 'joints' cut, the shaping of the centre piece can be carried out. Cut out the basic shape with a coping saw and remove the saw marks with a spokeshave.
5 Now shape up the top and bottom pieces of the clock, and glue and screw them in place.
6 Apply polyurethane or other finish to all three pieces of wood.
7 Now fit the zone dial. The one I used was self-adhesive, but just for safety I drilled two tiny holes at the top and bottom of the dial and secured it to the wood with panel pins. The electric movement is fitted into the housing and is held in place by a brass ferrule that tightens up and holds the mechanism firmly to the face of the clock.
8 The hands can now be fitted and the pendulum hung in place. The designers of the quartz movement have provided a built-in hanging bracket so all that remains is to fix a picture hook to the wall and hang the clock squarely.

■ Cotswold clock

This clock utilises exactly the same mechanism, the only difference being the case and the bezel with dial and glass. It is designed to complement the wall-mounted plate rack with deep chamfers on the top and base.

The method of housing the quartz movement and cutting the circular hole is the same as for the contemporary clock, but with this design the sides are fitted into rebates.

■ The rebate

A rebate is a step on the end or side of a piece of flat timber, which strengthens the joint when two pieces of timber have to be joined. The rebate provides extra gluing area and so this joint is much stronger than a butt joint. The rebate width is the same as the clock side pieces. To cut the joint you will have to buy a special rebate plane or an electric router which will do this job very quickly.
1 If you are using a hand plane, set the width and depth stops and start rebating at the front edge, working gradually backwards. It helps to rub a piece of old candle on the bottom of the plane.
2 Once both rebates have been cut it is time to cut the sides to length. As this clock case is considerably heavier than the other one a rail must be fitted onto the sides. The rail provides the suspension point if the clock is to be wall-hung. The joint is best cut with both sides held together in the vice and before they are glued in place.
3 Glue the sides in place and hold them with cramps.
4 Now shape the top and bottom pieces. The deep chamfer cut on the inside edge reflects the circular shape of the face. Shaping is done with the now familiar spokeshave and chisel.
5 Glue the two ends in place.
6 Before fixing any clock parts to the case apply the finish. Once this is done the various parts can be assembled as before.
7 The bezel dial and glass come as a complete unit. On the bezel you will find small fixing holes for panel pins. Before fixing the dial check that it is central and positioned correctly.

Photographs: opposite (contemporary-style clock); pages 8, 26-27 (Cotswold clock)

HOUSEHOLD SECTION

Contemporary style wall hanging clock

Main support	1 off	530 x 114 x 9 mm (20⅞ x 4½ x ⅜ in)	timber
Top block	1 off	178 x 105 x 22 mm (7 x 4⅛ x ⅞ in)	timber
Bottom block	1 off	156 x 67 x 12 mm (6 x 2⅝ x ½ in)	timber

Ancillaries

	1 off	Clock movement

Cotswold clock

Clock front	1 off	520 x 203 x 20 mm (20½ x 8 x ¾ in)	timber
Clock side	2 off	520 x 54 x 20 mm (20½ x 2⅛ x ¾ in)	timber
Top and bottom	1 of each	203 x 76 x 12 mm (8 x 3 x ½ in)	timber
Support rail	1 off	203 x 32 x 12 mm (8 x 1¼ x ½ in)	timber

Ancillaries

	1 off	Clock movement
	2 off	Decorative spikes

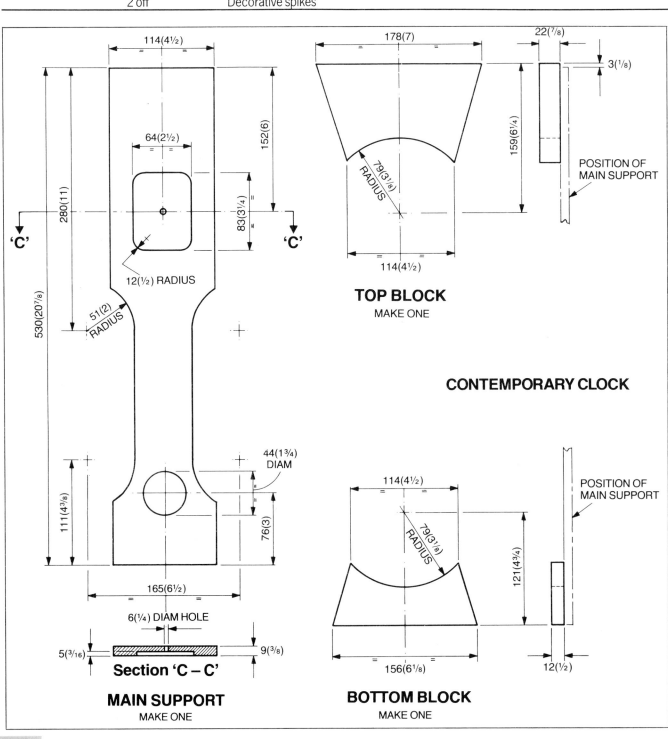

TOP BLOCK
MAKE ONE

CONTEMPORARY CLOCK

MAIN SUPPORT
MAKE ONE

BOTTOM BLOCK
MAKE ONE

Section 'C – C'

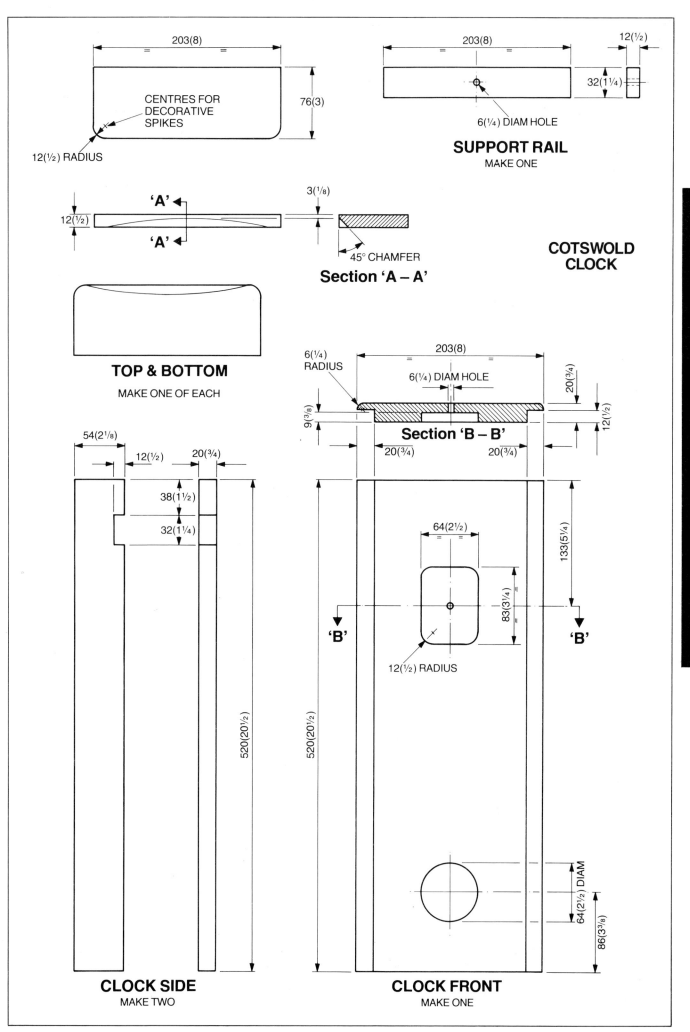

203(8)

CENTRES FOR
DECORATIVE
SPIKES

76(3)

12(½) RADIUS

203(8)

12(½)

32(1¼)

6(¼) DIAM HOLE

SUPPORT RAIL
MAKE ONE

12(½)

'A'

'A'

3(⅛)

45° CHAMFER

Section 'A – A'

**COTSWOLD
CLOCK**

TOP & BOTTOM

MAKE ONE OF EACH

6(¼)
RADIUS

203(8)

6(¼) DIAM HOLE

20(¾)

12(½)

9(⅜)

Section 'B – B'

20(¾)

20(¾)

54(2⅛)

12(½)

20(¾)

38(1½)

32(1¼)

520(20½)

64(2½)

133(5¼)

83(3¼)

12(½) RADIUS

520(20½)

'B'

'B'

64(2½) DIAM

86(3⅜)

CLOCK SIDE
MAKE TWO

CLOCK FRONT
MAKE ONE

For many hundreds of years man has practised the art of smoking herrings with oak shavings to produce the kipper, without which no English breakfast would be complete. The tannin-impregnated smoke infuses the herrings with a delicious flavour and turns them a golden brown colour. Oak has large quantities of tannin in its bark and heart-wood, and this is why when the timber is handled it leaves a black stain on your hands. Steak cooked on a platter of well seasoned oak thus acquires a unique and wonderful flavour.

■ Oak wooden platter

If you have always wanted to have a 'bash' at woodwork then this is an ideal starter as your only requirements are a gouge, a 'G' cramp, a wooden mallet and a large piece of oak.

Basically any shape will do, the only requirement being that it is well seasoned and sufficiently thick to allow for a portion to be gouged out of the middle.

1 Before you start, mark in pencil the area you want to cut out. It is best to keep some distance from the side as you may need this area to carve a decoration on the edge.

2 With the oak firmly cramped on the bench start gouging by taking fairly light cuts. Start each new cut from the pencil line at the edge, working the gouge towards the middle of the platter. Avoid letting the gouge dig in and try to keep the cuts to a fairly even depth overall. Once you have gouged out half the platter, turn it round on the bench and repeat the operation from the other side. At this stage if you feel things are a little uneven then one of the Surform shaver tools will be a great help to even things up before you take the next cut with the gouge. The 'U' shaped cut the gouge makes is particularly advantageous as we want the juices in the meat to flow towards the centre of the platter. As you gouge from the sides to the middle make the cut a little deeper towards the centre. Don't use the Surform shaver when you are going to take the 'last cut' across the platter as this will spoil the gouge marks.

3 The top of the platter can be given a very simple decoration or, if you prefer, just be rounded off with a spokeshave. You will probably find that your experience in using a gouge for the centre of the platter has given you one or two ideas for decorating the edges. It is a good idea to gouge out recesses on the underside of

the platter as these will assist the cook when taking it from a hot oven.

The exciting thing about woodcarving is that you don't have to buy dozens of tools to get started, and I am sure that if you only have a small number of chisels and gouges you will be more likely to explore their full potential for shaping wood before buying others.

■ Preparing the platter for the oven

The platter needs proving before you use it for cooking.

1 Rub it with cooking oil or dripping and a sprinkling of herbs (even garlic if you're brave).

2 Now put the platter into a cool oven (that should frighten a few woodworkers) and gently increase the heat to gas mark 6 or 400°F, and leave it at this high temperature for about 30 minutes. Turn off the oven and let the platter cool inside. The platter is now ready for use.

Inevitably there will be a few cracks, but don't worry as these will stabilise as the cooking oils penetrate the wood. I should stress that it is vital that the wood used is well seasoned and, if possible, kiln dried. Now at last we are ready to start cooking.

The meat

This method can be used for cooking steak (fillet, sirloin or rump), chops, sausages or even hamburgers.

1 Place the meat in the hollow of the platter and put a little oil or butter on top of the meat.

2 Place in a hot oven (gas mark 6, 400°F).

3 Turn the meat after 5 minutes and continue cooking for another 15 minutes or to taste.

4 If the meat is not top quality, you may need to marinade it and a quick and easy marinade can be made from Worcester Sauce, oil, salt, pepper and herbs. Leave the meat in this mixture for a few hours or overnight, then cook as described above.

To decorate and serve

1 Remove the platter of meat from the oven.

2 Put a pat of savoury butter (made from butter mixed with chopped fresh herbs, which has then been cooled in the refrigerator and sliced into portions) on top of the meat to melt, together with a small portion of Boursin cheese, if liked.

3 Garnish with some fresh tomatoes and watercress and serve.

NB Put the platter on a heat-resistant mat as it remains hot for some time.

For surf 'n turf

For a variation of this dish you will need some large cooked prawns (Dublin Bay prawns are best). These should be shelled, fried quickly in melted butter and served on top of the meat with the butter and cheese as above. You may also like to add some wedges of lemon.

■ HOUSEHOLD SECTION ■

Photographs: opposite and pages 8, 26-27

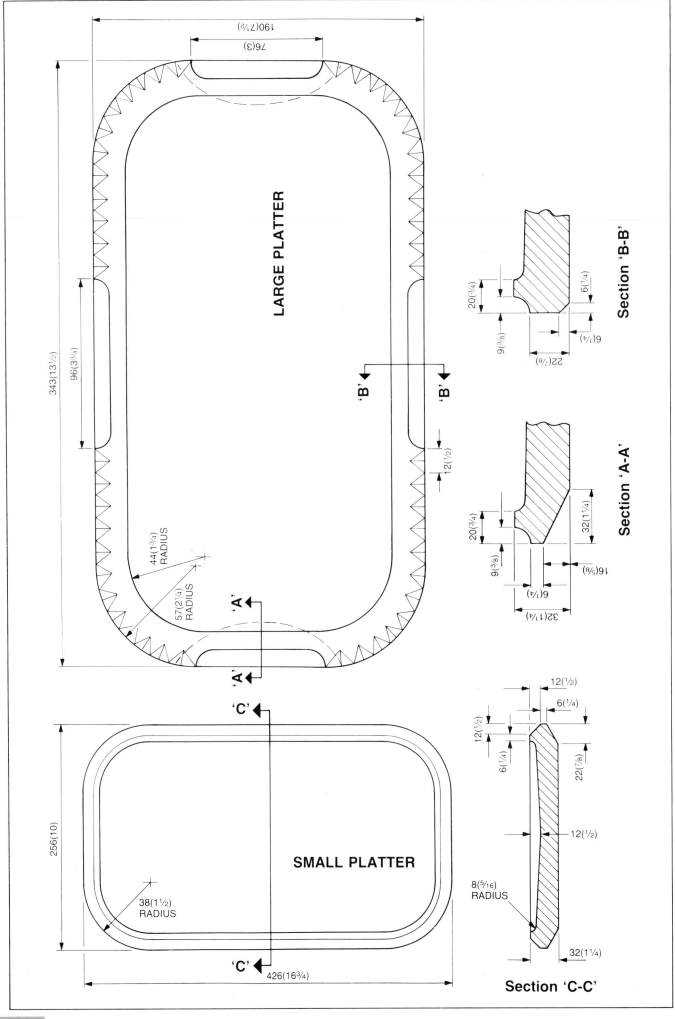

LARGE PLATTER

190(7½)
76(3)
343(13½)
96(3¾)
44(1¾) RADIUS
57(2¼) RADIUS
'A'
'A'
'B'
'B'
12(½)
'C'

Section 'B-B'
20(¾)
9(⅜)
6(¼)
6(¼)
22(⅞)

Section 'A-A'
20(¾)
9(⅜)
32(1¼)
6(¼)
16(⅝)
32(1¼)

SMALL PLATTER

256(10)
38(1½) RADIUS
'C'
'C'
426(16¾)

Section 'C-C'
12(½)
6(¼)
12(½)
6(¼)
22(⅞)
12(½)
8(⁵⁄₁₆) RADIUS
32(1¼)

STEAK KNIFE AND FORK CARVING SET AND BOARD

At first, the thought of making your own cutlery handles and fitting them to the 'steels' may seem a little daunting, but it really is quite a simple task which only requires patience. Of all the things in God's creation the human hand is perhaps the most wonderful, but when it comes to deciding what is the best shape to fit into it comfortably there seems to be a great diversity of opinion. For my part I like a knob on one end that fits into the palm of my hand and sufficient thickness of handle to get a firm hold. It really is a matter of choice, however, just how you carve and shape your handles.

The method for making handles is exactly the same for steak knives and forks and carving knives and forks. The first essential is to acquire a really dense hardwood (softwoods are completely unsatisfactory) and my favourite is yew. English yew is dense, has a magnificent colour and polishes very well.

1   Start by cutting the wood to be used to length. Sometimes you will be able to find a high-class joiner who will sell you offcuts which are ideal for this job.

2   With a sharp chisel clean up one end of the wood and mark with a pencil where the hole to take the blade shank will go.

3   Fix the wood in a vice and carefully drill a hole with a bit that is just a little wider in diameter than the blade shank. Now push the shank into the hole and get the 'bolster' at the end of the shank to fit tightly against the end of the wood. Sometimes it is helpful to use a countersink and slightly enlarge the entrance to the hole. Take time and be patient in order to get these two pieces to fit accurately.

4   Once this has been achieved push the blade shank right into the wood and mark with a pencil around the knife 'bolster'. Now you will have a mark to work to when shaping the handle. It is this part of the handle I shape first.

5   If this is the first time you have done any shaping and you are wondering just which tool to use, any sharp-edged tool will do. Obviously some are better than others, but great things have been achieved by the humble pen knife. I found myself using a variety of tools — a small bevel-edged chisel (always a favourite with me), two gouges and, very useful, the Surform shaver tool. Remember the golden rule and always cut away from yourself.

An awkward problem is how to hold the handle. It is not very large and if you start tightening the vice too much you will crush the wood. I always shape the portion adjacent to the steel 'bolster' first. Then I grip the handle in the middle and start carving the pommel. It is essential that your tools are razor sharp. A very sharp tool will cut with the minimum amount of pressure, but a blunt tool requires brute force and it's then that you will slip and injure your hands. I often stop three or four times just to re-sharpen my tools while completing one handle. The final shaping of the handle does present real problems as the vice jaws do tend to mark the wood.

6   At this stage I mix the epoxy resin (don't use anything else — it won't work) and prepare to fix the steel shanks in the wood. Epoxy resin is very strong but it won't work if it comes into contact with the oils left on the wood and metal by your fingers. It is therefore vital to clean the shank and bolster of the knife with methylated spirit to remove all traces of grease, and then don't touch the shank again. Wear a pair of gloves while handling the blades and fitting them into the handles.

7   Now, using a nail or similar object, make sure you get the resin well inside the pre-drilled hole in the handle. Apply the glue to the steel shank too.

8   As you bring the two objects together turn the handle on the steel shank to be sure that the glue is well worked onto all surfaces. To prevent water getting into the handle I leave a little residue of resin around the handle and the knife bolster.

9   The handles themselves are best finished using a polyurethane varnish which is highly resistant to hot water. I find the best method for getting a good finish is to 'cloth' the polyurethane onto the wood.

Using a piece of lint-free cloth, rub a little polyurethane into the wood and allow 24 hours to dry. Now, using a very fine glasspaper, rub the handle all over.

10   Repeat this process four times and it will give you a good finish resistant to water and grease.

■ Carving set and board

Your carving fork and knife should ideally be kept separate from all other cutlery, and a simple board takes care of this. The shape of it is really a matter of choice.

1   Make handles for the knife and fork first as described above.

2   When this is done, lay them both on a sheet of paper and you will have some idea of the length and shape of the board you need to cut for them. My board simply followed the outline shape of knife and handles.

3   Once you have cut out the board, glue and screw on the little wooden toggles to hold the knife and fork in place. It is advisable to use a fairly large screw to hold the toggle to the wood. The shaping of these two toggles will depend on the shape of the handles, so before fixing them to the board, do all the cutting and shaping necessary.

4   Finally, drill a hole in the top of the board so that it can be safely hung on the wall.

Photographs: pages 8, 26-27, 74 (carving set board not illustrated)

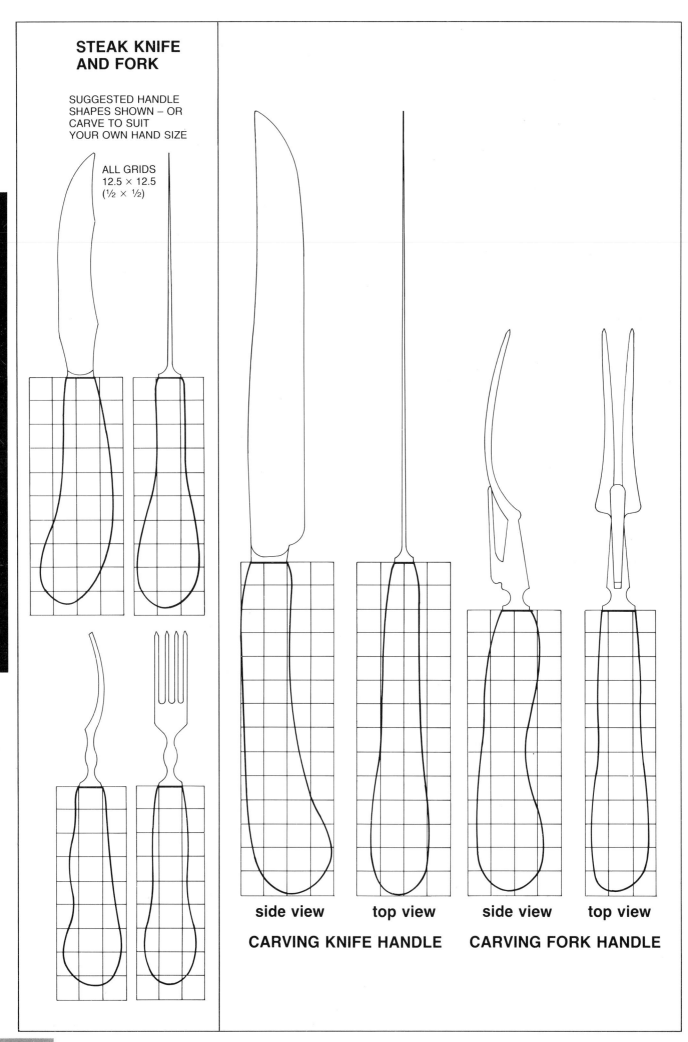

STEAK KNIFE
AND FORK

SUGGESTED HANDLE
SHAPES SHOWN – OR
CARVE TO SUIT
YOUR OWN HAND SIZE

ALL GRIDS
12.5 × 12.5
(½ × ½)

side view   top view

CARVING KNIFE HANDLE

side view   top view

CARVING FORK HANDLE

■ HOUSEHOLD SECTION ■

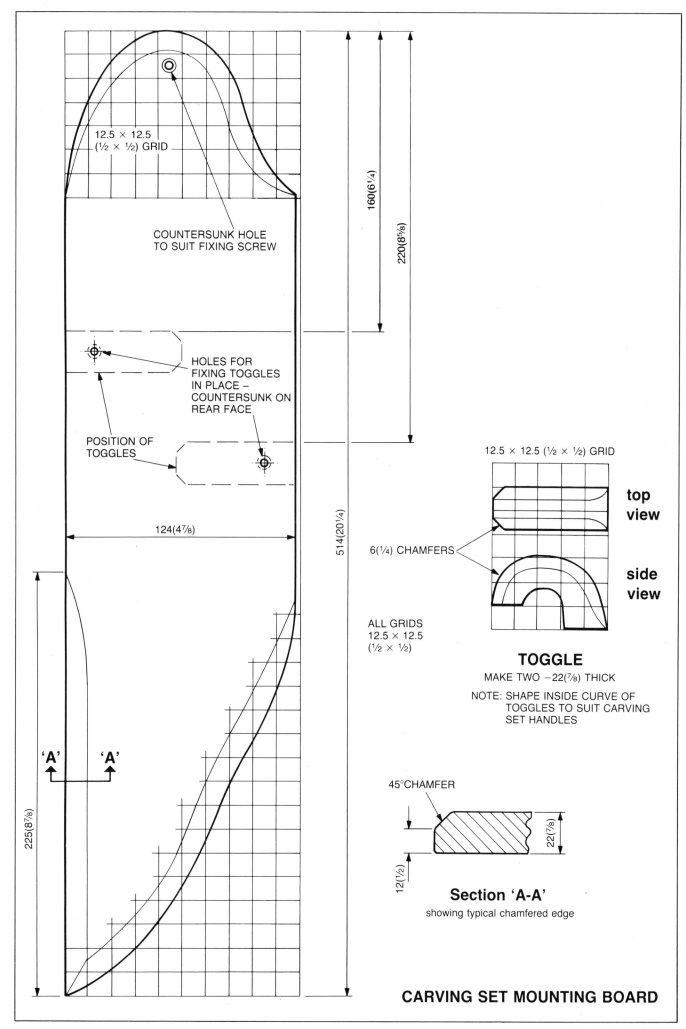

12.5 × 12.5
(½ × ½) GRID

COUNTERSUNK HOLE
TO SUIT FIXING SCREW

160(6¼)

220(8⅝)

HOLES FOR
FIXING TOGGLES
IN PLACE –
COUNTERSUNK ON
REAR FACE

POSITION OF
TOGGLES

124(4⅞)

514(20¼)

'A' 'A'

225(8⅞)

ALL GRIDS
12.5 × 12.5
(½ × ½)

12.5 × 12.5 (½ × ½) GRID

top
view

6(¼) CHAMFERS

side
view

TOGGLE

MAKE TWO −22(⅞) THICK

NOTE: SHAPE INSIDE CURVE OF
TOGGLES TO SUIT CARVING
SET HANDLES

45°CHAMFER

22(⅞)

12(½)

Section 'A-A'

showing typical chamfered edge

CARVING SET MOUNTING BOARD

TABLE LOOM

Weaving is undoubtedly one of the oldest crafts practised by mankind. Perhaps the most fascinating and indeed humbling aspect of the craft is that some of the finest cloth was woven on looms that would be considered primitive by today's technological standards. This 'four harness' table loom is not difficult to build and should really be considered as a means to an end. Once you have made it, a whole new skill has to be learned and indeed a new vocabulary mastered of terms such as heddles, healds, warping posts, beater rails, tenter hooks and raddles. The loom I have made is capable of weaving an almost infinitive variety of patterns, and there are several good books available to help you get started. Many counties have their own weaving guilds who may well be willing to help you 'set up'.

■ Frame

1   Start by cutting the two side pieces to length. These need to be substantial so that when you wind the warp threads up and keep a tension on them the frame doesn't warp or twist. If you don't use beech or oak, a good stout plywood is essential.

2   Four vertical columns which hold the breast beams must now be fitted onto the horizontal side pieces. These columns are 'notched' to fit onto the ends of the side pieces. This will prevent any possibility of them twisting when tension is applied via the warp threads.

3   Drill holes in the sides and ends to take the breast beams and the cloth/warp beams. The warp threads run over the breast beam and the cloth/warp beams unwind the warp threads and wind in the cloth as weaving progresses.

4   Drill holes for the square catapult elastic, which will be threaded through these holes and knotted. This will hold the harnesses taut.

5   Now drill holes for the beater bar legs. (You will find all hole-drilling easier before the two sides are fitted together.) Mark in pencil on the sides where the heddle holder columns are to be fitted.

6   The loom is held together by two pieces of wood underneath, which should both be notched, glued and screwed into the frame. After fitting these, glue the breast beams into the side columns. I found difficulty in obtaining sufficiently large diameter dowel rod for the breast beams and finally bought four hoe handles. Make sure that the grain runs straight and you will find these perfectly adequate.

7   Cramp up the loom until the glue sets.

8   Cut out the two columns which hold the heddle holders. Notch, glue and screw them to the side pieces.

9   Now cut out the heddle holders. To work efficiently I found it best to give each harness bar its own slot, with a recess in the top to hold it securely while weaving. By far the easiest way to cut such a deep slot is to mark out the wood first and, using a flat bit, drill a hole that corresponds to the width of the slot. Once the holes have been bored it is a simple task to cut straight down and remove the waste wood. Work these slots carefully with glasspaper, and make sure that the dowels that form the harnesses have sufficient slack to work smoothly.

10   Using a keyhole saw or jig-saw, cut slots in the heddle holders. Attach the holders to the uprights using coach bolts and wing nuts through the slots. These slots will enable you to adjust the height of the heddle holder, which is very useful when you are lining up the warp threads over the breast beams and through the string healds.

■ Beater Bar

During weaving the weft threads have to be firmed up or 'beaten' by a steel reed, which can be made or bought (see Useful Addresses, page 140). The reed has to be fitted into a framework that swings backwards and forwards.

1   Using a plough plane, groove out the top and bottom of the reed holder. (This can be done with a chisel but it's a pretty laborious task.)

2   Now notch, glue and screw these two channelled sections onto the two vertical 'legs' that fit on the outside of the loom sides.

3   The beater bar assembly is held to the loom sides by dowel rods. It is a good idea to drill a series of holes along the sides of the loom to accommodate the assembly in different positions on the loom. (Assembling the beater bar on a sliding mechanism would actually be better than a swing action.)

■ Alternative beater bar design

Some weavers prefer this simpler method of holding the steel reed for beating the weft threads. A groove is ploughed in a length of timber which is screwed across the frame. The reed simply rests in the groove until required. Both methods of construction are detailed in the plans.

■ Cloth/warp beams and tie rods

The loom has to be fitted with warp threads, which are held by the front cloth/warp beam and tie rod, and at the back by an identical beam and rod.

1   Drill holes in both the warp beams and tie rods.

2   Attach the tie rods using cord to the two warp beams (made from dowel rod) back and front.

3   Tie the warp threads in small bunches and pass them onto the warp beam. As the winding action takes place the tie rods trap the threads and hold them tightly against the beams.

■ Ratchets and stops

These wind on the cloth and control the letting out of the warp thread.

1   Mark out the ratchets carefully and drill the holes for the cloth warp/beams.

2   Now cut the ratchet teeth with a fine-toothed saw. The ratchets are best made out of plywood as there is no weakness with 'short grain shearing' as there is with hardwood. When finished, fit one on the front warp beam and one on the back warp beam.

3   Cut the stops and screw them onto the loom side so that they engage in the ratchets. Drill a hole through the other end of the two warp beams and push a turning bar through each hole.

■ Healds

Healds are basically lengths of cord in which loops are tied by means of knots.

HOUSEHOLD SECTION

This loom uses string healds. These are available ready tied (see Useful Addresses, page 140) and can be threaded straight onto the harness bars which hold them. Alternatively heald string is available if you would rather tie your own. If you decide to do this it is essential to make up a small jig with a spare piece of plywood and panel pins fixed at strategic places. The number of healds on each harness will vary according to the pattern being woven and also the width of cloth required.

Harness bars

The harness bars, both top and bottom, should be made from standard size dowel rod. Once the healds have been threaded onto both top and bottom bars some method of tensioning the whole harness must be used. To do this, screw two cup hooks under each bottom bar. Tension is achieved by threading a length of capapult elastic (available from sports shops) through the hooks and the loom sides and knotting each end. The amount of tension needed will have to be judged by experimenting.

Stick shuttle

Before you can start weaving you will need to make the shuttles. A different one is required for each colour, and ideally hardwood should be used. Drill a large diameter hole near each end of the shuttle. Then cut a narrow slot from the holes out to the ends of the shuttle so that you have a sort of keyhole in each end. The wool is then wound onto the shuttle by passing through the slots into the circular part of the 'keyholes' and can freely pass out again when you start weaving. Round off any sharp edges.

Warp board and tube stand

Before any weaving can start you have to 'warp up' the loom. To do this you have to make a tube stand to hold the warp yarn, and a warping board.
1   Following the diagram, drill and fit the base of the board with dowel rods.
2   Glasspaper all the surfaces, paying particular attention to the edges.
3   Make the tube stand from a block of hardwood. Drill and fit two dowel rods, being sure to use a small 'G' cramp to hold the stand to the table or bench where you are working.

Photograph: page 80

CUTTING LISTS

Loom

Sides	2 off	711 x 105 x 25 mm (28 x 4⅛ x 1 in)	timber
Breast beam column	4 off	203 x 64 x 25 mm (8 x 2½ x 1 in)	timber
Breast beam	2 off	571 mm (22½ in) long x 25 mm (1 in)	diam dowel
Bottom support	2 off	584 x 64 x 25 mm (23 x 2½ x 1 in)	timber
Cloth/warp beam	2 off	672 mm (26½ in) long x 25 mm (1 in)	diam dowel
Tie rods	2 off	522 mm (20½ in) long x 16 mm (⅝ in)	diam dowel
Turning bars	2 off	76 mm (3 in) long x 9 mm (⅜ in)	diam dowel
Ratchet	2 off	76 x 76 x 25 mm (3 x 3 x 1 in)	timber
Ratchet stop	2 off	79 x 32 x 25 mm (3⅛ x 1¼ x 1 in)	timber
Heddle holder head	2 off	254 x 203 x 25 mm (10 x 8 x 1 in)	timber
Heddle holder column	2 off	254 x 76 x 25 mm (10 x 3 x 1 in)	timber
Upper harness bar	4 off	794 mm (31¼ in) long x 20 mm (¾ in)	diam dowel
Lower harness bar	4 off	522 mm (20½ in) long x 20 mm (¾ in)	diam dowel
Beater frame leg	2 off	289 x 38 x 25 mm (11⅜ x 1½ x 1 in)	timber
Beater frame rail	2 off	635 x 32 x 25 mm (25 x 1¼ x 1 in)	timber
Beater frame pins	2 off	76 mm (3 in) long x 12 mm (½ in)	diam dowel
Alternative reed support	1 off	584 x 44 x 25 mm (23 x 1¾ x 1 in)	timber
Shuttle	1 off	647 x 35 x 9 mm (25½ x 1⅜ x ⅜ in)	timber

Ancillaries

		Wire or knotted healds as required	
		Steel reed	
		Strong nylon cord to form warp beam clamp	
	8 off	20 mm (¾ in) cup hooks	
		2440 mm (96 in) long square section catapult elastic	
		Assorted wood screws and cup washers	
		Wood glue	

Warping board

Board	1 off	988 x 304 x 12 mm (39 x 12 x ½ in)	plywood
Pegs	12 off	152 mm (6 in) long x 12 mm (½ in)	diam dowel

Warping post

Base	2 off	267 x 51 x 28 mm (10½ x 2 x 1⅛ in)	timber
Pegs	4 off	222 mm (8¾ in) long x 16 mm (⅝ in)	diam dowel

Ancillaries

	2 off	76 mm (3 in) 'G' clamps	

Shed or lease sticks

Sticks	2 off	711 x 22 x 9 mm (28 x ⅞ x ⅜ in)	timber

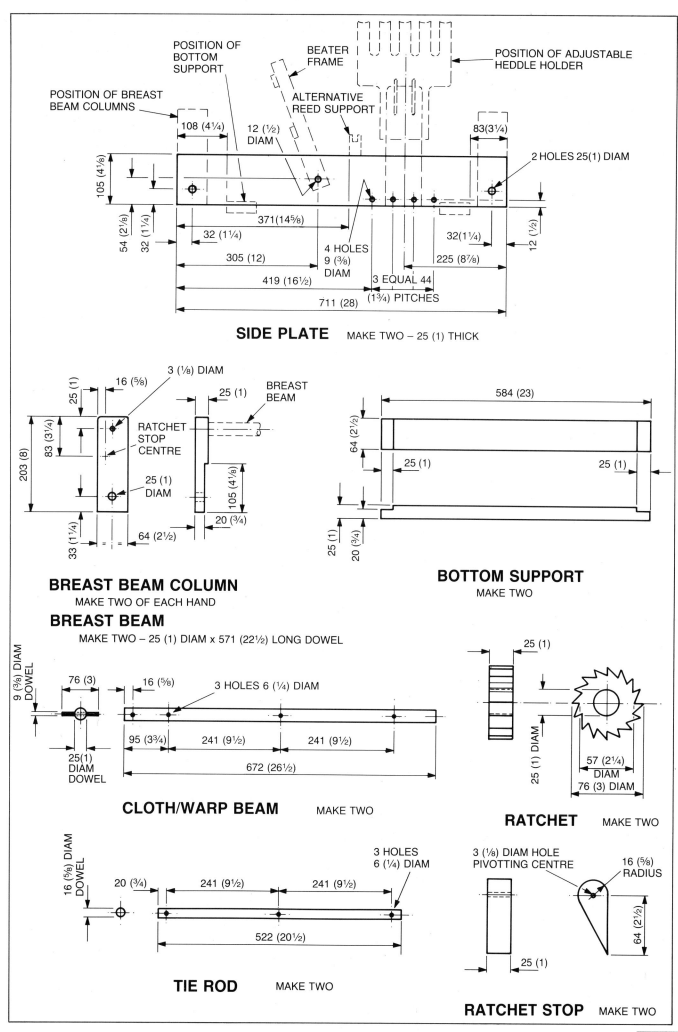

POSITION OF BREAST BEAM COLUMNS

POSITION OF BOTTOM SUPPORT

BEATER FRAME

POSITION OF ADJUSTABLE HEDDLE HOLDER

ALTERNATIVE REED SUPPORT

108 (4¼)

12 (½) DIAM

83 (3¼)

2 HOLES 25(1) DIAM

105 (4⅛)

54 (2⅛)

32 (1¼)

32 (1¼)

371 (14⅝)

12 (½)

305 (12)

225 (8⅞)

4 HOLES 9 (⅜) DIAM

419 (16½)

3 EQUAL 44 (1¾) PITCHES

711 (28)

SIDE PLATE MAKE TWO – 25 (1) THICK

3 (⅛) DIAM

16 (⅝)

25 (1)

25 (1)

BREAST BEAM

RATCHET STOP CENTRE

83 (3¼)

203 (8)

25 (1) DIAM

105 (4⅛)

33 (1¼)

64 (2½)

20 (¾)

584 (23)

64 (2½)

25 (1)

25 (1)

25 (1)

20 (¾)

BOTTOM SUPPORT
MAKE TWO

BREAST BEAM COLUMN
MAKE TWO OF EACH HAND

BREAST BEAM
MAKE TWO – 25 (1) DIAM x 571 (22½) LONG DOWEL

9 (⅜) DIAM DOWEL

76 (3)

16 (⅝)

3 HOLES 6 (¼) DIAM

25 (1)

95 (3¾)

241 (9½)

241 (9½)

25 (1) DIAM

25(1) DIAM DOWEL

672 (26½)

25 (1) DIAM

57 (2¼) DIAM

76 (3) DIAM

CLOTH/WARP BEAM MAKE TWO

RATCHET MAKE TWO

16 (⅝) DIAM DOWEL

3 HOLES 6 (¼) DIAM

20 (¾)

241 (9½)

241 (9½)

3 (⅛) DIAM HOLE PIVOTTING CENTRE

16 (⅝) RADIUS

64 (2½)

522 (20½)

25 (1)

TIE ROD MAKE TWO

RATCHET STOP MAKE TWO

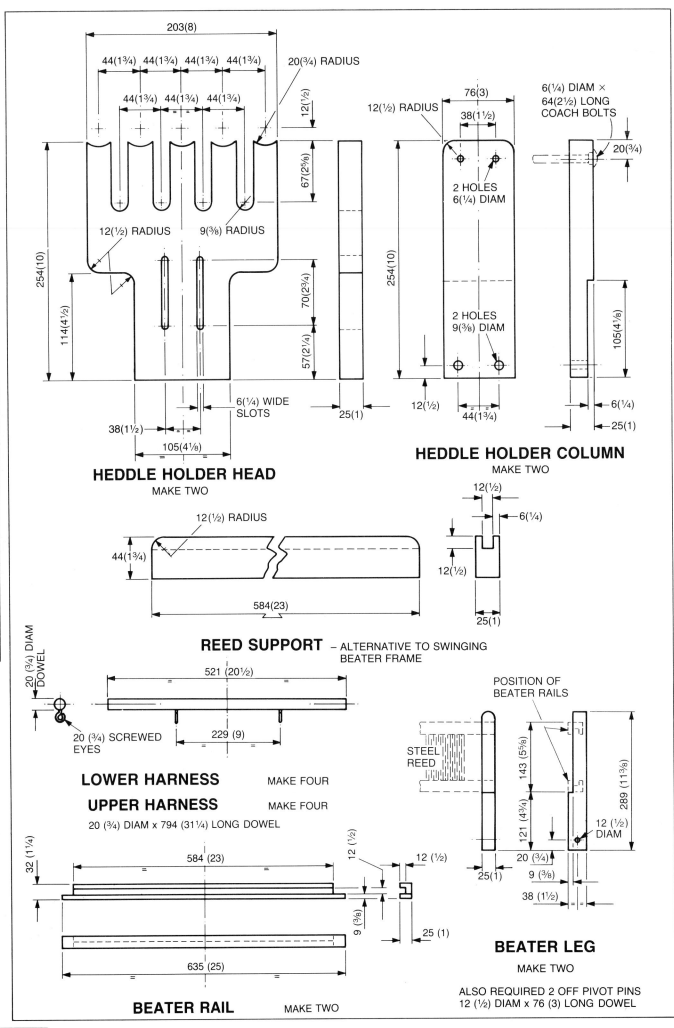

203(8)

44(1¾) 44(1¾) 44(1¾) 44(1¾)

20(¾) RADIUS

12(½)

44(1¾) 44(1¾) 44(1¾)

67(2⅝)

12(½) RADIUS   9(⅜) RADIUS

254(10)

114(4½)

70(2¾)

57(2¼)

6(¼) WIDE SLOTS

38(1½)

105(4⅛)

HEDDLE HOLDER HEAD

MAKE TWO

25(1)

76(3)

12(½) RADIUS

38(1½)

6(¼) DIAM × 64(2½) LONG COACH BOLTS

20(¾)

2 HOLES 6(¼) DIAM

254(10)

105(4⅛)

2 HOLES 9(⅜) DIAM

12(½)

44(1¾)

6(¼)

25(1)

HEDDLE HOLDER COLUMN

MAKE TWO

12(½)

6(¼)

12(½) RADIUS

44(1¾)

12(½)

584(23)

25(1)

REED SUPPORT – ALTERNATIVE TO SWINGING BEATER FRAME

20 (¾) DIAM DOWEL

521 (20½)

229 (9)

20 (¾) SCREWED EYES

LOWER HARNESS   MAKE FOUR

UPPER HARNESS   MAKE FOUR

20 (¾) DIAM x 794 (31¼) LONG DOWEL

POSITION OF BEATER RAILS

STEEL REED

143 (5⅝)

289 (11⅜)

121 (4¾)

12 (½) DIAM

32 (1¼)

584 (23)

12 (½)

12 (½)

9 (⅜)

25 (1)

635 (25)

20 (¾)

25(1)

9 (⅜)

38 (1½)

BEATER LEG

MAKE TWO

BEATER RAIL   MAKE TWO

ALSO REQUIRED 2 OFF PIVOT PINS
12 (½) DIAM x 76 (3) LONG DOWEL

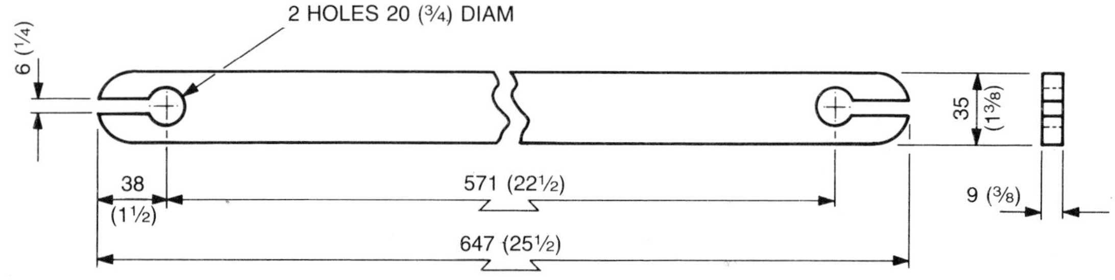
2 HOLES 20 (¾) DIAM
6 (¼)
35 (1⅜)
38 (1½)
571 (22½)
9 (⅜)
647 (25½)

SHUTTLE MAKE AS REQUIRED TO SUIT PATTERN COLOURS

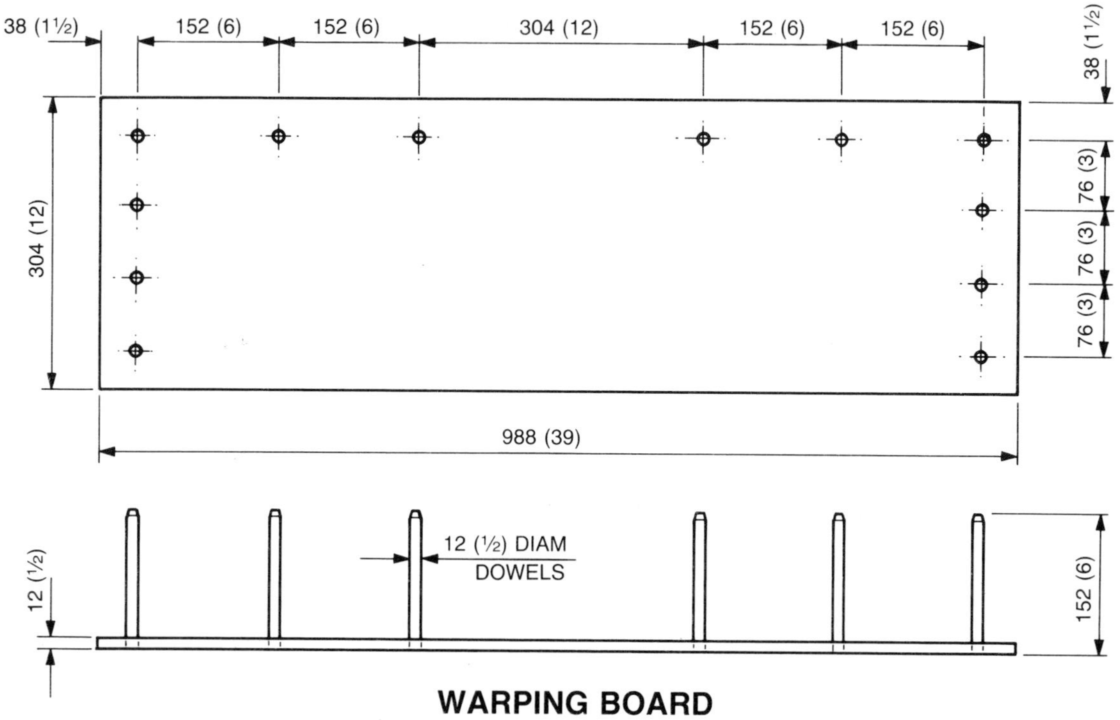
38 (1½)
152 (6)
152 (6)
304 (12)
152 (6)
152 (6)
38 (1½)
304 (12)
76 (3)
76 (3)
76 (3)
988 (39)
12 (½) DIAM
DOWELS
12 (½)
152 (6)

WARPING BOARD

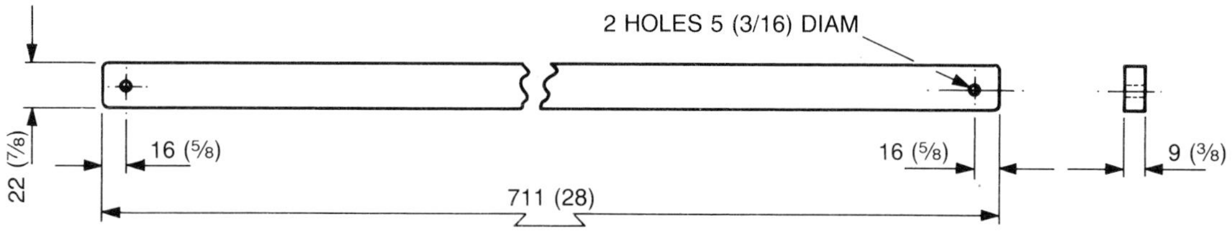
2 HOLES 5 (3/16) DIAM
22 (⅞)
16 (⅝)
16 (⅝)
9 (⅜)
711 (28)

SHED OR LEASE STICK MAKE TWO

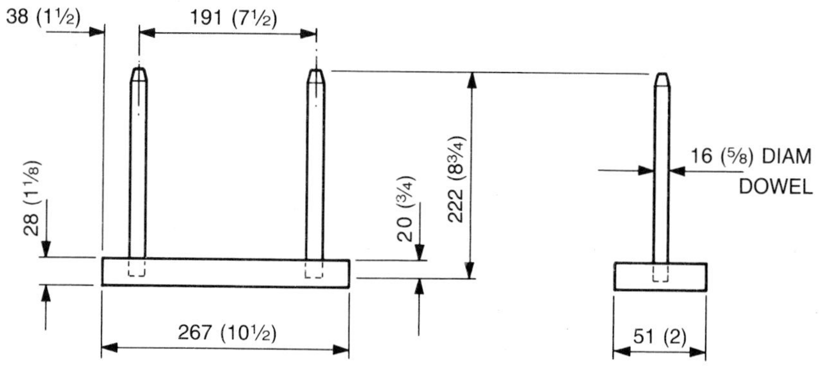
38 (1½)
191 (7½)
28 (1⅛)
20 (¾)
222 (8¾)
16 (⅝) DIAM
DOWEL
267 (10½)
51 (2)

WARPING POST MAKE TWO

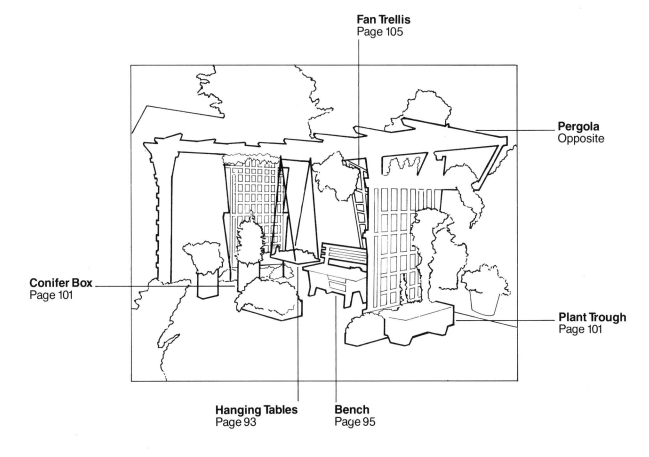

Fan Trellis
Page 105

Pergola
Opposite

Conifer Box
Page 101

Plant Trough
Page 101

Hanging Tables
Page 93

Bench
Page 95

PATIO ARRANGEMENT
PERGOLA

Life in the Western world goes at a great pace and many of us look forward to just relaxing and being quiet in our own gardens. Of course you don't have to have a huge estate to enjoy growing flowers and plants. I am frequently amazed at the ingenuity that city dwellers display with their window boxes, flower tubs and hanging baskets. There are those who simply have 'green fingers' and are able to make even the most unlikely places beautiful with their love of growing things.

In the past few years we have seen more and more garden centres appearing where you can buy not only plants, shrubs, fruit trees etc. but also garden tables, chairs, pergolas, plant boxes and so on. Unfortunately the prices of some of these latter items are fairly high and however keen you may be to add them to your garden, the cost may well prove to be prohibitive.

I have designed and made many such items, some of which involve the very minimum of skills, namely the ability to measure, cut and wield a hammer. Once you have acquired a little confidence with these projects I am sure that you will then go on to tackle the more ambitious ones, such as this large rose pergola, which can be made to any dimensions to fit the space desired. Many gardens already have an area of paving slabs and for these I have adapted the bottoms of the posts to form flower boxes. This will save you the trouble of taking up the paving slabs and fixing in the posts with concrete. The design is very adaptable, so before you start, measure the area you wish to cover and amend the design to fit. When buying timber do ask the merchant to select straight timbers with no twists, otherwise you will have difficulties. You will need only a few tools and a lot of willing neighbours to help hold the pergola up while you bolt the legs on!

■ Main structure

Large objects always look more difficult to construct than smaller items, but if you have already made all three trellises on page 105 then you have already practised the only joint necessary.

1 Cramp together both longitudinal timbers and pencil in on them where the cross-pieces will go.
2 Keep the timbers together and, using a fine-toothed saw, cut the notches out. A good firmer chisel is essential to chisel out the middle portion. Don't forget to chisel from both sides.
3 Now cut the cross-pieces to length. Cramp them all together and mark the position of the notches. Saw and chisel out the middle portion.
4 Draw on in pencil the shaping of the ends and cut them to shape using the same fine-toothed saw. Plane off the saw marks with a plane.
5 The 'notches' on both longitudinal battens and cross-pieces hold the structure rigid, but you also need to screw the framework together. Drill pilot holes through the cross-pieces, followed by a

large drill which counter-bores the hole. A counter-bore hole allows the head of the screw to go into the timber; this means the threaded portion will penetrate well into the longitudinal batten below.

You will need very long screws and the gauge should be 10 or 12. Don't buy a box full but just the number you need because they are expensive (very). It is important to use zinc-plated screws throughout, if possible, as these will not rust. However, the larger screw sizes are not always available plated and then the only alternative is to grease them before screwing them into the wood.

Sometimes people experience difficulty when trying to get screws into wood and, as they struggle, the head of the screw becomes more and more damaged ending in a broken screw slot and no means of getting the screw in or out. The secret is always to drill pilot holes first and if the screw goes 'tight' remove it and drill a slightly deeper hole or use a larger drill. Large screws need a fairly large screwdriver, otherwise you simply won't get sufficient torque to drive the screw in.

6 Glue and screw the cross-pieces to the longitudinal timbers.

■ The legs and flower box feet

If you have no patio area already laid down then simply dig holes and after the legs have been bolted to the framework set them in concrete.

If you do already have a concrete or paved area on which the pergola is to be sited, you will probably not want to start digging things up, so with this in mind I have designed flower box feet for the bottom of the legs. The unevenness of some gardens may also give rise to concern, but with this design you can fix the main structure, then cut some legs shorter than others to compensate for the line of the ground. Ideally the flower box feet want to be let a little way into the ground to give the structure stability. They can then be filled with soil and used for climbing plants etc.

1 Make all the feet first before starting to attach them to the legs. They are made from the same timber as the flower boxes (see page 101), and the sections should be fixed together with glue and nails at all corners.
2 It is important when attaching the feet to the legs that the legs are fixed on at right angles, so you will need a spirit level which gives readings in both vertical and horizontal positions. Find a flat surface, place the foot on it and fit the leg, holding it in place with a large 'G' cramp. Check that it is vertical with the spirit level.
3 Now lie leg and foot down and nail through into the leg from both sides of the foot. Repeat this for all the legs and feet.
4 Turn the pergola onto its back and, with the help of 'G' cramps, position the legs onto the main framework. Admittedly it looks a little strange lying on its back with its legs in the air, but this is the easiest way of drilling the bolt holes!
5 A powerful electric drill is necessary to drill holes for the coach bolts. Coach bolts are available from most builders' merchants and hardware shops in a variety of sizes and lengths. Drill two holes for each leg, positioning the holes at opposite sides of the leg. I always drill a slightly oversize hole to take the bolt. Check that the bolts will go in and that there is sufficient thread on the end of the bolt to fit a washer and nut.

6 Repeat this operation for all the legs, but don't bolt them onto the main structure yet. Number each leg to the place on the main frame where it fits and then remove all the legs. Turn the structure the right way up.

■ Lifting the framework and attaching the legs

Even if you are an independent type be warned that the next part needs a minimum of two people, lengths of timber, 'G' cramps and a step ladder, and if you have a bad back get other people to do it for you!

1 Start by lifting one end of the framework partway off the ground and resting it on a suitable platform—a 'workmate' is ideal for this.

2 Now lift the other end of the framework a little way off the ground and, while one person holds it steady, the other helper attaches a stout length of wood on either side of the framework with a 'G' cramp. The frame is thus supported while you rest and get ready for the next lift.

3 Have two longer lengths of timber to hand, also the step ladder and 'G' cramps. Both lift again, and while one holds the structure, the other attaches the longer temporary legs with 'G' cramps.

4 Now check that the two 'real' legs are to hand, also the bolts, washers, nuts and a suitable spanner. Both lift once more, leaving the last temporary legs attached, just in case! The assistant has to be quick and attach the real legs with bolts. Once this has been achieved remove all the cramps and temporary legs.

5 Raising the other end is a similar operation. Make sure when lifting this that the two legs already attached don't skid along the ground. When you have raised it, attach the bolts.

Obviously the more hands there are to hold and lift, the easier this stage will be. The legs will be a little wobbly still as they are not braced, which is the next job.

6 Using the spirit level check that the legs are vertical. When you are sure they are, cramp two long pieces of spare batten diagonally across from corner to corner to hold them rigid until you have attached the trellises.

7 Screw (using zinc-plated screws) three horizontal battens across the legs—one at the top, middle and bottom.

8 Now cut more roofing battens and attach them vertically to the three horizontal pieces that are already in place. I only used screws at top, middle and bottom. Once this has been done at each end of the framework the legs are held rigidly apart.

9 Cut and fit bracing pieces from the legs to the main longitudinal timbers. At one end this is a feature and provides for flower baskets to be held on a shelf constructed of battens. All the bracing pieces are coach-bolted for strength.

If you build this structure in the way illustrated then each leg relies on the battens for its rigidity. There are many variations possible but it is a good idea to keep the main 'walk through' area free of bracing spars. You may even wish to add sheets of translucent plastic sheet to keep off the odd summer shower. Be brave — have a go!

Photographs: pages 86, 98-99

■ CUTTING LIST

Pergola

Main longitudinal beams	2 off	4375 x 95 x 44 mm (172¼ x 3¾ x 1¾ in)	timber
Extension longitudinal beams	2 off	3048 x 95 x 44 mm (120 x 3¾ x 1¾ in)	timber
Main cross-beams	5 off	1829 x 95 x 44 mm (72 x 3¾ x 1¾ in)	timber
Extension cross-beams	3 off	1130 x 95 x 44 mm (44½ x 3¾ x 1¾ in)	timber
Verticals 'A' and 'B'	4 off	2286 x 95 x 44 mm (90 x 3¾ x 1¾ in)	timber
Vertical 'C'	1 off	2375 x 95 x 44 mm (93½ x 3¾ x 1¾ in)	timber
Bracing strutt	2 off	1016 x 44 x 44 mm (40 x 1¾ x 1¾ in)	timber
Flower box sides	10 off	610 x 222 x 22 mm (24 x 8¾ x ⅞ in)	timber
Flower box ends	10 off	140 x 133 x 22 mm (5½ x 5¼ x ⅞ in)	timber
Shelf support	2 off	724 x 95 x 44 mm (28½ x 3¾ x 1¾ in)	timber
Tie member	2 off	686 x 38 x 22 mm (27 x 1½ x ⅞ in)	timber
Shelf	4 off	1525 x 44 x 22 mm (60 x 1¾ x ⅞ in)	timber
	3 off	457 x 44 x 22 mm (18 x 1¾ x ⅞ in)	timber
Verticals bracing	6 off	1473 x 38 x 22 mm (58 x 1½ x ⅞ in)	timber
'A' and 'B' trellis	14 off	1820 x 38 x 22 mm (71½ x 1½ x ⅞ in)	timber
	12 off	1067 x 38 x 22 mm (42 x 1½ x ⅞ in)	timber
	8 off	991 x 38 x 22 mm (39 x 1½ x ⅞ in)	timber
'C' trellis	2 off	406 x 44 x 22 mm (16 x 1¾ x ⅞ in)	timber
	2 off	2034 x 38 x 22 mm (80 x 1½ x ⅞ in)	timber
	1 off	1264 x 38 x 22 mm (49¾ x 1¾ x ⅞ in)	timber
	6 off	406 x 38 x 22 mm (16 x 1½ x ⅞ in)	timber
	1 off	610 x 38 x 22 mm (24 x 1½ x ⅞ in)	timber
	1 off	812 x 38 x 22 mm (32 x 1½ x ⅞ in)	timber
	1 off	1016 x 38 x 22 mm (40 x 1½ x ⅞ in)	timber
	2 off	876 x 38 x 22 mm (34½ x 1½ x ⅞ in)	timber

Ancillaries

	Assorted length 9mm (⅜ in) diam coach bolts
	No 8 and No 12 galvanised wood screws
	Wood preservative
	Waterproof wood glue

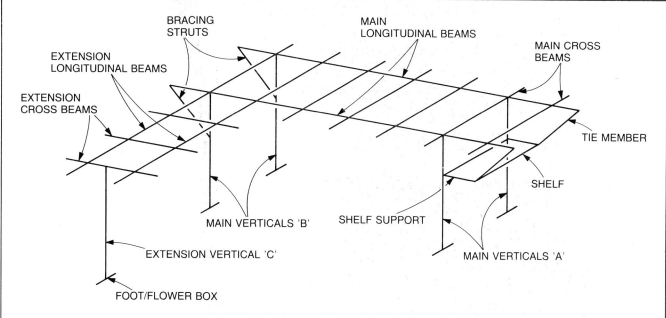

SCHEMATIC LAYOUT OF PERGOLA

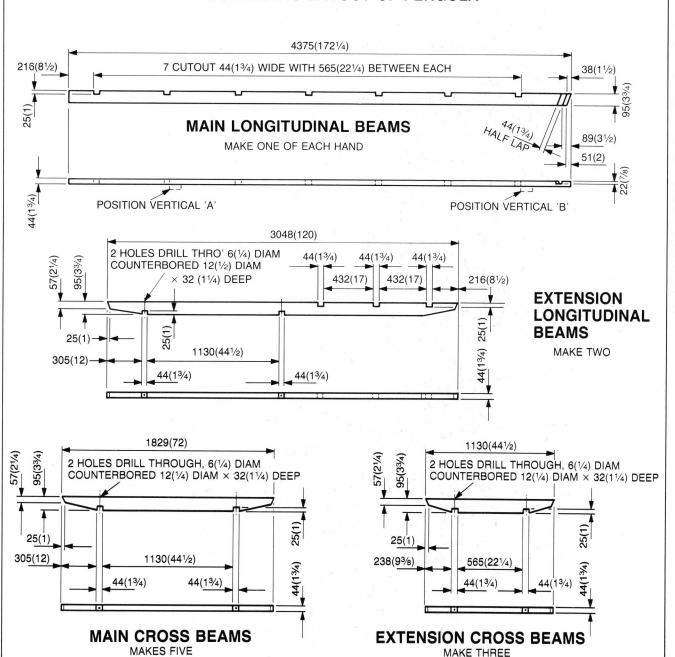

MAIN LONGITUDINAL BEAMS

MAKE ONE OF EACH HAND

4375(172¼)

7 CUTOUT 44(1¾) WIDE WITH 565(22¼) BETWEEN EACH

216(8½)　38(1½)　95(3¾)　44(1¾) HALF LAP　89(3½)　51(2)　22(⅞)

25(1)

44(1¾)

POSITION VERTICAL 'A'　POSITION VERTICAL 'B'

EXTENSION LONGITUDINAL BEAMS

MAKE TWO

3048(120)

2 HOLES DRILL THRO' 6(¼) DIAM COUNTERBORED 12(½) DIAM × 32 (1¼) DEEP

57(2¼)　95(3¾)

44(1¾)　44(1¾)　44(1¾)

432(17)　432(17)　216(8½)

25(1)

25(1)

305(12)　1130(44½)　44(1¾)　25(1)

44(1¾)

44(1¾)

MAIN CROSS BEAMS

MAKES FIVE

1829(72)

2 HOLES DRILL THROUGH, 6(¼) DIAM COUNTERBORED 12(¼) DIAM × 32(1¼) DEEP

57(2¼)　95(3¾)

25(1)

305(12)　1130(44½)

44(1¾)　44(1¾)

25(1)

44(1¾)

EXTENSION CROSS BEAMS

MAKE THREE

1130(44½)

2 HOLES DRILL THROUGH, 6(¼) DIAM COUNTERBORED 12(¼) DIAM × 32(1¼) DEEP

57(2¼)　95(3¾)

25(1)

238(9⅜)　565(22¼)

44(1¾)　44(1¾)

25(1)

44(1¾)

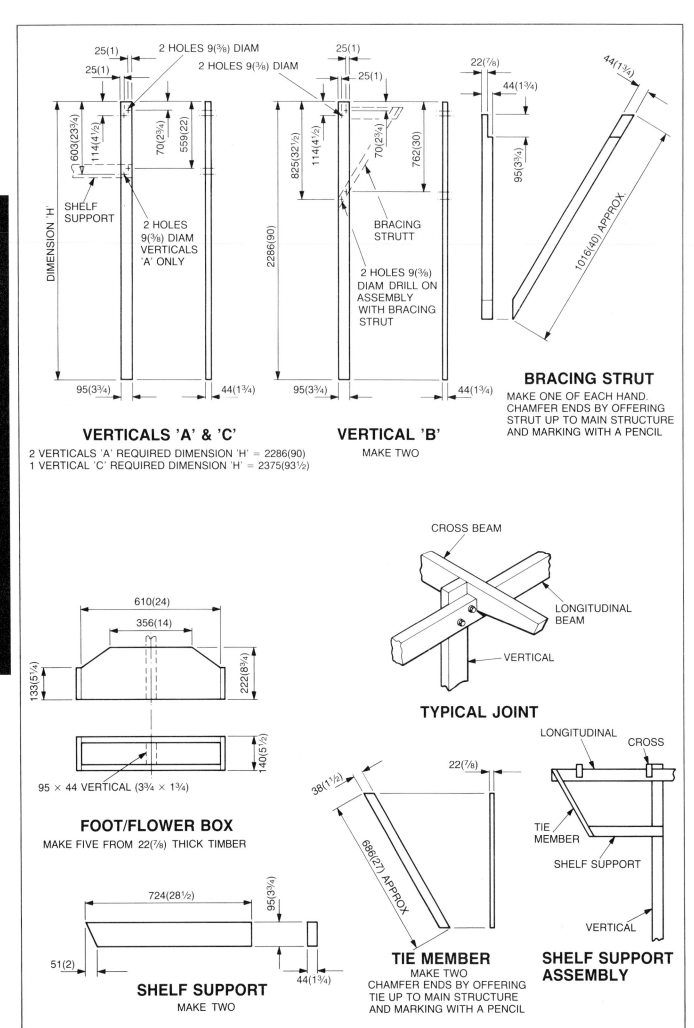

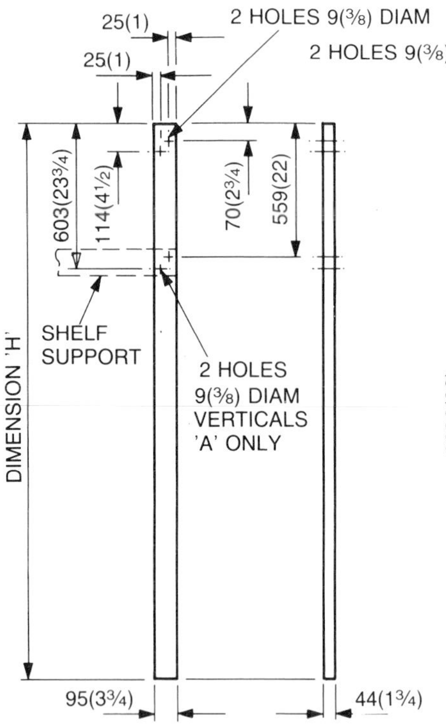
25(1)
2 HOLES 9(⅜) DIAM
25(1)
603(23¾)
114(4½)
70(2¾)
559(22)
DIMENSION 'H'
SHELF SUPPORT
2 HOLES 9(⅜) DIAM VERTICALS 'A' ONLY
95(3¾)
44(1¾)

VERTICALS 'A' & 'C'

2 VERTICALS 'A' REQUIRED DIMENSION 'H' = 2286(90)
1 VERTICAL 'C' REQUIRED DIMENSION 'H' = 2375(93½)

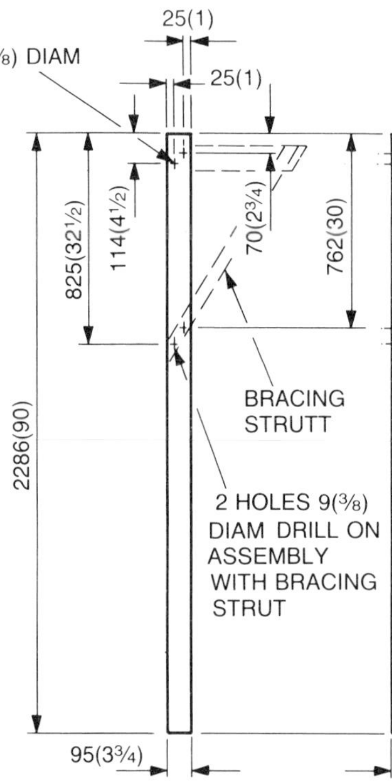
25(1)
2 HOLES 9(⅜) DIAM
25(1)
825(32½)
114(4½)
70(2¾)
762(30)
2286(90)
BRACING STRUTT
2 HOLES 9(⅜) DIAM DRILL ON ASSEMBLY WITH BRACING STRUT
95(3¾)
44(1¾)

VERTICAL 'B'

MAKE TWO

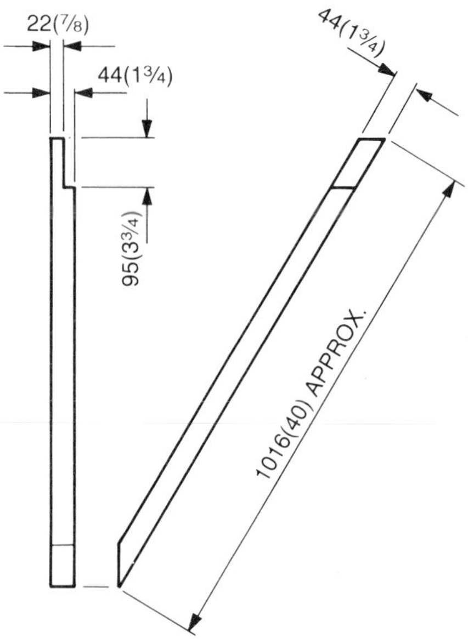
22(⅞)
44(1¾)
95(3¾)
44(1¾)
1016(40) APPROX.

BRACING STRUT

MAKE ONE OF EACH HAND.
CHAMFER ENDS BY OFFERING STRUT UP TO MAIN STRUCTURE AND MARKING WITH A PENCIL

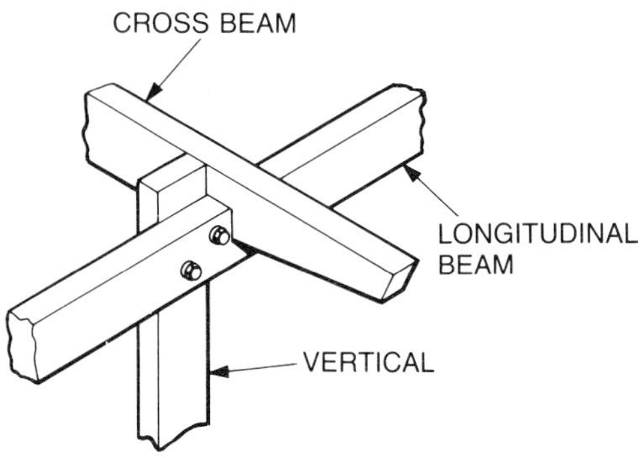
CROSS BEAM
LONGITUDINAL BEAM
VERTICAL

TYPICAL JOINT

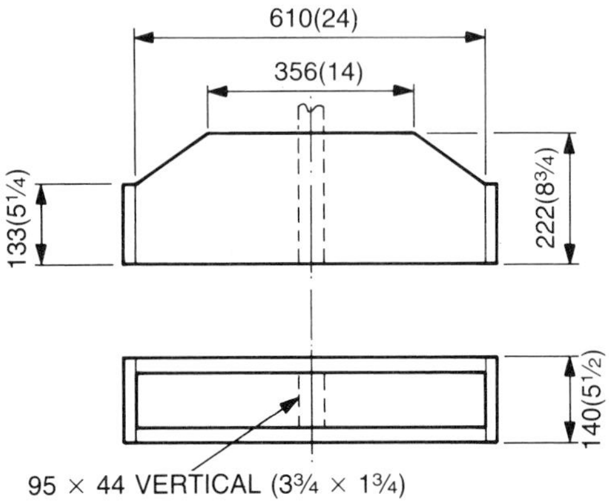
610(24)
356(14)
133(5¼)
222(8¾)
140(5½)
95 × 44 VERTICAL (3¾ × 1¾)

FOOT/FLOWER BOX

MAKE FIVE FROM 22(⅞) THICK TIMBER

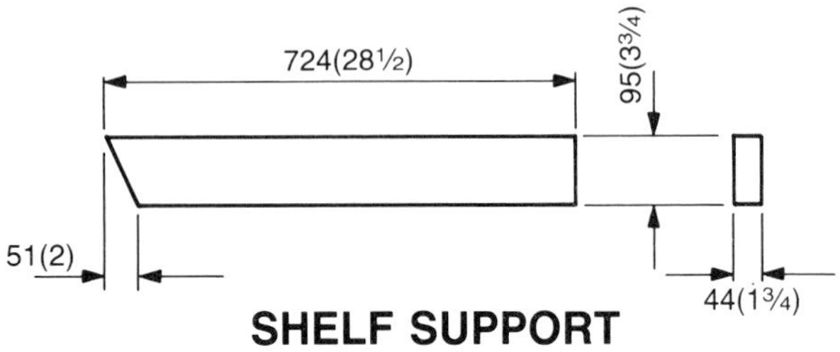
724(28½)
95(3¾)
51(2)
44(1¾)

SHELF SUPPORT

MAKE TWO

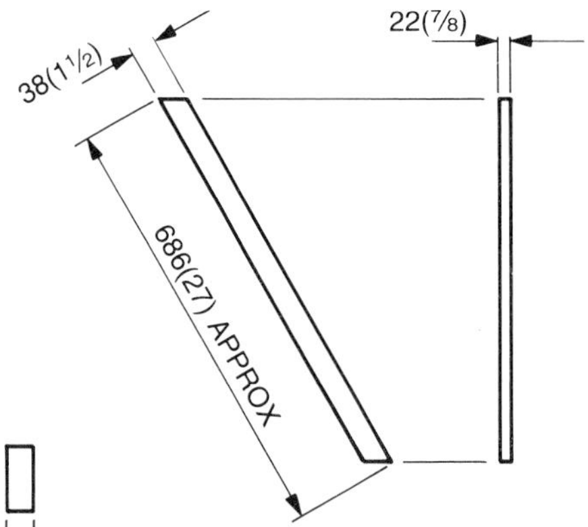
22(⅞)
38(1½)
686(27) APPROX

TIE MEMBER

MAKE TWO
CHAMFER ENDS BY OFFERING TIE UP TO MAIN STRUCTURE AND MARKING WITH A PENCIL

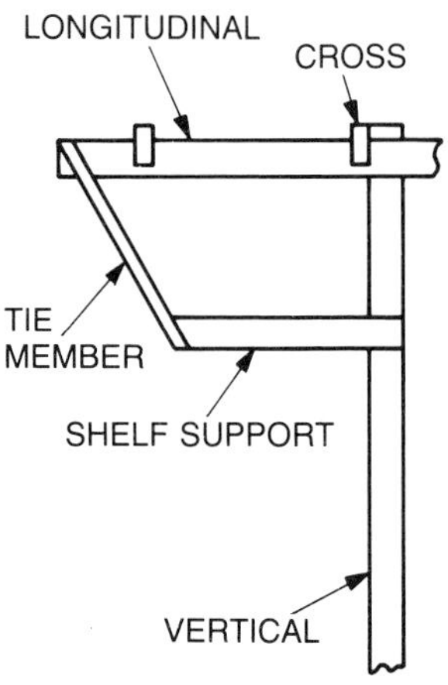
LONGITUDINAL
CROSS
TIE MEMBER
SHELF SUPPORT
VERTICAL

SHELF SUPPORT ASSEMBLY

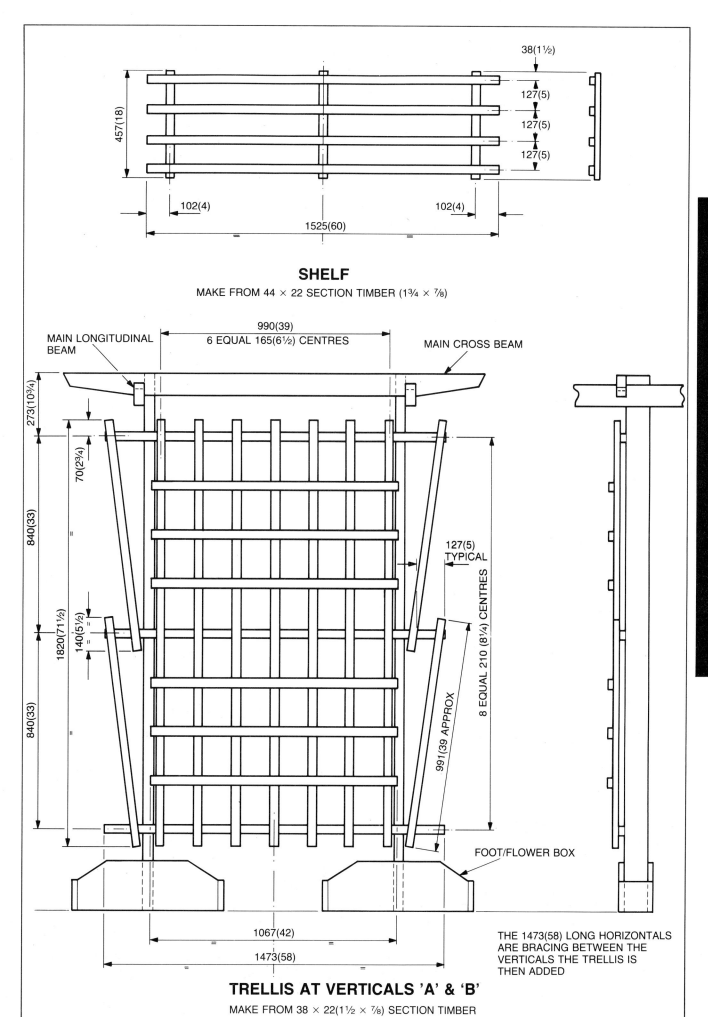

38(1½)

127(5)

127(5)

127(5)

457(18)

102(4)

1525(60)

102(4)

SHELF

MAKE FROM 44 × 22 SECTION TIMBER (1¾ × ⅞)

MAIN LONGITUDINAL
BEAM

990(39)
6 EQUAL 165(6½) CENTRES

MAIN CROSS BEAM

273(10¾)

70(2¾)

840(33)

1820(71½)

140(5½)

127(5)
TYPICAL

8 EQUAL 210 (8¼) CENTRES

840(33)

991(39 APPROX

FOOT/FLOWER BOX

1067(42)

1473(58)

THE 1473(58) LONG HORIZONTALS
ARE BRACING BETWEEN THE
VERTICALS THE TRELLIS IS
THEN ADDED

TRELLIS AT VERTICALS 'A' & 'B'

MAKE FROM 38 × 22(1½ × ⅞) SECTION TIMBER

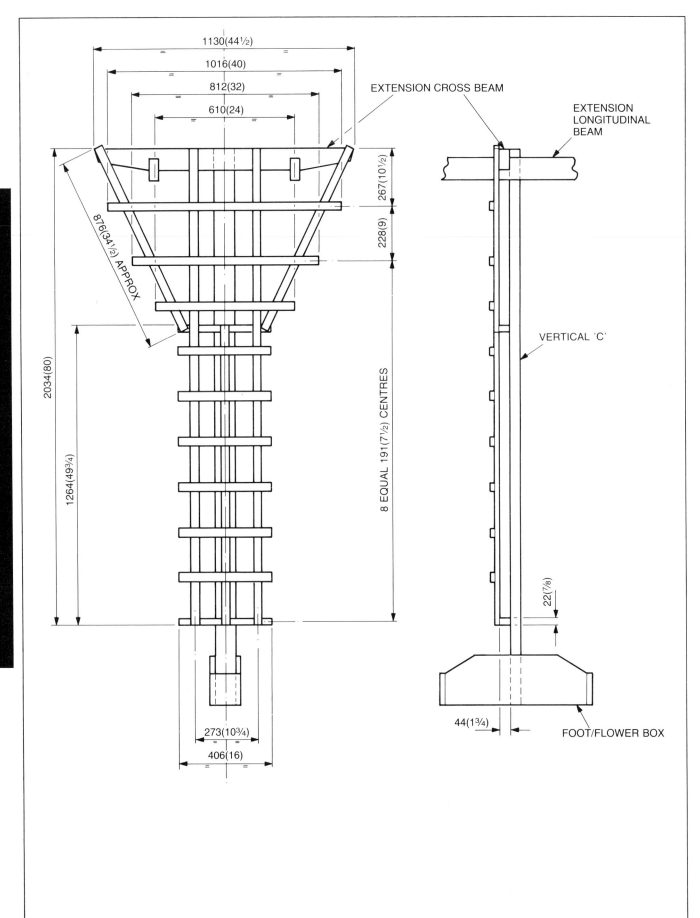

1130(44½)

1016(40)

812(32)

610(24)

EXTENSION CROSS BEAM

EXTENSION LONGITUDINAL BEAM

876(34½) APPROX

267(10½)

228(9)

2034(80)

1264(49¾)

8 EQUAL 191(7½) CENTRES

VERTICAL 'C'

22(⅞)

273(10¾)

406(16)

44(1¾)

FOOT/FLOWER BOX

TRELLIS ON VERTICAL 'C'

MAKE FROM 38 × 22(1½ × ⅞) SECTION TIMBER,
EXCEPT FIXING STRIPS WHICH ARE 44 × 22(1¾ × ⅞)

PERGOLA

Once you have taken the trouble to build the pergola, it will take only a very little extra time and effort to build this hanging table, and after all what could be more useful!

1 Start by cutting two planks to the same length and glue them together. It's very helpful to have a pair of cramps to hold the planks together while the glue is drying.
2 Now glue and screw a small strip of wood across the edges of the planks at both ends. These will help to hold the planks together. Glue and screw another strip of wood down each side of the planks as well, leaving a gap at one corner. This 'rail' will prevent things from rolling off but allow you to sweep crumbs away through the gap.
3 A useful safety feature is a holder for glasses and bottles. This can be made from a length of plank slightly wider than the table, into which circular holes of the appropriate size are cut to take these items. Circular-hole saws are available for electric drills which will cut very clean holes. Larger holes can be cut with a jig-saw or a keyhole saw if you don't have a power tool. Glue and screw a strip of wood across each end of the plank. Then turn it over and you have a 'tray' which will slot over your table.
4 Now fit the table with large screw eyes and thread rope or strong cord through them. Position screw hooks in several places on the pergola, so that the table can be hung in different positions.

Photographs: pages 86, 98-99

GARDEN SECTION

■ CUTTING LIST

Hanging table

Table top	2 off	762 x 222 x 20 mm (30 x 8¾ x ¾ in)	timber
	2 off	380 x 44 x 22 mm (15 x 1¾ x ⅞ in)	timber
	2 off	660 x 44 x 22 mm (26 x 1¾ x ⅞ in)	timber

Ancillaries

	4 off	20 mm (¾ in) screwed eyes	
		Strong nylon cord	
		Assorted No 8 galvanised wood screws	
		Waterproof wood glue	
		Wood preservative	

Glass and bottle holder

	1 off	508 x 213 x 16 mm (20 x 8⅜ x ⅝ in)	timber
	2 off	213 x 38 x 20 mm (8⅜ x 1½ x ¾ in)	timber

Ancillaries

		Assorted No 8 galvanised wood screws	
		Wood preservative	
		Waterproof wood glue	

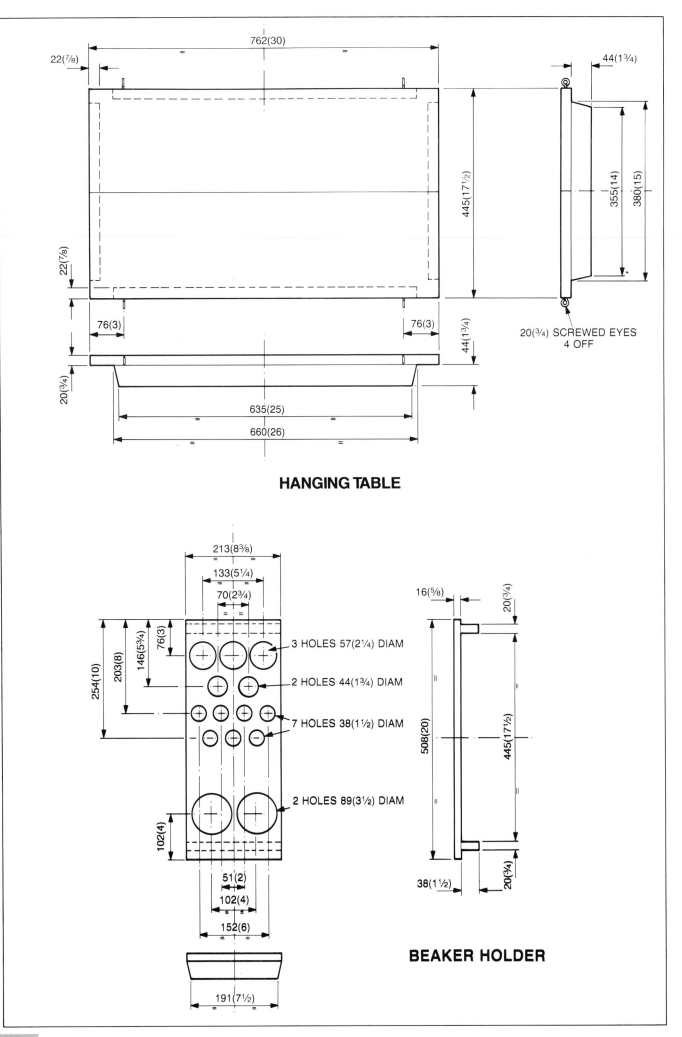

762(30)

22(⁷/₈)

44(1³/₄)

445(17½)

355(14)

380(15)

22(⁷/₈)

76(3)

76(3)

44(1³/₄)

20(³/₄) SCREWED EYES
4 OFF

20(³/₄)

635(25)

660(26)

HANGING TABLE

213(8³/₈)

133(5¼)

70(2³/₄)

76(3)

146(5³/₄)

203(8)

254(10)

3 HOLES 57(2¼) DIAM

2 HOLES 44(1³/₄) DIAM

7 HOLES 38(1½) DIAM

2 HOLES 89(3½) DIAM

102(4)

16(⁵/₈)

20(³/₄)

508(20)

445(17½)

51(2)

102(4)

152(6)

38(1½)

20(³/₄)

191(7½)

BEAKER HOLDER

PATIO ARRANGEMENT BENCH

Even if you don't build a pergola I hope you will be sufficiently inspired to build this garden bench. It has no joints at all – ideal for your first garden project – and the only 'skill' you will need is the ability to use a handsaw, drill, chisel and screwdriver. You should countersink all screws otherwise torn clothes and scratches will result.

1   Study the drawing of the end of the bench carefully. It may even be a good idea to re-draw this full size on a sheet of card or hardboard before cutting out the pieces of timber.
2   Glue and screw two of the legs onto a cross-piece, and then screw a back support on. Repeat this procedure for the other bench end.

3   Now cut battens to fix the two bench ends together, and glue and screw them into place. To give the bench just a little shape I cut the battens on an angle at the ends.
4   After all the battens have been attached, turn the bench upside down and, with a chisel or spokeshave, cut a chamfer on the bottoms of all the legs.

This prevents the wood 'splitting out' if at some time the bench is dragged across the ground.
5   The bench should be treated with wood preservative each year.

Photographs: pages 86, 98-99

■ CUTTING LIST

Bench

End brace plate	2 off	432 x 208 x 22 mm (17 x 8 x 7/8 in)	timber
Legs	4 off	457 x 95 x 44 mm (18 x 3¾ x 1¾ in)	timber
Tie bars	2 off	875 x 44 x 22 mm (34½ x 1¾ x 7/8 in)	timber
Back support	2 off	578 x 44 x 44 mm (22¾ x 1¾ x 1¾ in)	timber
Back and seat slats	9 off	1220 x 44 x 32 mm (48 x 1¾ x 1¼ in)	timber

Ancillaries

Assorted No 10 galvanised wood screws	
Wood preservative	
Waterproof wood glue	

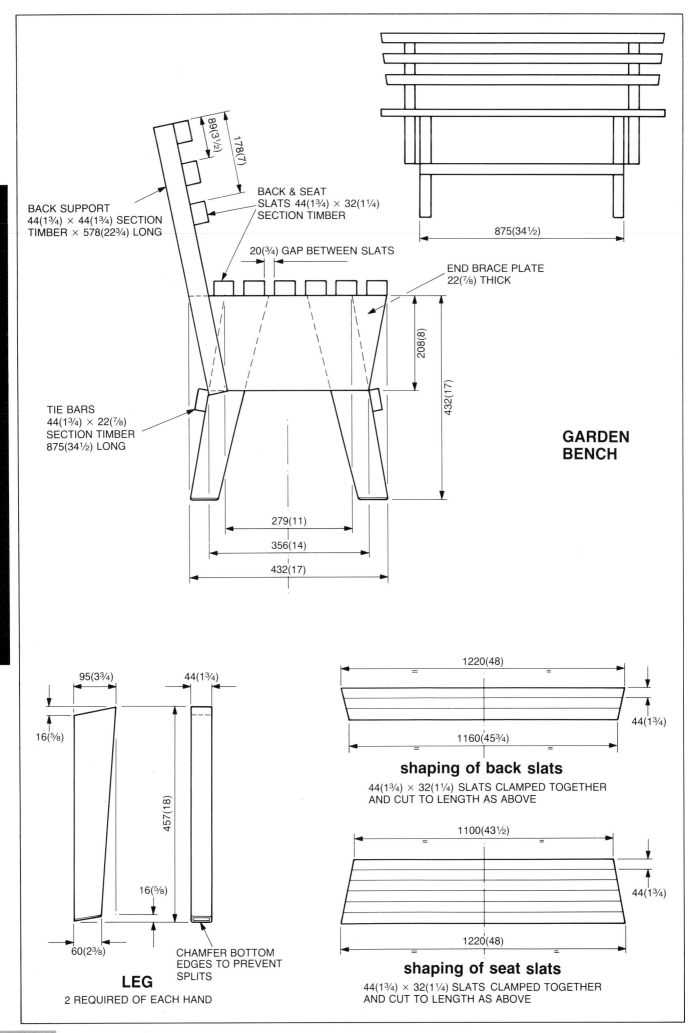

BACK SUPPORT
44(1¾) × 44(1¾) SECTION
TIMBER × 578(22¾) LONG

89(3½)

178(7)

BACK & SEAT
SLATS 44(1¾) × 32(1¼)
SECTION TIMBER

20(¾) GAP BETWEEN SLATS

END BRACE PLATE
22(⅞) THICK

208(8)

432(17)

TIE BARS
44(1¾) × 22(⅞)
SECTION TIMBER
875(34½) LONG

279(11)

356(14)

432(17)

875(34½)

**GARDEN
BENCH**

95(3¾)

44(1¾)

16(⅝)

457(18)

16(⅝)

60(2⅜)

CHAMFER BOTTOM
EDGES TO PREVENT
SPLITS

LEG
2 REQUIRED OF EACH HAND

1220(48)

1160(45¾)

44(1¾)

shaping of back slats
44(1¾) × 32(1¼) SLATS CLAMPED TOGETHER
AND CUT TO LENGTH AS ABOVE

1100(43½)

44(1¾)

1220(48)

shaping of seat slats
44(1¾) × 32(1¼) SLATS CLAMPED TOGETHER
AND CUT TO LENGTH AS ABOVE

PICNIC TABLE
PAGE 119

FLOWER BOXES

GARDEN SECTION

For these all you need is a rule, pencil, nails, hammer and a saw. They can be any length you like to fit any place in the garden. The wood is best bought from a builders' merchant. You only need a low grade board, and if you are not fussy about splinters the sawn board is very much cheaper. I bought the widest sawn board available and then planed the timber (I don't like splinters!).

All woodwork is difficult if you don't have a firm surface to work on—even the concrete path in your garden will do at a pinch. The boxes are simply nailed and glued together, but make sure you use a glue that is water-proof. The easiest way to make the box is to cut the ends sufficiently wide to allow the bottom of the box to fit between the sides. If you are not too accurate here it won't matter as you have to drill holes in the base anyway to allow for drainage.

■ Plant trough

1 First nail one end onto a side and then do the same with the other side and end. Now put the two sides and ends together. (It is much easier this way as it prevents all the bits getting 'out of hand'.)

Nails can be a problem since they sometimes split the wood and by the time six nails have been driven into one end it's all in bits. There are ways of overcoming this problem:

i Drill a small pilot hole for the nail.

ii Use oval nails as these nails are specially shaped to prevent the wood splitting. However, the professionals have another trick. They use a big round nail, but before they drive it into the wood they thump the sharp end with the hammer and blunt it. Then when they bang it in the wood doesn't split. Try it—it works!

2 The base of the box should now be nailed in and the feet fixed to the bottom by nails driven through the base.

3 Drill a series of random holes in the base to allow for drainage.

■ Conifer box

The size of the box you make for your conifer is very important as it is this which will determine the ultimate size of the tree. Sawn board from a builder's merchant would be a suitable timber to use.

1 Cut four equal lengths of board and nail them together to form the box.

2 Fix the base on and drill holes for drainage.

3 Use a few spare lengths of roofing batten to make the feet and handles. Nail and glue these in place.

4 Finish off with wood preservative.

Photographs: pages 86, 98-99

■ CUTTING LISTS

Plant trough—short

Sides	2 off	762 x 222 x 22 mm (30 x 8¾ x ⅞ in)	timber
Ends	2 off	266 x 222 x 22 mm (10½ x 8¾ x ⅞ in)	timber
Base	1 off	806 x 222 x 22 mm (31¾ x 8¾ x ⅞ in)	timber
Feet	2 off	304 x 73 x 47 mm (12 x 2⅞ x 1⅞ in)	timber

Plant trough—long

Sides	2 off	914 x 222 x 22 mm (36 x 8¾ x ⅞ in)	timber
Ends	2 off	266 x 222 x 22 mm (10½ x 8¾ x ⅞ in)	timber
Base	1 off	958 x 222 x 22 mm (37¾ x 8¾ x ⅞ in)	timber
Feet	2 off	304 x 73 x 47 mm (12 x 2⅞ x 1⅞ in)	timber

Ancillaries

Nails or assorted No 10 galvanised wood screws
Waterproof wood glue
Wood preservative

Conifer Box

Sides	4 off	406 x 216 x 22 mm (16 x 8½ x ⅞ in)	timber
Base	1 off	304 x 216 x 22 mm (12 x 8½ x ⅞ in)	timber
Handle	2 off	260 x 35 x 22 mm (10¼ x 1⅜ x ⅞ in)	timber
Feet	2 off	248 x 35 x 22 mm (9¾ x 1⅜ x ⅞ in)	timber

Ancillaries

Nails or assorted No 8 galvanised wood screws
Waterproof wood glue
Wood preservative

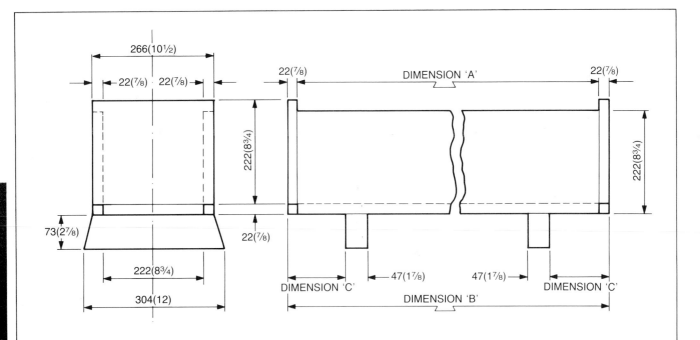

	DIMENSION 'A'	DIMENSION 'B'	DIMENSION 'C'
LONG BOX	914(36)	958(37¾)	152(6)
SHORT BOX	762(30)	806(31¾)	127(5)

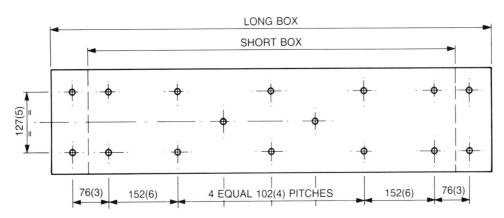

detail of base drainage hole drillings

12(½) DIAM – 12 IN THE SHORT BOX AND 16 IN THE LONG

PLANT TROUGH

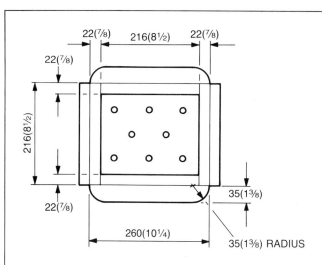

22(⅞) 216(8½) 22(⅞)

22(⅞)

216(8½)

22(⅞)

35(1⅜)

260(10¼)

35(1⅜) RADIUS

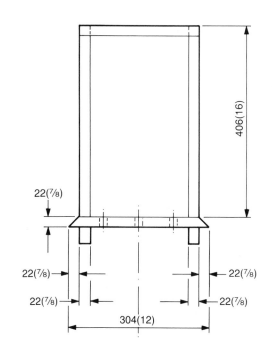

406(16)

22(⅞)

22(⅞) 22(⅞)

22(⅞) 22(⅞)

304(12)

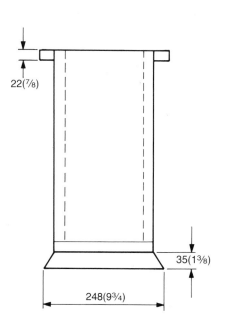

22(⅞)

35(1⅜)

248(9¾)

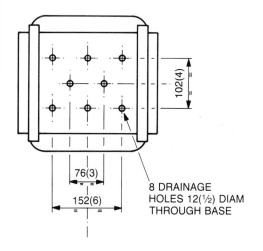

102(4)

76(3)

152(6)

8 DRAINAGE
HOLES 12(½) DIAM
THROUGH BASE

CONIFER BOX

When looking around garden centres I have noticed that trellises are very expensive, although they are very simple to construct. I made all the trellises shown here from roofing batten, which is the strip of wood that holds a roof tile or slate in place. It is available in bundles and can be obtained in different lengths. Batten is sawn to size so it is rather rough and has to be planed. It is best to buy the 'un-treated' variety as you will want to choose your own colour preservative when you have made the trellis. If you have not made a trellis before start with the simplest one shown to get used to the method of construction.

Basic trellis

1   First clamp together the two longitudinal battens and mark in pencil where the cross-pieces go. Now mark in the pencil lines with a marking knife.
2   Cut down the edges with a tenon saw and then remove the waste in the middle with a firmer chisel. Work from both sides of the wood and only take 'light' cuts.
3   Cut the cross-pieces to length and glue and nail them into the 'slots' you have cut. On this trellis there are only slots on the longitudinal battens.

Wall trellis

This trellis has a curved bottom end and looks well on a wall. It is only a little more complicated to make than the basic type.
1   Select some knot-free lengths for the carved longitudinal pieces. Cramp these together and mark with a pencil the

position of the two top cross-pieces only.
2   It is best to cut 'notches' in both the longitudinal battens and the cross-pieces for this trellis. By 'notching' both pieces the battens are held far more securely. If you are in doubt about cutting this joint, practise on an off-cut first.
3   Once the top two cross-pieces have been fitted, the bottom two can be marked. Gently tie the bottom battens together with a length of cord. Don't be tempted to pull the cord too tight, but get a gentle and even curve on all four battens. Now position the two cross-pieces and mark where the notches have to be cut with a pencil. Because of the bends in the longitudinal battens the notches will have to be cut individually and not clamped together as in the basic trellis.
4   Glue and nail the cross-pieces in place.

Fan trellis

1   Select two longitudinal battens that are as knot-free as possible (not always an easy thing with roofing battens). Cramp one end of both battens together to form the part that will be sunk into the ground.
2   At the top of the trellis fix a batten to hold both longitudinal pieces apart. Don't be tempted to overdo the curve — roofing batten is not the most flexible wood available!
3   Now lay all the cross-pieces onto the longitudinal battens and mark where to cut the notch with a pencil mark. Remember that the cross-pieces not only hold the trellis together but also hold the longitudinal battens apart to form the fan. Use glue and oval nails to secure the cross-pieces.
4   To help the plant climb up cut and fit 'criss cross' spans.
5   Now that the framework is complete, nail the bottom battens together and shape off the end into a spike, which will make it easier to drive into the ground.

Photographs: opposite (wall trellis); pages 86, 98-99 (fan trellis)

CUTTING LISTS

Wall trellis

Verticals	5 off	1830 x 32 x 22 mm (72 x 1¼ x ⅞ in)	timber
Horizontals	2 off	890 x 32 x 22 mm (35 x 1¼ x ⅞ in)	timber
	1 off	812 x 32 x 22 mm (32 x 1¼ x ⅞ in)	timber
	1 off	686 x 32 x 22 mm (27 x 1¼ x ⅞ in)	timber

Fan trellis

Verticals	2 off	2800 x 32 x 22 mm (110 x 1¼ x ⅞ in)	timber
	1 off	1752 x 32 x 22 mm (69 x 1¼ x ⅞ in)	timber
Horizontals	1 off	356 x 32 x 22 mm (14 x 1¼ x ⅞ in)	timber
	3 off	380 x 32 x 22 mm (15 x 1¼ x ⅞ in)	timber
	1 off	406 x 32 x 22 mm (16 x 1¼ x ⅞ in)	timber
	1 off	457 x 32 x 22 mm (18 x 1¼ x ⅞ in)	timber
	1 off	533 x 32 x 22 mm (21 x 1¼ x ⅞ in)	timber
	1 off	711 x 32 x 22 mm (28 x 1¼ x ⅞ in)	timber
Stringers	make from	3500 x 20 x 12 mm (140 x ¾ x ½ in)	timber

Ancillaries

	Nails or assorted No 8 galvanised wood screws
	Wood preservative. Waterproof wood glue

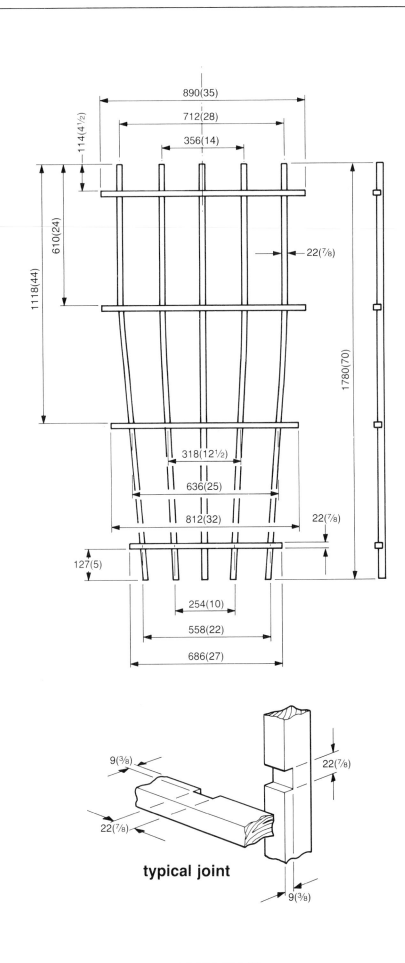

890(35)
712(28)
356(14)
114(4½)
610(24)
1118(44)
22(⅞)
1780(70)
318(12½)
636(25)
812(32)
22(⅞)
127(5)
254(10)
558(22)
686(27)

9(⅜)
22(⅞)
22(⅞)
9(⅜)

typical joint

WALL TRELLIS

CONSTRUCTED IN 32(1¼) × 22(⅞) SECTION TIMBER

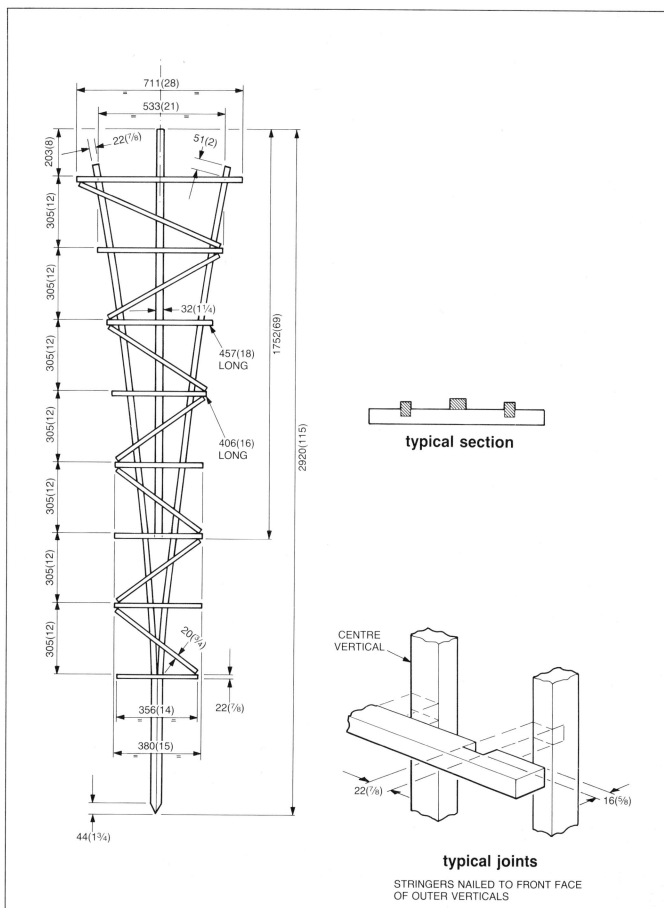

711(28)

533(21)

22(⅞)

51(2)

203(8)

305(12)

305(12)

305(12)

32(1¼)

457(18)
LONG

305(12)

1752(69)

305(12)

406(16)
LONG

305(12)

2920(115)

305(12)

305(12)

20(¾)

356(14)

22(⅞)

380(15)

44(1¾)

typical section

CENTRE
VERTICAL

22(⅞)

16(⅝)

typical joints

STRINGERS NAILED TO FRONT FACE
OF OUTER VERTICALS

FAN TRELLIS

VERTICALS & HORIZONTALS 32(1¼) × 22(⅞) TIMBER
STRINGERS 20(¾) × 12(½) TIMBER

This box is made in exactly the same way as the flower boxes attached to the pergola feet only with the addition of legs. The legs can be made from any reasonably stout timber you may have or can find at the builder's merchant. Frequently you will find there that an explanation of what you are making will help the assistant to sort out something suitable and often you can buy short lengths that are quite cheap.

1   After making up the box as described on page 101, glue and nail on the legs. It is probably advisable to use oval nails for this to prevent the wood from splitting. Other ways of preventing splitting are described in the Hints and Tips section on page 135.

2   Before fixing the two trellis pieces drill holes in them to take the nylon cord, then nail them to the end of the box.
3   Thread nylon cord through the holes to assist the plants to climb. (Nylon cord is best for this job as it won't rot.)

Photograph: opposite

■ CUTTING LIST

Flower trough and trellis

Sides	2 off	482 x 222 x 22 mm (19 x 8¾ x ⅞ in)	timber
Ends	2 off	266 x 222 x 22 mm (10½ x 8¾ x ⅞ in)	timber
Base	1 off	526 x 222 x 22 mm (20¾ x 8¾ x ⅞ in)	timber
Foot support frame	make from	1830 x 44 x 20 mm (72 x 1¾ x ¾ in)	timber
Head legs	2 off	560 x 44 x 20 mm (22 x 1¾ x ¾ in)	timber
Head legs tie	1 off	394 x 44 x 20 mm (15½ x 1¾ x ¾ in)	timber
Trellis	2 off	915 x 44 x 20 mm (36 x 1¾ x ¾ in)	timber

Ancillaries

	3 metres (120 in) long nylon cord	
	Nails or assorted No 8 and No 10 galvanised wood screws	
	Waterproof wood glue	
	Wood preservative	

FLOWER BOX WITH TRELLIS

SIDES, ENDS & BASE IN 22(⅞) THICK TIMBER
LEGS, FEET & TRELLIS FROM 44 × 20(1¾ × ¾)
SECTION TIMBER

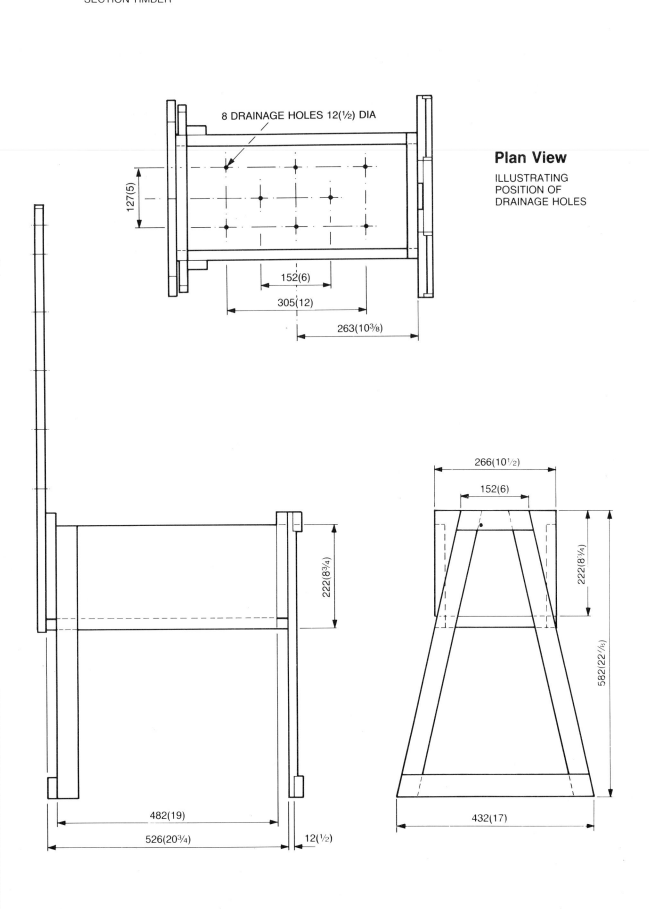

8 DRAINAGE HOLES 12(½) DIA

127(5)

152(6)

305(12)

263(10⅜)

Plan View

ILLUSTRATING
POSITION OF
DRAINAGE HOLES

222(8¾)

482(19)

526(20¾)

12(½)

266(10½)

152(6)

222(8¾)

582(22⅞)

432(17)

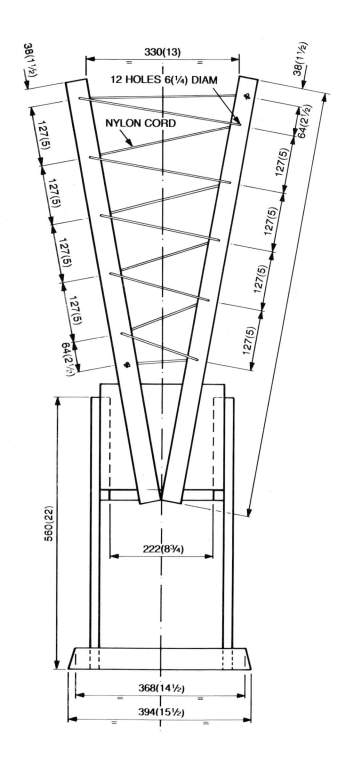

330(13)

12 HOLES 6(¼) DIAM

NYLON CORD

38(1½)

38(1½)

127(5)

127(5)

127(5)

127(5)

64(2½)

64(2½)

127(5)

127(5)

127(5)

127(5)

560(22)

222(8¾)

368(14½)

394(15½)

BONSAI CENTRE

The Japanese word *Bonsai* simply means a plant that has been grown in a tray or a pot. It is thought that it was the Chinese who first started planting small wild trees in pots but there is no doubt that it is the Japanese who have perfected the gentle art of miniaturising trees. The gardener is not restricted to any particular variety of tree, any sapling will do, and visiting a Bonsai centre will give you some idea of just how interesting a pursuit miniature-tree culture can be.

The work centre shown here has provision not only for potting plants and pruning miniature trees, but also displaying them on the rack shelving. The work area of the centre has a slatted roof to give shade to the gardener and the plants, while the front area has a corrugated PVC roof which provides a valuable collecting area for rainwater. The work centre is self-contained and makes a most useful and attractive addition to the garden. It is also ideal for growing alpines, as it protects the leaves from rain.

1 Start by cutting the two legs and feet to length. A recess must then be cut in the feet to take the legs, and the two then glued and screwed together.
2 Now cut all the cross-pieces that support the slatted shelves. These cross-pieces, unlike the feet, will only be bolted in position, therefore allowing for the whole centre to be dismantled if necessary.
3 Cut recesses in the cross-pieces, marking them out carefully to fit the width of the legs. Using a hand or tenon saw, cut down the sides and then, using a firmer chisel, cut the 'waste' out to form the recess. Only take light cuts out when you get near the bottom of the recess.
4 Clamp the cross-pieces to the legs and drill through for the coach bolts.

■ **Slatted shelving**

Once all the joints have been cut and all cross-pieces bolted to the legs, the next stage is the slatted shelving. I have found that roofing batten is very useful for this, especially if you don't possess a circular saw for cutting plank into strips.
Battens are sold in bundles at builder's merchants. It is worth examining the bundles carefully before you buy as some will be more rough sawn than others and require planing before use.
1 Build one shelf unit at a time by fixing the battens onto the cross-pieces with zinc-plated screws and glue. As you work towards the top shelves you will be surprised at how stable the whole unit becomes.

2 The work shelf is the only one which requires extra support, so I have designed a wooden framework that slides in between the bottom shelf and the work shelf. This gives the work shelf extra rigidity and eliminates any 'bounce' from it when plants are being re-potted etc.

■ **Roof sections**

The roof is in two sections, a wooden slatted one at the back and a corrugated PVC one at the front. If you wish to use the centre for growing alpines you may consider it worth covering the whole roof in PVC and you can do this over the top of the slatted roof section which will give you cover as well as shade. The rainwater gutter and down-pipe provide you with your own water supply, which is very handy for daily watering.
1 Glue and screw the frameworks together for the two roof sections
2 Fix the slats onto one framework in the same way as for the slatted shelves.
3 Cut the PVC for the other roof framework to size using a fine-toothed tenon saw. This can be quite tricky so either get someone to hold it steady for you, or cramp it to a table top. Don't apply to much pressure while cutting and don't worry about the terrible squeaking noise it makes!
4 Screw the PVC to the framework. You will need to buy special screws and plastic cups from a D.I.Y. shop for this. Ideally you should fix the screws at the top of the corrugation, which means

that you will have to find a piece of broom handle to support the sheet as you drill through, otherwise it will split. It is very important to drill holes through the corrugated sheet before you try to put the screws in. Fix the screws with the plastic cup in place and then 'snap on' the top which prevents the rain getting in.
5 Now bolt the two roof sections onto the top of the uprights.
6 The guttering and down-pipe should be fixed onto the centre with special clips. All these are available from builder's merchants. Then fix a small plastic tub on a shelf next to the work bench to collect the rainwater.
7 As with all garden furniture, the garden centre should be finished with a wood preservative. After the wood preservative has been applied, allow a few days for it to dry thoroughly before putting plants on it.

Photographs: opposite and page 97

GARDEN SECTION

Bonsai centre

Vertical support	2 off	2135 x 95 x 44 mm (84 x 3¾ x 1¾ in)	timber
Support 'A'	2 off	717 x 70 x 44 mm (28¼ x 2¾ x 1¾ in)	timber
Support 'B'	2 off	717 x 70 x 44 mm (28¼ x 2¾ x 1¾ in)	timber
Support 'C'	2 off	914 x 95 x 44 mm (36 x 3¾ x 1¾ in)	timber
Support 'D'	2 off	546 x 70 x 44 mm (21½ x 2¾ x 1¾ in)	timber
Foot 'E'	2 off	1220 x 95 x 44 mm (48 x 3¾ x 1¾ in)	timber
Longitudinals	2 off	1511 x 70 x 44 mm (59½ x 2¾ x 1¾ in)	timber
Glazed roof section	3 off	1727 x 44 x 32 mm (68 x 1¾ x 1¼ in)	timber
	2 off	1067 x 44 x 44 mm (42 x 1¾ x 1¾ in)	timber
	2 off	1625 x 44 x 32 mm (64 x 1¾ x 1¼ in)	timber
Slatted roof section	3 off	1143 x 38 x 35 mm (45 x 1½ x 1⅜ in)	timber
	2 off	1372 x 44 x 44 mm (54 x 1¾ x 1¾ in)	timber
	16 off	1727 x 44 x 22 mm (68 x 1¾ x ⅞ in)	timber
Deck 'A' 'B' and 'C' slats	31 off	1511 x 32 x 22 mm (59½ x 1¼ x ⅞ in)	timber
Deck 'D' slats	20 off	546 x 32 x 22 mm (21½ x 1¼ x ⅞ in)	timber
Tool holder	2 off	228 x 32 x 22 mm (9 x 1¼ x ⅞ in)	timber
	3 off	203 x 32 x 22 mm (8 x 1¼ x ⅞ in)	timber
Water tub support	2 off	457 x 32 x 22 mm (18 x 1¼ x ⅞ in)	timber
	3 off	267 x 32 x 22 mm (10½ x 1¼ x ⅞ in)	timber
Main decking support	1 off	864 x 44 x 44 mm (34 x 1¾ x 1¾ in)	timber
Frame	1 off	546 x 44 x 44 mm (21½ x 1¾ x 1¾ in)	timber
	2 off	470 x 44 x 38 mm (18½ x 1¾ x 1½ in)	timber

Ancillaries

	Corrugated plastic sheeting
	Assorted 9mm (⅜ in) diam coach bolts
	Assorted No 8 and No 10 galvanised wood screws
	76 mm (3 in) diam rainwater guttering and down-pipe
	Water tub – modified plastic cider barrel
	Wood preservatives
	Waterproof wood glue
	Plastic sheet fixing screws and sealing caps and washers

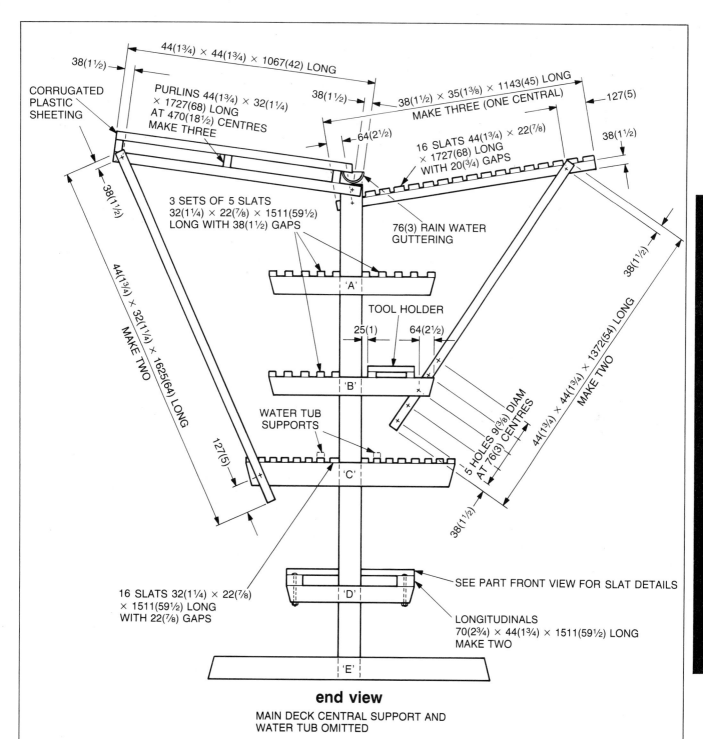

44(1¾) × 44(1¾) × 1067(42) LONG

38(1½)

CORRUGATED
PLASTIC
SHEETING

PURLINS 44(1¾) × 32(1¼)
× 1727(68) LONG
AT 470(18½) CENTRES
MAKE THREE

38(1½)

38(1½) × 35(1⅜) × 1143(45) LONG
MAKE THREE (ONE CENTRAL)

127(5)

64(2½)

16 SLATS 44(1¾) × 22(⅞)
× 1727(68) LONG
WITH 20(¾) GAPS

38(1½)

38(1½)

3 SETS OF 5 SLATS
32(1¼) × 22(⅞) × 1511(59½)
LONG WITH 38(1½) GAPS

76(3) RAIN WATER
GUTTERING

'A'

38(1½)

44(1¾) × 32(1¼) × 1625(64) LONG

MAKE TWO

TOOL HOLDER

25(1)   64(2½)

'B'

44(1¾) × 44(1¾) × 1372(54) LONG

MAKE TWO

WATER TUB
SUPPORTS

5 HOLES 9(⅜) DIAM
AT 76(3) CENTRES

44(1¾) × 44(1¾)

127(5)

'C'

38(1½)

16 SLATS 32(1¼) × 22(⅞)
× 1511(59½) LONG
WITH 22(⅞) GAPS

'D'

SEE PART FRONT VIEW FOR SLAT DETAILS

LONGITUDINALS
70(2¾) × 44(1¾) × 1511(59½) LONG
MAKE TWO

'E'

end view

MAIN DECK CENTRAL SUPPORT AND
WATER TUB OMITTED

SUPPORT 'A' 70(2¾) × 44(1¾) × 717(28¼) LONG
SUPPORT 'B' 70(2¾) × 44(1¾) × 717(28¼) LONG
SUPPORT 'C' 95(3¾) × 44(1¾) × 914(36) LONG
SUPPORT 'D' 70(2¾) × 44(1¾) × 546(21½) LONG
FOOT 'E' 95(3¾) × 44(1¾) × 1220(48) LONG

CROSS MEMBERS
ALL WITH 15° CHAMFER AT EACH END
MAKE TWO OF EACH

BONSAI CENTRE

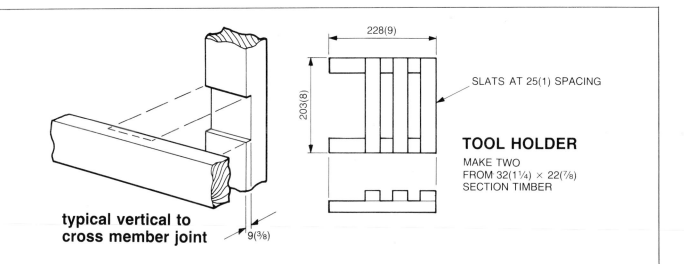

typical vertical to cross member joint

9(³⁄₈)

228(9)

203(8)

SLATS AT 25(1) SPACING

TOOL HOLDER

MAKE TWO
FROM 32(1¼) × 22(⅞)
SECTION TIMBER

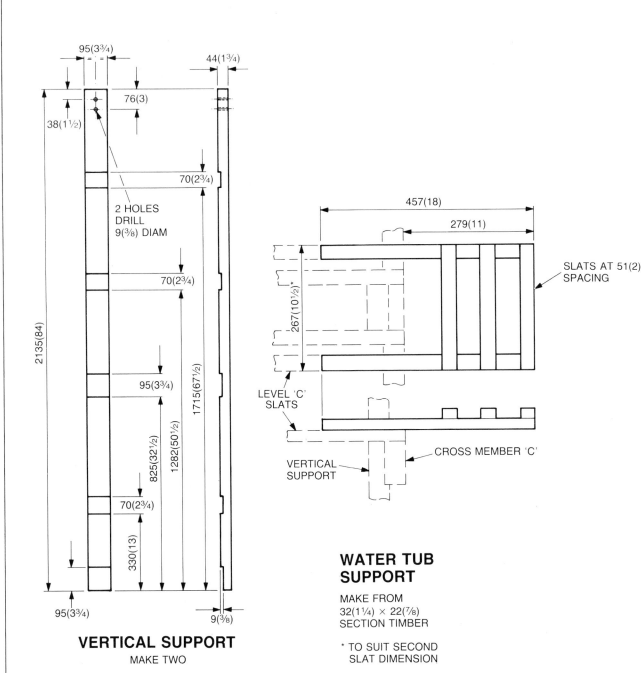

95(3¾)

44(1¾)

76(3)

38(1½)

70(2¾)

2 HOLES
DRILL
9(³⁄₈) DIAM

70(2¾)

95(3¾)

2135(84)

1715(67½)

1282(50½)

825(32½)

70(2¾)

330(13)

95(3¾)

9(³⁄₈)

VERTICAL SUPPORT

MAKE TWO

457(18)

279(11)

267(10½)*

SLATS AT 51(2)
SPACING

LEVEL 'C'
SLATS

CROSS MEMBER 'C'

VERTICAL
SUPPORT

WATER TUB SUPPORT

MAKE FROM
32(1¼) × 22(⅞)
SECTION TIMBER

* TO SUIT SECOND
SLAT DIMENSION

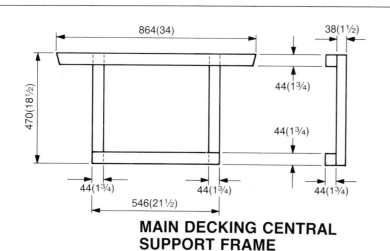

**MAIN DECKING CENTRAL
SUPPORT FRAME**

864(34)   38(1½)

470(18½)

44(1¾)

44(1¾)

44(1¾)   44(1¾)   44(1¾)

546(21½)

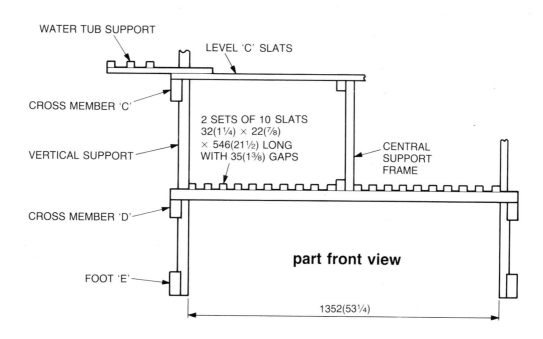

WATER TUB SUPPORT

LEVEL 'C' SLATS

CROSS MEMBER 'C'

VERTICAL SUPPORT

2 SETS OF 10 SLATS
32(1¼) × 22(⅞)
× 546(21½) LONG
WITH 35(1⅜) GAPS

CENTRAL
SUPPORT
FRAME

CROSS MEMBER 'D'

part front view

FOOT 'E'

1352(53¼)

Next to sitting in the garden doing nothing, sitting there eating must be the most pleasurable occupation I know! This table is very sturdy and no traditional woodwork joints are used—in fact it could be described as 'wood engineering'.

1 From the drawings you can see that there are a number of angles on the main frames. By far the simplest and easiest way to mark these angles correctly is to draw them full size on a sheet of old hardboard. Draw the table frame full size in pencil, and then place the timber on the drawing and mark off the various angles.

2 Now cramp the pieces together and drill the holes for the coach bolts. Some hardware shops and builder's merchants stock square metal plates as well as coach bolts. If you can get these they are ideal as they allow you to do the bolts up very tight and put tremendous pressure on the joints. If you can't get a plate you will need to use a washer under the nut head.

3 Once the bolts have been done up a rigid framework is formed. The ends of the bolts, however, are a hazard and can give some very nasty scratches. To

prevent this buy a length of plastic pipe (obtainable from shops that sell wine-making kits), cut off short lengths and fit them onto the bolt ends.

These plastic 'sleeves' serve a dual purpose as they can be packed with grease, which stops rusting and makes for easy dismantling of the table in the winter time. It is very important that the ends of the bolts are covered as described or by some other method.

4 The two frames are now fitted together by a rail on the lower cross-piece. This rail should be bolted onto the cross-pieces and provides a fixing point for the two children's chairs.

5 Once the rail has been fitted, you should fit the table top spars. To get the semi-circular shaping on the ends I cramped all the spars together and used a jig-saw to cut the ends to shape. The spars should then be glued and screwed onto the top of the table.

6 Now make the bench tops. These are planks, which must be screwed to longitudinal pieces underneath for greater rigidity.

7 Fix the benches to the table with long coach bolts which must pass through the bench top and cross-pieces.

8 The children's chairs are an optional extra, but if you do make them it is important to fit spars around them to prevent adults sitting in them. The reason for this is that, although the seat will take the weight of an adult, the balance of the table will be upset—unless adults sit at both ends simultaneously! The chairs are bolted onto the lower rail and, even though the bolt is tight, it will allow the seat to swivel from side to side. It is very important to use metal plates with these two bolts, otherwise it is possible that the nut and washer might pull through the wood.

Photographs: opposite and page 100

■ CUTTING LIST

Picnic table

Main cross member	2 off	1245 x 95 x 44 mm (49 x 3¾ x 1¾ in)	timber
Top cross member	2 off	730 x 95 x 44 mm (28¾ x 3¾ x 1¾ in)	timber
Leg	4 off	813 x 95 x 44 mm (32 x 3¾ x 1¾ in)	timber
Table top	10 off	1524 x 44 x 32 mm (60 x 1¾ x 1¼ in)	timber
Bench seat assembly	2 off	1524 x 219 x 22 mm (60 x 8⅝ x ⅞ in)	timber
	4 off	1398 x 44 x 44 mm (55 x 1¾ x 1¾ in)	timber
Horizontal tie rail	1 off	990 x 76 x 51 mm (39 x 3 x 2 in)	timber
Children's chair assembly	2 off	800 x 51 x 41 mm (31½ x 2 x 1⅝ in)	timber
	2 off	368 x 228 x 20 mm (14½ x 9 x ¾ in)	timber
	4 off	165 x 35 x 22 mm (6½ x 1⅜ x ⅞ in)	timber
	4 off	178 x 35 x 22 mm (7 x 1⅜ x ⅞ in)	timber
	4 off	247 x 35 x 22 mm (9¾ x 1⅜ x ⅞ in)	timber
	4 off	292 x 35 x 22 mm (11½ x 1⅜ x ⅞ in)	timber
	4 off	412 x 35 x 22 mm (16¼ x 1⅜ x ⅞ in)	timber
Pivot spacer	2 off	44 x 38 x 38 mm (1¾ x 1½ x 1½ in)	timber

Ancillaries

	Assorted 9mm (⅜ in) diam coach bolts	
	9mm (⅜ in) bore plastic tube	
	Assorted No 8 and No 10 galvanised wood screws	
	Wood preservative	
	Waterproof wood glue	

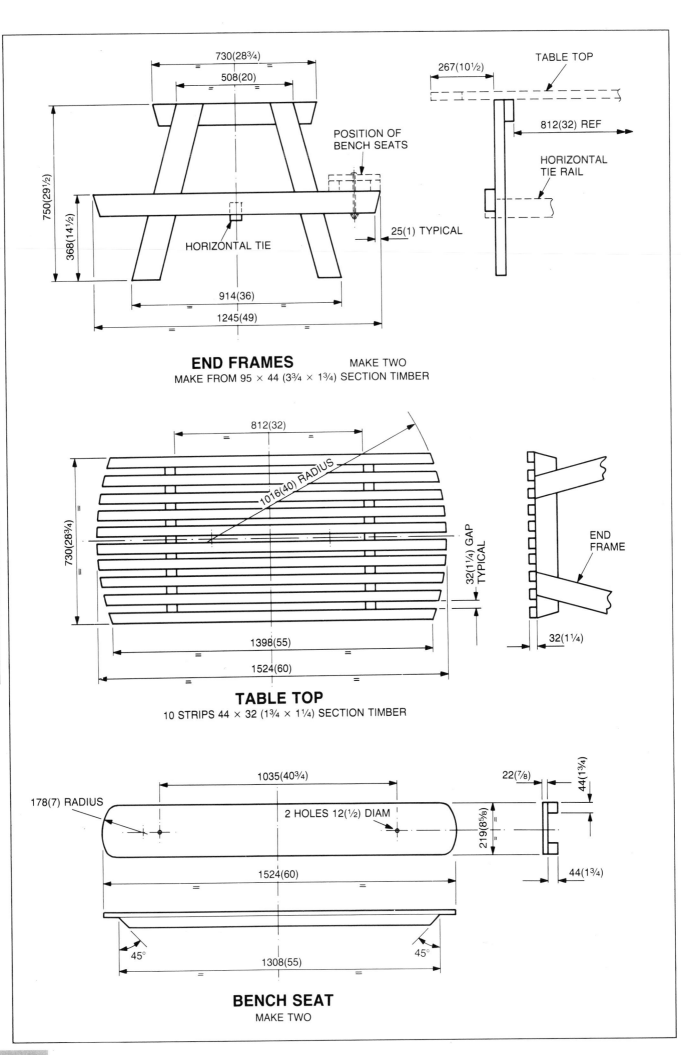

END FRAMES MAKE TWO
MAKE FROM 95 × 44 (3¾ × 1¾) SECTION TIMBER

730(28¾)
508(20)
750(29½)
368(14½)
914(36)
1245(49)

POSITION OF BENCH SEATS
HORIZONTAL TIE
25(1) TYPICAL

267(10½)
TABLE TOP
812(32) REF
HORIZONTAL TIE RAIL

TABLE TOP
10 STRIPS 44 × 32 (1¾ × 1¼) SECTION TIMBER

812(32)
1016(40) RADIUS
730(28¾)
32(1¼) GAP TYPICAL
1398(55)
1524(60)
32(1¼)
END FRAME

BENCH SEAT
MAKE TWO

1035(40¾)
178(7) RADIUS
2 HOLES 12(½) DIAM
22(⅞)
44(1¾)
219(8⅝)
1524(60)
44(1¾)
1308(55)
45°
45°

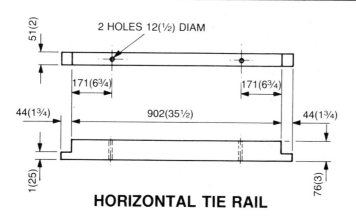

HORIZONTAL TIE RAIL

2 HOLES 12(½) DIAM

51(2)

171(6¾)   171(6¾)

44(1¾)   902(35½)   44(1¾)

1(25)   76(3)

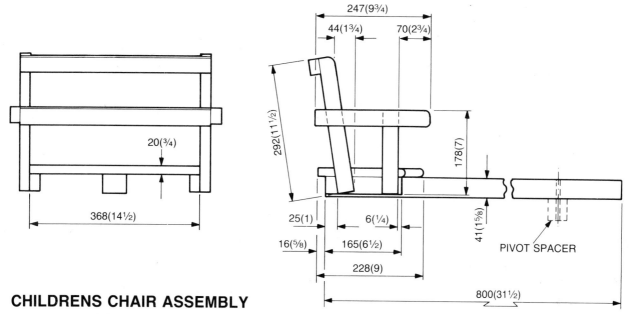

247(9¾)

44(1¾)   70(2¾)

292(11½)

178(7)

41(1⅝)

PIVOT SPACER

25(1)   6(¼)

16(⅝)   165(6½)

228(9)

800(31½)

20(¾)

368(14½)

CHILDRENS CHAIR ASSEMBLY

MAKE TWO FROM 35 × 22(1⅜ × ⅞) SECTION
TIMBER, UNLESS DETAILED OTHERWISE

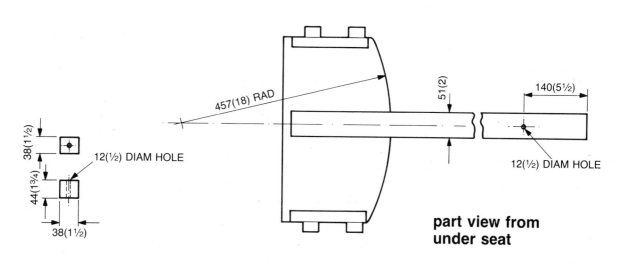

457(18) RAD

51(2)

140(5½)

12(½) DIAM HOLE

part view from
under seat

38(1½)

44(1¾)

12(½) DIAM HOLE

38(1½)

PIVOT SPACER
MAKE TWO

FLOWER WAGON

Anyone who has made a flower box will know that carrying it to site is a heavy task, but with four wheels on your wagon the problem is solved and it is possible to move it anywhere in the garden quite easily. None of the sizes in this design is critical and the use of nails as a means of fixing planks together is not frowned upon!

1 Start by cutting two lengths of plank and fastening them together by two cross-pieces.
2 Screw blocks of wood, into which holes have been drilled to take the axles for the wheels, onto the bottoms of the cross-pieces.
3 Now drill holes in the base to allow water to drain away.
4 Glue and nail the sides of the wagon together. To prevent any possibility of splitting, pre-drill small pilot holes for the nails.

5 Place the sides on the base and, with a pencil, mark the position of the sides and ends. Remove the sides and drill pilot holes for the screws. Screw the sides to the base.
6 Most plants need some support as they grow and therefore trellises are provided at the ends of the wagon. Screw these together and then fit them into the sides of the wagon.
7 The handle and mounting block should ideally be made from hardwood — an offcut of oak would be ideal.

Attach the handle to the mounting block with a dowel rod that runs right through handle and block. Then screw the block onto the bottom of the cart.
8 Fit steel axle rods and spring clips to keep the wheels on. The ends of the axle rod will need chamfering with a file before you can push the clips into place.
9 To prevent the wagon rotting a good wood preservative should be applied. This is best done several weeks before you intend putting plants into the wagon as otherwise the preservative may damage the plants.
(In any event it is always sensible to read the instructions on the tin carefully before use).

Photograph: opposite

■ GARDEN SECTION ■

■ CUTTING LIST

Flower wagon

End	2 off	360 x 149 x 22 mm (14⅛ x 5⅞ x ⅞ in)	timber
Side	2 off	610 x 149 x 22 mm (24 x 5⅞ x ⅞ in)	timber
Floor/chassis	2 off	654 x 149 x 22 mm (25¾ x 5⅞ x ⅞ in)	timber
	2 off	300 x 70 x 35 mm (11¾ x 2¾ x 1⅜ in)	timber
	4 off	108 x 70 x 35 mm (4¼ x 2¾ x 1⅜ in)	timber
Handle mounting block	1 off	117 x 76 x 70 mm (4⅝ x 3 x 2¾ in)	timber
Handle	1 off	712 x 44 x 24 mm (28 x 1¾ x ¹⁵⁄₁₆ in)	timber
	1 off	9 mm (⅜ in) diam x 165 mm (6½ in)	long dowel
Pivot pin	1 off	9 mm (⅜ in) diam x 117 mm (4⅝ in)	long dowel
Trellis (pair)	4 off	418 x 38 x 20 mm (16½ x 1½ x ¾ in)	timber
	4 off	495 x 22 x 20 mm (19½ x ⅞ x ¾ in)	timber
	2 off	457 x 22 x 20 mm (18 x ⅞ x ¾ in)	timber
	2 off	418 x 22 x 20 mm (16½ x ⅞ x ¾ in)	timber
	4 off	370 x 22 x 20 mm (14½ x ⅞ x ¾ in)	timber

Ancillaries

4 off	203 mm (8 in) diam road wheels
4 off	9 mm (⅜ in) diam x 171 mm (6¾ in) long steel axles
8 off	Spring dome caps to suit 9 mm (⅜ in) diameter axles

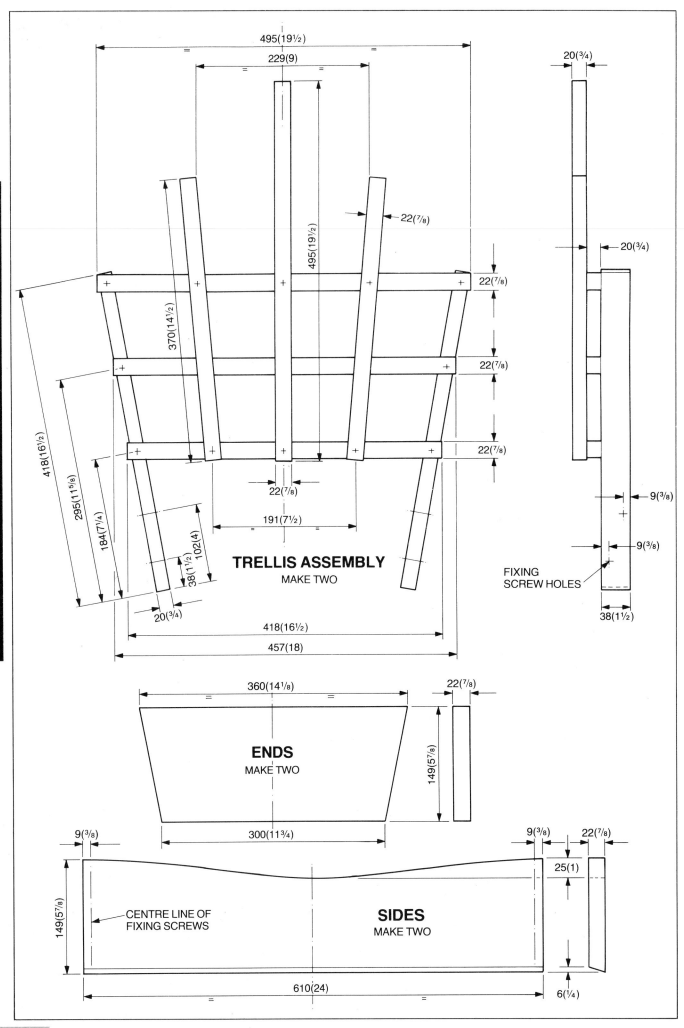

495(19½)

229(9)

22(⅞)

495(19½)

370(14½)

418(16½)

295(11⅝)

184(7¼)

38(1½) 102(4)

20(¾)

22(⅞)

22(⅞)

22(⅞)

22(⅞)

191(7½)

TRELLIS ASSEMBLY
MAKE TWO

418(16½)

457(18)

20(¾)

20(¾)

9(⅜)

9(⅜)

FIXING
SCREW HOLES

38(1½)

360(14⅛)

22(⅞)

ENDS
MAKE TWO

149(5⅞)

300(11¾)

9(⅜)

9(⅜)

22(⅞)

25(1)

149(5⅞)

CENTRE LINE OF
FIXING SCREWS

SIDES
MAKE TWO

610(24)

6(¼)

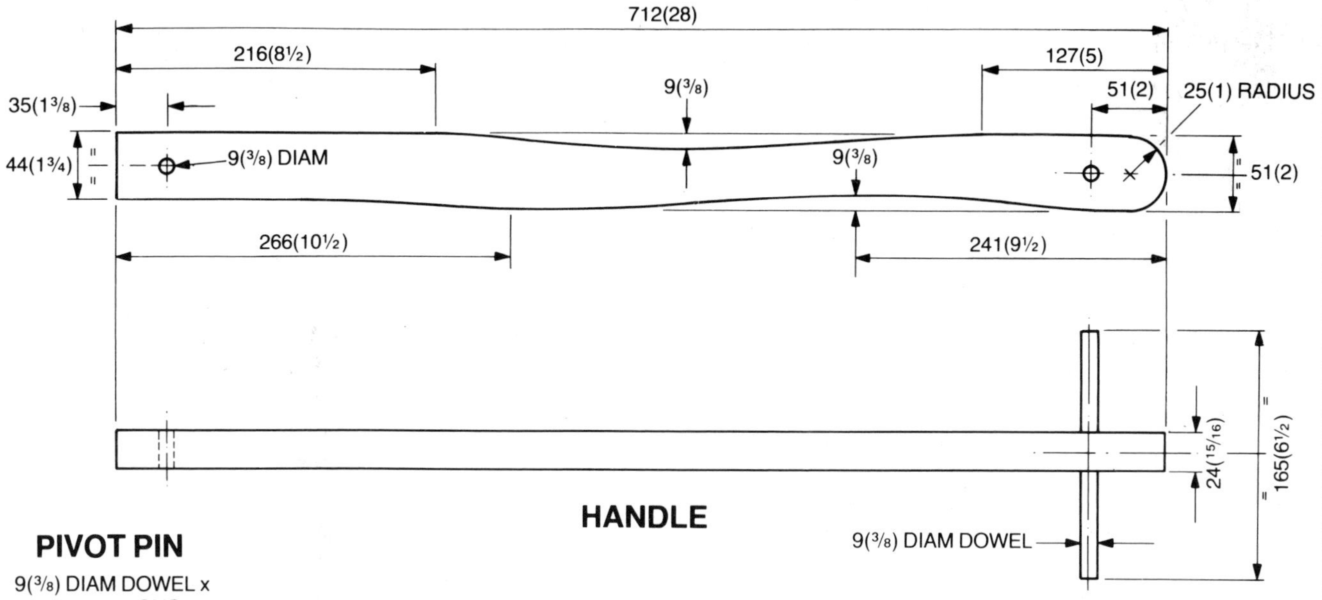
712(28)
216(8½)
127(5)
35(1⅜)
9(⅜)
51(2)
25(1) RADIUS
44(1¾)
9(⅜) DIAM
9(⅜)
51(2)
266(10½)
241(9½)
24(15/16)
165(6½)
9(⅜) DIAM DOWEL

HANDLE

PIVOT PIN

9(⅜) DIAM DOWEL x 117(4⅝) LONG

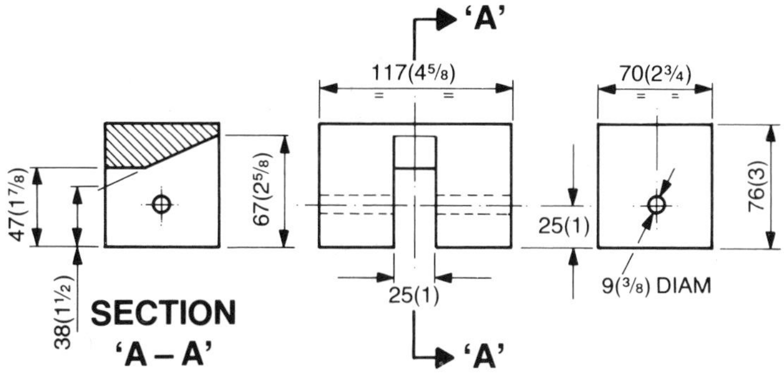
'A'
117(4⅝)
70(2¾)
47(1⅞)
67(2⅝)
25(1)
76(3)
9(⅜) DIAM
25(1)
38(1½)
'A'

SECTION 'A – A'

HANDLE MOUNTING BLOCK

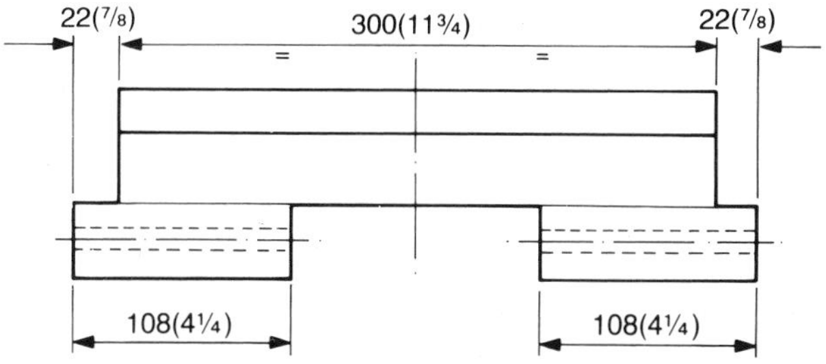
22(⅞)
300(11¾)
22(⅞)
108(4¼)
108(4¼)

View on arrow 'B'

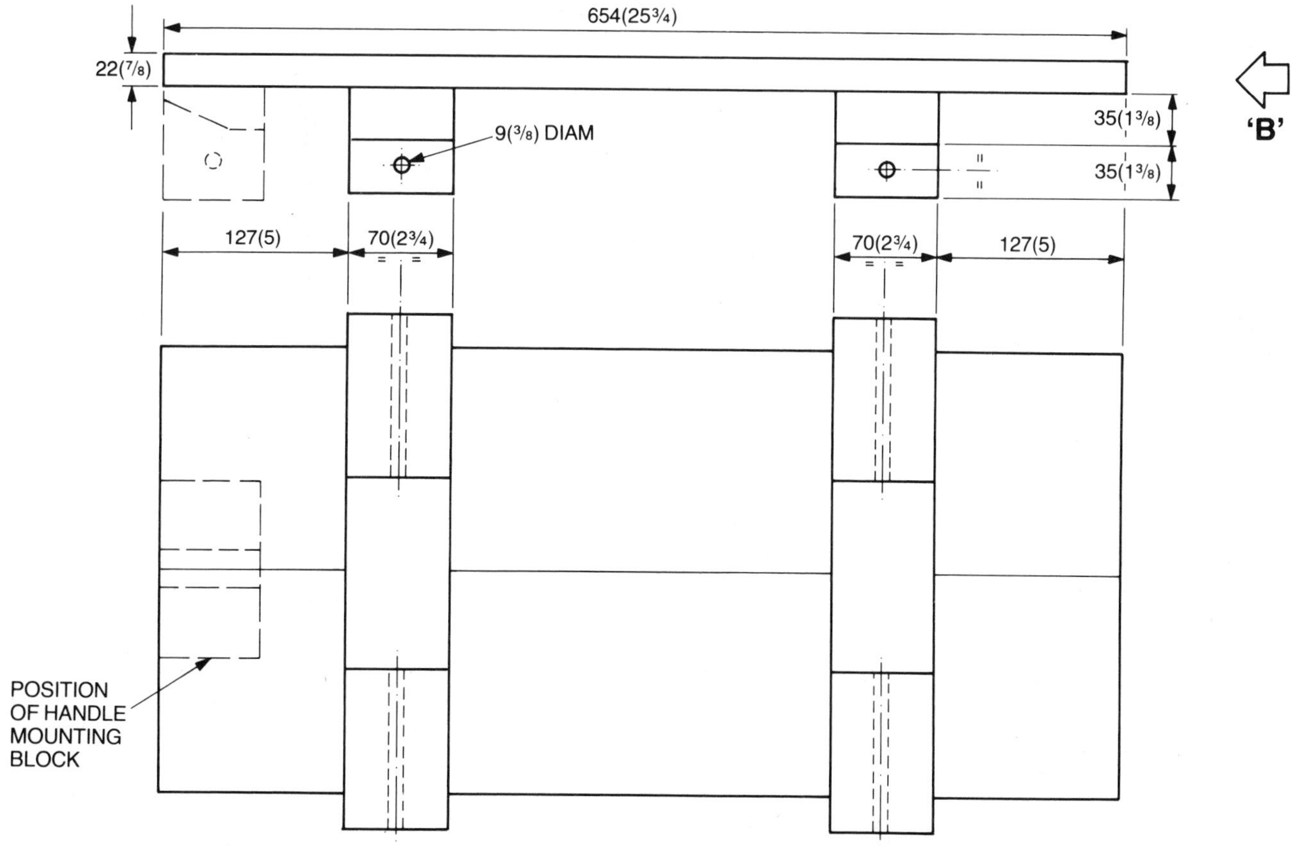
654(25¾)
22(⅞)
9(⅜) DIAM
35(1⅜)
35(1⅜)
'B'
127(5)
70(2¾)
70(2¾)
127(5)
POSITION
OF HANDLE
MOUNTING
BLOCK

FLOOR/CHASSIS ASSEMBLY

The word 'dilly' is an interesting one. Originally it meant the local stage coach, but later it came to mean an 'agricultural cart', which is what this dilly is. How many of us arrive at the bottom of the garden only to realise that we have forgotten something. Or, even if we have remembered all the tools, we still have to go back for the bag of compost as well! This 'cart' should take care of such problems.

1   The body is formed from plywood which is glued and screwed together. The screws should be of the type especially designed for fixing chipboard and plywood. These new 'supa screws' have a different kind of thread from the traditional wood screw and get a better hold in the plywood. Fit each screw with a cup-washer as this provides extra pressure on the sides and helps hold the body firmly together.
2   Once you have made the body, two blocks of wood are needed to fit the axles into. Drill axle holes into the two blocks. Now turn the body of the dilly over and carefully mark the positions of the blocks in pencil. What is important here is that the blocks are attached parallel with one another and not one slightly in front or behind the other.
3   Now drill holes for the screws, bearing in mind that the axle runs through the middle of the block. Turn the dilly body over and countersink the axle block holes from the inside.

4   Glue and screw the blocks to the body of the dilly.
5   Now make the handles. These need to be of sufficient length to be able to support your garden fork and spade handles, so it is well worth measuring your tools and increasing or decreasing the given measurements to suit your own needs. Screw the handles onto the sides.
6   Cut the cross-pieces and shape the hand-holds with a spokeshave. Since a great deal of strain will be imposed on the side handles I cut and shaped two blocks to fit at the bottom where the handle joins the body. The blocks should be screwed and glued onto the side of the body, one long screw passing right through block, handle and body, thus giving the handles great strength.

■ Tool tidy

Now don't just dump your tools in the dilly, take the trouble to make a tidy!

1   Using a piece of card, draw around the end profile of the tools and cut this out to test if the tools fit.
2   Once you have got a good fit for each tool, transfer the shapes to a piece of plywood and, using a key-hole saw or jigsaw, cut the shapes out.
3   Screw the tidy to the dilly and arrange the tools.
4   Fix the wheels on, but before attaching the spring caps 'run' a fine cut metal file around the edges of the axle rod and make a chamfer, otherwise you will be unable to get the spring caps on. Whatever sort of finish you intend to put on the wood should be done before the wheels are attached.

Photograph: opposite

■ CUTTING LIST

Garden dilly

Container section	2 off	610 x 228 x 12 mm (24 x 9 x ½ in)	marine plywood
	1 off	330 x 210 x 12 mm (13 x 8¼ x ½ in)	marine plywood
	1 off	330 x 248 x 12 mm (13 x 9¾ x ½ in)	marine plywood
	2 off	140 x 95 x 44 mm (5½ x 3¾ x 1¾ in)	timber
Handle assembly	2 off	826 x 47 x 35 mm (32½ x 1⅞ x 1⅜ in)	timber
	1 off	622 x 47 x 35 mm (24½ x 1⅞ x 1⅜ in)	timber
	1 off	426 x 32 x 22 mm (16¾ x 1¼ x ⅞ in)	timber
Leg	2 off	235 x 44 x 44 mm (9¼ x 1¾ x 1¾ in)	timber
Tool tidy	1 off	432 x 89 x 9 mm (17 x 3½ x ⅜ in)	marine plywood
Mudguard/handle support	2 off	203 x 95 x 44 mm (8 x 3¾ x 1¾ in)	timber

Ancillaries

	2 off	241 mm (9½ in) diam road wheels
	2 off	230 mm (9 in) long x 12 mm (½ in) diam steel stub axles
	4 off	Spring dome caps to suit 12 mm (½ in) diam axles
	3 off	12 mm (½ in) terry clips
		Assorted No 8 galvanised wood screws and cup washers
		Wood preservative
		Waterproof wood glue

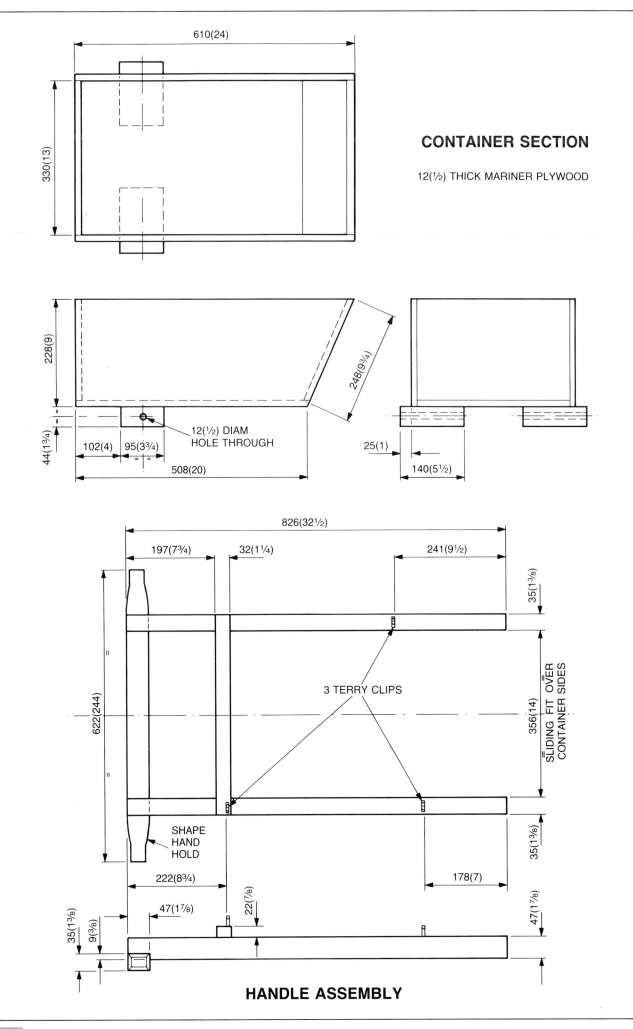

610(24)

330(13)

CONTAINER SECTION

12(½) THICK MARINER PLYWOOD

228(9)

248(9¾)

44(1¾)

12(½) DIAM
HOLE THROUGH

102(4)   95(3¾)

508(20)

25(1)

140(5½)

826(32½)

197(7¾)   32(1¼)   241(9½)

35(1⅜)

622(244)

3 TERRY CLIPS

356(14)

SLIDING FIT OVER
CONTAINER SIDES

SHAPE
HAND
HOLD

35(1⅜)

222(8¾)

178(7)

47(1⅞)

22(⅞)

35(1⅜)
9(⅜)

47(1⅞)

47(1⅞)

HANDLE ASSEMBLY

GARDEN SECTION

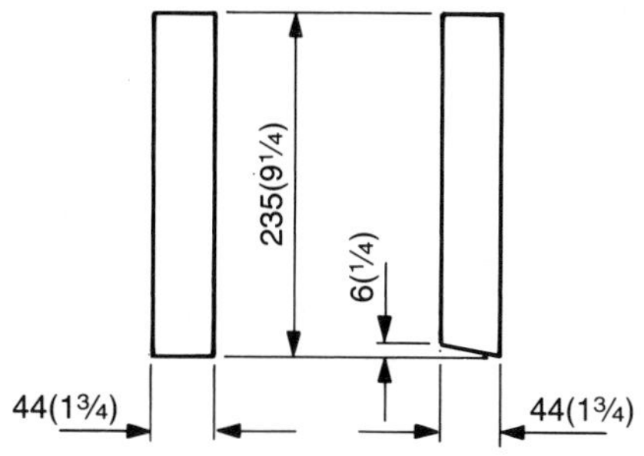
235(9¼)
6(¼)
44(1¾)
44(1¾)

LEG
MAKE TWO

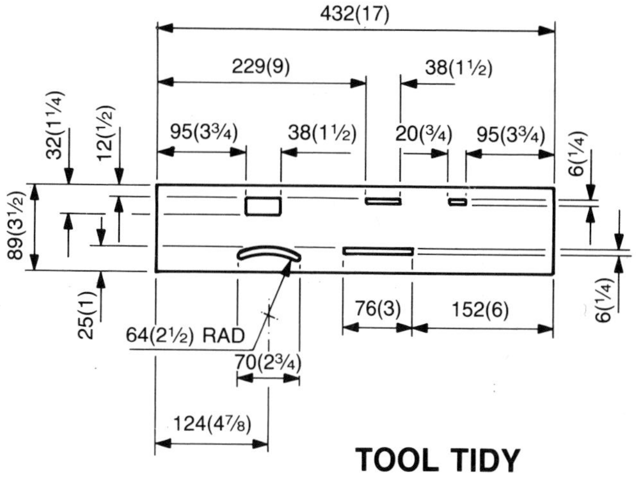
432(17)
229(9)
38(1½)
32(1¼)
12(½)
95(3¾)
38(1½)
20(¾)
95(3¾)
6(¼)
89(3½)
25(1)
64(2½) RAD
70(2¾)
76(3)
152(6)
6(¼)
124(4⅞)

TOOL TIDY
9(⅜) THICK PLYWOOD

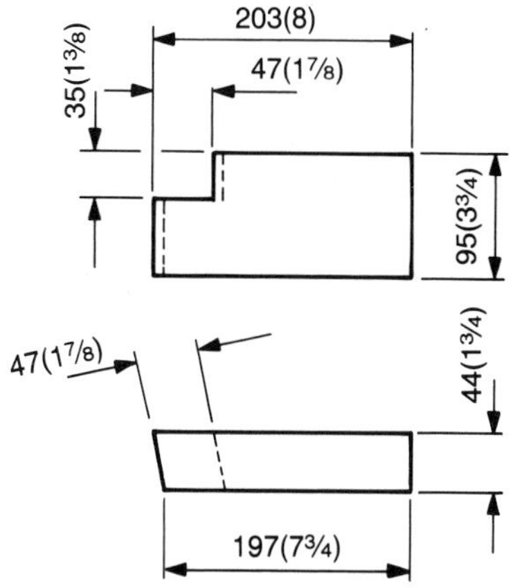
203(8)
35(1⅜)
47(1⅞)
95(3¾)
47(1⅞)
44(1¾)
197(7¾)

MUDGUARD/ HANDLE SUPPORT
MAKE ONE OF EACH HAND

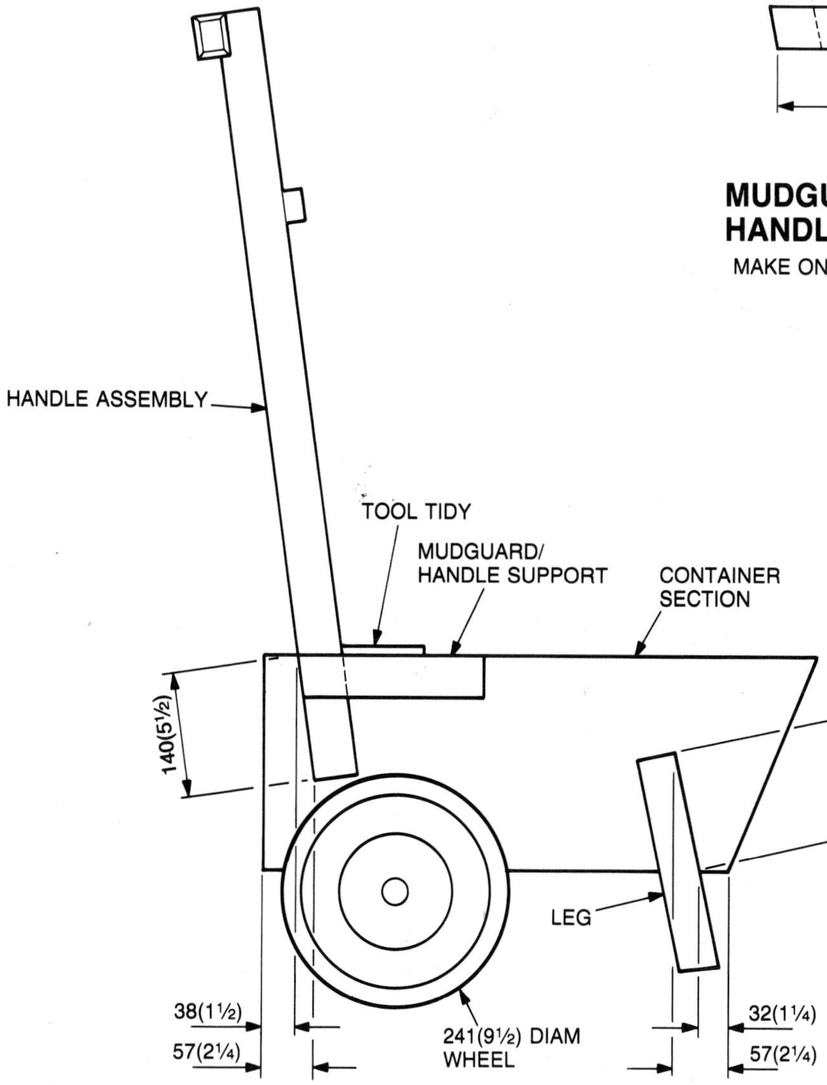
HANDLE ASSEMBLY
TOOL TIDY
MUDGUARD/
HANDLE SUPPORT
CONTAINER
SECTION
140(5½)
127(5)
LEG
38(1½)
57(2¼)
241(9½) DIAM
WHEEL
32(1¼)
57(2¼)

A cloche is very useful for protecting and encouraging the growth of young or delicate plants in the garden. Frequently the weak point of such a structure is the covering material, which often rips after very little use. With my design you are guaranteed a five-year life using a rigid PVC sheet. Aluminium is the best material to use for the wire hoop as it won't rust. Aluminium rod is available from a number of sources (check the Yellow Pages for your area) and will bend very easily.

1 Bend a length of aluminium rod into a hoop. Drill two holes in a piece of roofing batten and poke the ends of the hoop through these holes. This will be your cloche support. How many of these you need to make will depend on how long you want your cloche to be.
2 Insert your length of PVC sheeting through the support hoops and push the battens up to fit tightly against the bottom of the sheeting. Place the cloche in position in the garden and push the ends of the aluminium hoops into the ground to secure it.
3 Cut two ends out of plywood. Fix one end of an offcut of roofing batten onto each piece of plywood and sharpen the other end into a spike so that it can be driven into the ground.

Photograph: opposite

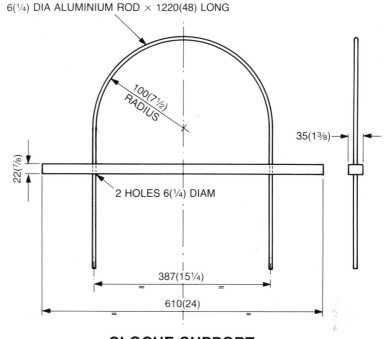

CLOCHE SUPPORT

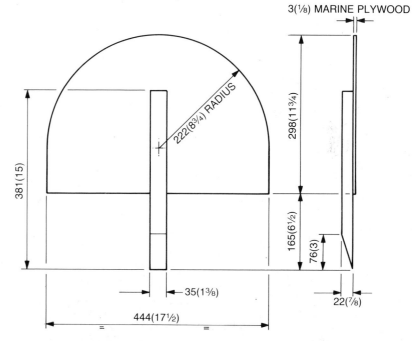

CLOCHE END BLANKING PLATE

■ CUTTING LIST

Cloche items per cloche			
Support	2 off	610 x 35 x 22 mm (24 x 1⅜ x ⅞ in)	timber
Blanking plate	2 off	444 x 298 x 3 mm (17½ x 11¾ x ⅛ in)	marine plywood
	2 off	381 x 35 x 22 mm (15 x 1⅜ x ⅞ in)	timber

Ancillaries	
	Corrugated P.V.C. sheeting
	1220 mm (48 in) length of 6 mm (¼ in) diam aluminium rod
	Assorted No 8 galvanised wood screws
	Wood preservative. Waterproof wood glue.

This must be one of the most useful structures in this section and a must for any garden. I have kept the construction as simple as possible and no hinges are involved! Don't forget to use waterproof glue on all the joins.

1 Cramp the two pieces of board for the back together. Screw and glue strips of wood across the inside edges. These strips of wood have a dual purpose: they hold the back together and provide support for the lid framework. Note from the drawings that the top-edge strip is 'set down' and that the end blocks are 'set in' from the side edges.

2 To make the sides you will need three pieces of plank, one cut diagonally in half. Once again, glue and screw strips of wood across them to hold the pieces together.

3 Fit two blocks on the inside of the front board 'set back' from the edges to allow the sides to fit.

4 Now glue and screw the sides to the back and front, and treat the entire structure with wood preservative.

■ Lid

This is formed from translucent corrugated P.V.C. sheeting. The frame is designed so that if you cut your sheet in half, the two pieces will adequately cover the whole box.

1 Make the lid framework by gluing and screwing roofing battens together. Treat with wood preservative.

2 Cut the corrugated sheet in half. This is far easier than it looks and, providing that you use a fine-toothed saw (tenon saw), you shouldn't have any problems. It is a good idea to have someone else to help hold the material as it is slippery. Saw gently and you will find that it cuts easily. The only unpleasant part is the dreadful squealing sound made by the saw.

3 Position the two halves over the framework and attach the sheeting to the battens. This should be done by first using an ordinary hand drill to drill a small pilot hole through the plastic wherever you wish to fit a screw. Then use the special screws and plastic caps available to fix the sheeting to the wood.

4 Fit an extra length of batten on the outside edge of the framework to use for lifting the lid. The framework should fit snugly inside the cold frame box and the corrugated sheet rests on the sides.

Photograph: opposite

■ CUTTING LIST

Cold frame

Front	1 off	1220 x 203 x 22 mm (48 x 8 x 7/8 in)	timber
Back	2 off	1220 x 222 x 22 mm (48 x 8¾ x 7/8 in)	timber
Ends	3 off	864 x 222 x 22 mm (34 x 8¾ x 7/8 in)	timber
Front corner blocks	2 off	203 x 44 x 44 mm (8 x 1¾ x 1¾ in)	timber
Back corner blocks	2 off	400 x 44 x 44 mm (15¾ x 1¾ x 1¾ in)	timber
Back reinforcing strips	3 off	400 x 44 x 32 mm (15¾ x 1¾ x 1¼ in)	timber
Lid	2 off	1212 x 35 x 22 mm (47¾ x 1⅜ x 7/8 in)	timber
	5 off	864 x 35 x 22 mm (34 x 1⅜ x 7/8 in)	timber
	1 off	635 x 35 x 22 mm (25 x 1⅜ x 7/8 in)	timber

Ancillaries

	Corrugated P.V.C. sheeting	
	Nails or assorted No 8 and 10 galvanised wood screws	
	Wood preservative. Waterproof wood glue	
	P.V.C. sheeting fixing screws and sealing caps and washers	

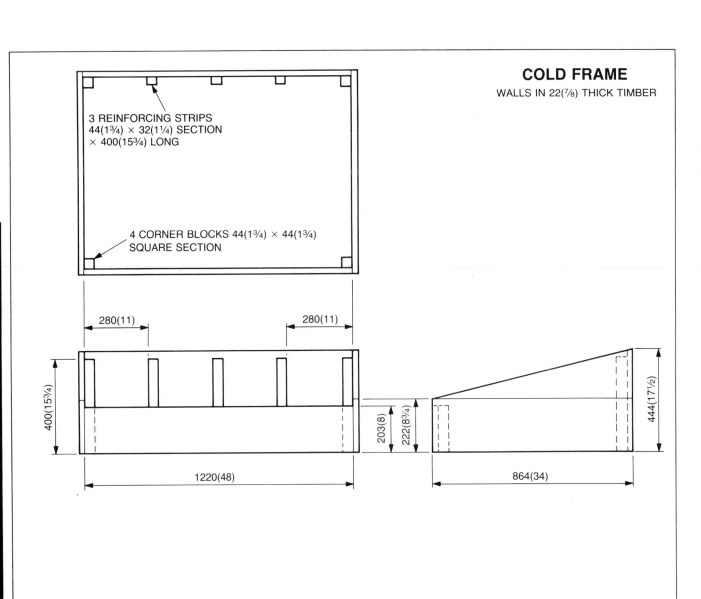

COLD FRAME
WALLS IN 22(⁷⁄₈) THICK TIMBER

3 REINFORCING STRIPS
44(1¾) × 32(1¼) SECTION
× 400(15¾) LONG

4 CORNER BLOCKS 44(1¾) × 44(1¾)
SQUARE SECTION

280(11)

280(11)

400(15¾)

203(8)

222(8¾)

1220(48)

444(17½)

864(34)

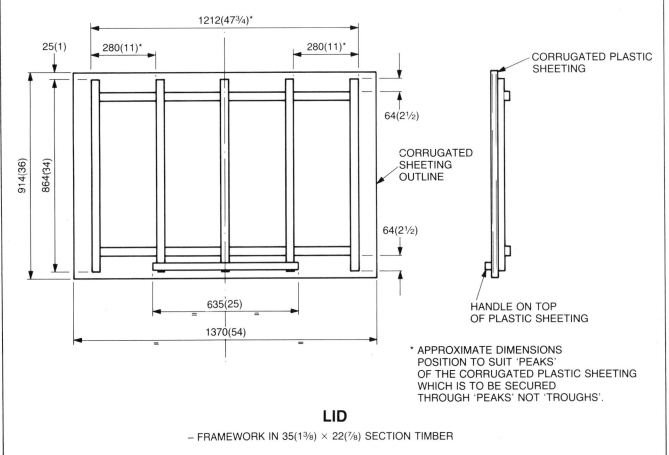

1212(47¾)*

25(1)

280(11)*

280(11)*

914(36)

864(34)

64(2½)

CORRUGATED PLASTIC
SHEETING

CORRUGATED
SHEETING
OUTLINE

64(2½)

635(25)

1370(54)

HANDLE ON TOP
OF PLASTIC SHEETING

* APPROXIMATE DIMENSIONS
POSITION TO SUIT 'PEAKS'
OF THE CORRUGATED PLASTIC SHEETING
WHICH IS TO BE SECURED
THROUGH 'PEAKS' NOT 'TROUGHS'.

LID
– FRAMEWORK IN 35(1⅜) × 22(⁷⁄₈) SECTION TIMBER

USEFUL INFORMATION

■ Man – made board

Within the last 20 years there has been an ever increasing range of 'man-made' boards available to the practical amateur. These do have some advantages over traditional woods. Firstly they tend to be very stable since movement is reduced to a minimum. The second great advantage is that if the project in mind is planned carefully then there is very little wastage.

For a number of the items featured in this book I used a blockboard with veneer on both sides, but there are plenty of alternatives, so it is a case of visiting your local D.I.Y. shop and looking at what's available. You will also find that there are many different plastic corner blocks available for joining boards together. Many of these need fitting at both back, front, top and bottom. Now for wardrobes these are ideal, but in a book case they would stop the books from fitting flush against the sides. However, if you have never attempted any sort of wood jointing before then use these blocks on a small project, get used to their potential and, when you are confident, try something larger.

It is essential to have the right tools when cutting man-made boards. The first essential is a fine tooth saw. Electric power tools will do a good job providing they are fitted with the correct blades. Many tool makers have recognised the problems cutting man-made board and make special blades for this. If you have a jig-saw then a metal cutting blade will cut plywood without splintering it. With a circular saw a teflon-coated fine ground blade is very useful. Another useful tip is to tape over the area to be cut. This will help stop the veneer or ply surface breaking out and leaving a jagged edge.

Make sure before you start cutting that you have sufficient room to finish the cut. The work should be well supported and be sure that the piece being cut off from the main board is supported too. Don't let it fall off, otherwise you will damage both boards at the edges.

On the right are drawings of some procedures you may need to use when making the projects in this book.

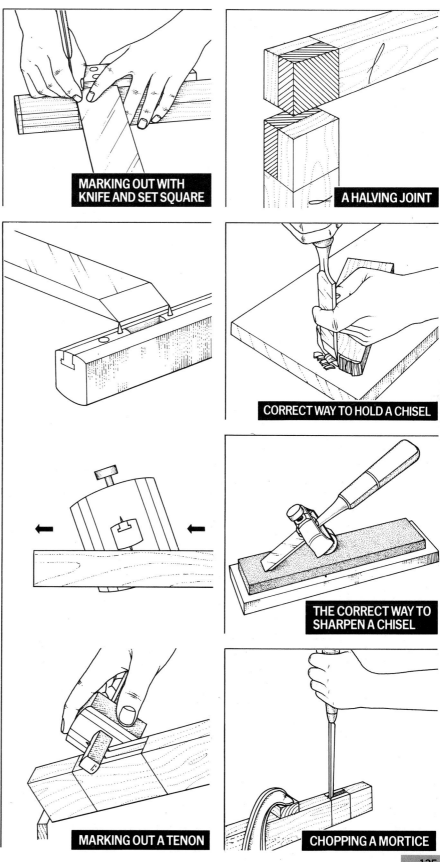

MARKING OUT WITH KNIFE AND SET SQUARE

A HALVING JOINT

CORRECT WAY TO HOLD A CHISEL

THE CORRECT WAY TO SHARPEN A CHISEL

MARKING OUT A TENON

CHOPPING A MORTICE

■ HINTS AND TIPS ■

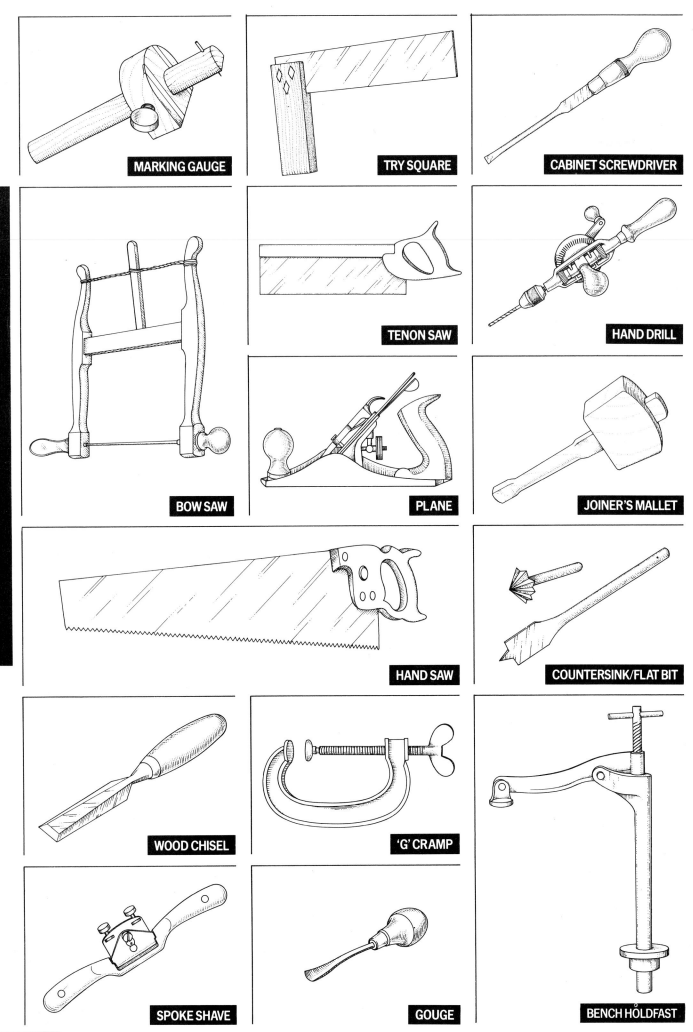

MARKING GAUGE

TRY SQUARE

CABINET SCREWDRIVER

BOW SAW

TENON SAW

HAND DRILL

PLANE

JOINER'S MALLET

HAND SAW

COUNTERSINK/FLAT BIT

WOOD CHISEL

'G' CRAMP

SPOKE SHAVE

GOUGE

BENCH HOLDFAST

Marking gauges

Two gauges are really essential – one with a single spur for marking timber width and thickness, and a twin spur gauge (known as a mortice gauge) for marking the mortice hole and tenons accurately.

Try square

This tool is essential for accurate marking out.

Cabinet screwdriver

In spite of all the mechanical aids which exist for screw-driving it is still necessary to have a small cabinet screwdriver for all the small, delicate jobs.

Tenon saw

This saw, with its brass or steel back to stiffen the blade, is necessary for the accurate cutting of tenons etc.

Hand drill

In spite of having an electric drill, I still use a hand drill for many jobs on the workbench.

Bow saw

Although this saw has changed little since Noah made the Ark it is still a very useful tool with which to cut shapes in large thick pieces of timber.

Plane

Wood planes come in many shapes and sizes. If I had to choose just one then I think the Jack plane is the most useful. The Jack is longer than the smoothing plane and its name obviously comes from the fact that it is so useful in so many different situations.

Joiner's mallet

Never be tempted to hit chisel handles with a hammer. Get a mallet and save the handles!

Hand saw

For those without a power saw this is obviously an essential tool.

Flat bits

These comparatively inexpensive drilling bits have been especially developed for the electric drill. They are not suitable for use in a hand drill.

Countersink

If you use countersink screws it is important to have a countersink to widen the top of the screw hole. This allows the screw head to finish up 'flush' with the surface.

Wood chisels

My favourite general purpose chisel is the bevel-edged chisel. However, it is also essential to have a firmer or mortice chisel for cutting mortice holes. An ash-handled firmer chisel with a leather washer to absorb shock and a steel ferrule at the end of the handle is a very good buy.

'G' Cramp

For working in safety it is always a good idea to hold down the wood you are cutting or shaping firmly with a 'G' cramp.

Spokeshave

Metal and wood spokeshaves are available with either a convex or concave sole.

Gouge

This is a more specialised wood tool and not essential for the beginner.

Bench holdfast

This is a useful tool if you need to hold a piece of timber or board flat on the bench top for drilling or sawing. It is more versatile than a 'G' cramp as it can be used in the centre of a bench where a 'G' cramp could not reach.

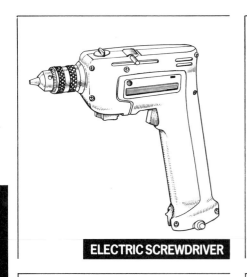

ELECTRIC SCREWDRIVER

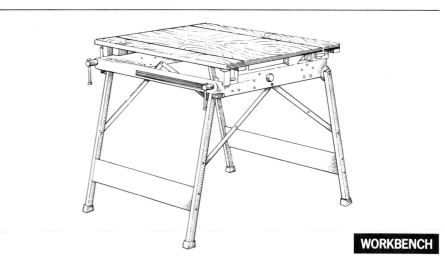

WORKBENCH

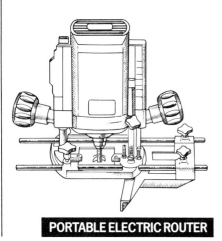

PORTABLE ELECTRIC ROUTER

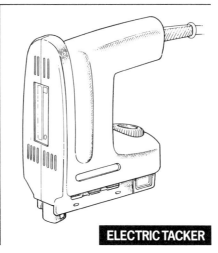

ELECTRIC TACKER

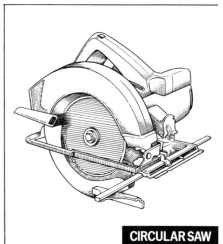

CIRCULAR SAW

JIG-SAW

SANDER

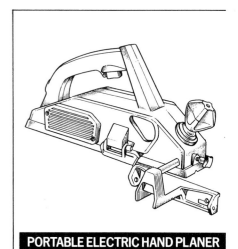

PORTABLE ELECTRIC HAND PLANER

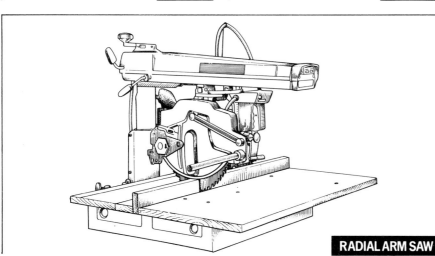

RADIAL ARM SAW

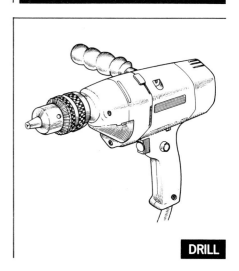

DRILL

■ Electric screwdriver

A most valuable addition to the tool kit, this will save your arm muscles if you have a large quantity of screws to fix. Most models are rechargeable so you don't need to trail a long length of flex around with you.

■ Work bench

It is essential to have a firm surface to work on when using power tools. An old strong table is quite sufficient, but even more useful is a 'workmate' with adjustable jaws.

■ Router

This tool will revolutionise the way you work in wood. A vast variety of cutters are available for different shapes, and it will also cut many joints. It is not until you have one to use in the workshop that you really begin to appreciate just what a versatile tool it is. I believe its capabilities are limited only by the user's imagination. There are many accessories available, but the one I find most interesting is the one that holds the router in a pantograph. It can then carve pictures on the wood while the pantograph follows a master drawing.

■ Electric tacker

This tool can be used for fixing fabric to hard surfaces as well as for building garden trellises. An attachment is available which allows you to use nails instead of staples in it.

■ Circular saw

This tool will speed up all straight-line cutting operations dramatically. If you decide to 'convert' the larger standard sheets of plywood, plastic-coated chipboard and blockboard into smaller sections for your projects, then this will certainly make the task much easier. There is a good selection of blades available; use a very fine-toothed, teflon-coated blade when cutting veneered blockboard.

■ Jig-saw

This tool is very undervalued. It can do almost anything that a circular saw can do, but more slowly. It is particularly useful for internal shapes, curves etc. Pendulum jig-saws are capable of cutting much thicker wood and very much more quickly.

■ Sander

The great advantage an orbital sander has over a disc sander is that it doesn't score the surface of the board being finished. However, the very fine wood-dust given off is a nuisance and possible health hazard unless you have a dust bag attached. Most standard makes are now available with a dust bag, and models where the dust is extracted through holes in the sanding pad are particularly efficient.

■ Portable electric hand planer

This tool will save you its cost in a short while since sawn timber is much cheaper to buy than ready-planed. Most models are available with a stand, which is very useful when dealing with thick pieces of wood. If you decide to save even more money by using reclaimed wood, there is now a useful electronic gadget on the market to use when planing. It detects nails and staples embedded in the wood which might damage your planer if not removed.

■ Radial arm saw

For the enthusiastic woodworker this tool really does make ambitious woodworking projects possible. The radial arm saw is more versatile than the traditional bench saw as it is capable not only of cross-cutting, but also rip-sawing. Large sheets of plywood and chipboard can easily be 'converted' using these machines. Besides the normal range of saw cuts, it can perform in addition plough, compound mitre and dish contour cuts. The range of bolt-on accessories is very comprehensive and includes a disc sander, sabre saw, router and drill/borer. Perhaps the most useful one is a dado head which will cut wide grooves in boards.

■ Drill

Besides drilling holes rapidly and cleanly, this tool can also usually be adapted with a whole range of bolt-on attachments, such as a jig-saw, circular saw and sander.

Frequently those who want to make things are frustrated by the great difficulties they experience in getting the necessary raw materials. If you are unable to get the basics for any of the projects in this book the following addresses may be useful. Do first enquire in your own area, however, as there may well be local suppliers who are willing to help:

■ Timber

John Boddy Timber Ltd, Riverside
Sawmills, Broughbridge,
North Yorkshire YO5 9LJ
This company can supply a vast range of
quality hardwoods through mail order.
Write for list enclosing an SAE.

■ Weaving equipment, yarn, wool, cotton, loom parts etc.

Dryad, P.O. Box 38, Northgates,
Leicester LE1 9BW
Write, enclosing an SAE, for catalogue.

■ Rocking chair upholstery

Chalford Chairs, Chalford, Stroud,
Gloucestershire
This company hand-made the
upholstery for the rocking chair. Write,
enclosing an SAE, for information.

■ Steak knives and forks, carving set and oak platter 'blank'

Blades and forks with wood blanks ready
for fitting and carving are available; also
an oak 'blank' for carving into a steak
platter. Write for list enclosing an SAE to:
R. Blizzard (Wheels), P.O. Box 5,
Gloucester GL3 4RJ

■ Weaving loom

A complete kit of loom parts is available
– all you have to do is glue and screw
them together. Write, enclosing an SAE,
for information to:
R. Blizzard (Wheels), P.O. Box 5,
Gloucester GL3 4RJ

■ Electronic clock mechanisms

For further information send an SAE to:
R. Blizzard (Wheels), P.O. Box 5,
Gloucester GL3 4RJ

■ Wheels for garden dilly

Write for information, enclosing an SAE, to:
R. Blizzard (Wheels), P.O. Box 5,
Gloucester GL3 4RJ

■ Overseas enquiries

If you live outside the UK and would like
to obtain any of the items mentioned on
this page, please write for information
and prices to:
R. Blizzard (Wheels), P.O. Box 5,
Gloucester GL3 4RJ, UK
Regrettably no enquiries can be dealt
with unless a self-addressed, reply-paid,
airmail envelope is enclosed.